INSPIRING
TEACHING

INSPIRING TEACHING

Carnegie Professors of the Year Speak

John K. Roth
General Editor
Claremont McKenna College

Anker Publishing Company, Inc.
Bolton, MA

Inspiring Teaching
Carnegie Professors of the Year Speak

ISBN 1-882982-14-2

Composition by Deerfoot Studios
Cover design by Deerfoot Studios

Anker Publishing Company, Inc.
176 Ballville Road
P.O. Box 249
Bolton, MA 01740-0249

To the Memory

of

Ernest L. Boyer

1928–1995

"In the end, inspired teaching keeps the flame of scholarship alive. Almost all successful academics give credit to creative teachers—those mentors who defined their work so compellingly that it became, for them, a lifelong challenge. Without the teaching function, the continuity of knowledge will be broken and the store of human knowledge dangerously diminished."

Ernest L. Boyer

Scholarship Reconsidered

About the General Editor

Fresh from graduate study at Yale University, John Roth joined the Claremont McKenna College faculty in 1966. CMC has been his academic home ever since, but he has also taught in Switzerland, Austria, Japan, Israel, and Norway. Roth's honors at CMC include the Huntoon Senior Teaching Award, the Crocker Award for Excellence, which he has received three times, and the President's Award. Dedicated to writing, Roth has published more than twenty books and hundreds of essays, many of them focused on the Holocaust. His writings include the text for the permanent exhibition at Holocaust Museum Houston, which opened in that Texas city in March 1996. From 1992 to 1994, Roth chaired the California Council for the Humanities. Presently he serves on the United States Holocaust Memorial Council, which governs the United States Holocaust Memorial Museum in Washington, D.C. The Council for Advancement and Support of Education (CASE) and the Carnegie Foundation for the Advancement of Teaching named Roth the 1988 U.S. National Professor of the Year.

Contributors

MARTHA ANDRESEN, Department of English, Pomona College (1992 California Carnegie Professor of the Year)

PETER G. BEIDLER, Department of English, Lehigh University (1983 U.S. Carnegie Professor of the Year)

HARVEY D. BLANKESPOOR, Department of Biology, Hope College (1991 U.S. Carnegie Professor of the Year)

DIANA COOPER-CLARK, Department of English and Humanities, York University (1995 Canadian Carnegie Professor of the Year)

JOHN DAVID DAWSON, Department of Religion, Haverford College (1994 Pennsylvania Carnegie Professor of the Year)

MICHAEL FLACHMAN, Department of English, California State University–Bakersfield (1995 Outstanding Master's Degree Universities Carnegie Professor of the Year)

J. DENNIS HUSTON, Department of English, Rice University (1989 U.S. Carnegie Professor of the Year)

RALPH KETCHAM, Department of History, Syracuse University (1987 U.S. Carnegie Professor of the Year)

ANTHONY J. LISSKA, Department of Philosophy, Denison University (1994 Outstanding Baccalaureate Colleges Carnegie Professor of the Year)

JOHN R. LOUGH, Department of Management, University of Georgia

VASHTI U. MUSE, Department of Reading, Hinds Community College (1994 Mississippi Carnegie Professor of the Year)

PATRICK PARKS, Department of English, Elgin Community College (1994 Outstanding Community Colleges Carnegie Professor of the Year)

BARBARA PAUL-EMILE, Department of English, Bentley College (1994 Massachusetts Carnegie Professor of the Year)

SALLY PHILLIPS, School of Nursing, University of Colorado Health Sciences Center (1994 Colorado Carnegie Professor of the Year)

JOHN K. ROTH, Department of Philosophy, Claremont McKenna College (1988 U.S. Carnegie Professor of the Year)

TEOFILO F. RUIZ, Department of History, Brooklyn College (1994 Outstanding Master's Universities and Colleges Carnegie Professor of the Year)

MARK C. TAYLOR, Department of Religion, Williams College (1995 Outstanding Baccalaureate Colleges Carnegie Professor of the Year)

ROSEMARIE TONG, Department of Medical Humanities, Davidson College (1986 U.S. Carnegie Professor of the Year)

JAMES W. VARGO, Department of Rehabilitative Medicine, University of Alberta (1994 Canadian Carnegie Professor of the Year)

JOHN ZUBIZARRETA, Department of English, Columbia College (1994 South Carolina Carnegie Professor of the Year)

Contents

PART THREE
Teaching Philosophies

Foreword

ERNEST L. BOYER AND THE SCHOLARSHIP OF TEACHING

Ernest L. Boyer, president of The Carnegie Foundation for the Advancement of Teaching, passed away in December of 1995, at the time that the essays in this volume were being completed and compiled. He had intended to write this foreword himself. In his absence, however, we thought it appropriate to draw on his writings and speeches to present his influential view of teaching as scholarly work.

It is in the Carnegie Foundation report *Scholarship Reconsidered: Priorities of the Professoriate* (1990) that Ernest Boyer explores in most depth what it means to be a teacher and a scholar in a college or university. The goal of this report was to move beyond the old debate about "teaching versus research" as faculty priorities, and give to scholarship a broader, more efficacious meaning.

In *Scholarship Reconsidered*, we propose a new paradigm of scholarship, one with four separate yet interlocking parts: the discovery of knowledge, the integration of knowledge, the application of knowledge, and the scholarship of teaching. The first two kinds of scholarship—the discovery and integration of knowledge—reflect the investigative and synthesizing traditions of academic life. The third element, the application of knowledge, moves toward engagement as the scholar asks: "How can knowledge be responsibly applied to real-world problems?" Finally, the scholarship of teaching recognizes that the work of the scholar becomes consequential only as it is shared with others.

Scholarship Reconsidered argues that the academy needs to encourage and reward all four categories of scholarship. The scholarship of discovery—the category that comes closest to what is meant when academics speak of research—should be reaffirmed. But we must also recognize that without integration, knowledge may become pedantry; without application, knowledge may become irrelevant; and without sharing through teaching, the continuity of scholarship may be lost. If higher education is to be enriched by exchange among these different forms of scholarship, a more inclusive view of what it means to be a scholar is needed.

Ernest Boyer recognized that teaching, especially, had become undervalued in recent years. Teaching, we note in *Scholarship Reconsidered*, is too often viewed as a routine function, tacked on, something almost anyone can do. When defined as scholarship, however, teaching both educates and entices future scholars. In the end, we concluded, "inspired teaching keeps the flame of scholarship alive. Almost all successful academics give credit to creative teachers—those mentors who defined their work so compellingly that it became, for them, a lifetime challenge. Without the teaching function, the continuity of knowledge will be broken and the store of human knowledge dangerously diminished."

The importance of the scholarship of teaching is given vivid and compelling expression by the contributors to this important new volume, *Inspiring Teaching: Carnegie Professors of the Year Speak*. The authors are faculty members who have over the years demonstrated their capacity not only to convey knowledge but to inspire and motivate their students to excel both in their college years and beyond. These scholar-teachers are well informed, steeped in the knowledge of their fields. But they also understand that teaching is a dynamic endeavor, requiring the scholar to build bridges between the teacher's understanding and student learning. These award-winning teachers are also learners, learning from their experience with students how to extend their own knowledge in creative new directions.

All forms of scholarship involve sharing. Our academic system readily affirms the value of delivering a paper at a convention; it affirms, too, the value of sharing knowledge through publication. But there remains much work to be done before the scholarship in teaching is recognized and full weight is given to teaching those new to scholarship—those who might multiply its impact far more in years to come than colleagues and peers. Robert Oppenheimer, in a lecture at the 200th anniversary of Columbia University in 1954, spoke eloquently of the teacher as mentor and placed teaching at the very heart of the scholarly endeavor: "It is proper to the role of the scientist that he not merely find new truth and communicate it to his fellows, but that he teach, that he try to bring the most honest and intelligible account of new knowledge to all who will try to learn." Most assuredly, this includes teaching future scholars in the classroom.

Ultimately, quality in the undergraduate experience is defined by quality in teaching. The reward system in higher education simply must recognize professors who are effective in the classroom, who spend time with students, and who engage their colleagues in talk about teaching. Without such a commitment, fine words about strengthening undergraduate education will be simply a diversion. Yet teaching and learning have become more challenging than ever, as our society and our students become more diverse, and as our educational institutions attempt to make good use of new information technology. Looking ahead, it is clear that the scholarship of teaching must be powerfully affirmed.

This is why Ernest L. Boyer and The Carnegie Foundation for the Advancement of Teaching have been especially pleased to join with the Council for Advancement and Support of Education in the Professors of the Year program. We are convinced that the provocative essays published in *Inspiring Teaching* will serve to stimulate discussion of teaching among scholars and to further recognize and encourage excellence in teaching on the nation's campuses. Nothing could be more important for our students and our future.

Robert Hochstein
The Carnegie Foundation for the Advancement of Teaching

Preface

On May 16, 1995, my Claremont McKenna College mail contained a letter from Anker Publishing Company. "We're very interested," the letter said, "in putting together a volume of teaching strategies compiled by the winners of the Carnegie Professor of the Year award." Having received that award in 1988, I had long believed that such a book would be fascinating, useful, and provocative. Now a publisher was inviting us Carnegie professors to create it.

Would I be interested in contributing an essay, the letter asked. Did I have any interest in serving as the general editor for the project, or could I suggest someone who might fill that role? Minutes after reading the letter, I replied by fax. Yes, I would gladly write an essay. More than that, I would be delighted to edit the book as well. One step led to another: *Inspiring Teaching* exists.

The Carnegie Professor of the Year awards recognize exemplary teaching. As Susan Anker and I refined the approach that this book should take, we invited prospective contributors to reflect on the exemplary practices that characterize their teaching successes. These reflections, we suggested, should be personal, practical, and philosophical. The personal background ought to reveal *who* these particular professors are and how they got to be that way. The practical information should provide material or ideas that teachers can readily apply in their classes; it ought to stress *what* the Carnegie professors do, not just the theory but the practice. The philosophical slant should indicate *why* the practices are so important; it ought to offer "food for thought," presenting ideas that cause professors to pause and consider broad educational issues.

In addition to honoring American professors nationally and state-by-state, the Carnegie awards recognize Canadian professors as well. We invited contributions from men and women representing all three of those categories. Some of them were unable to write for the book, but collected here are nineteen essays by Carnegie Professors of the Year who proposed themes, drafted reflections, responded to editorial comments, revised their work, and polished the writing amidst busy schedules. While each essay exhibits the author's particularity—for example, disciplinary perspective and institutional affiliation—all of them contain the personal, practical, and philosophical elements that I requested.

The book has three major parts: "Teaching Characteristics," "Teaching Practices," and "Teaching Philosophies." Like the book's title, those headings contain a rhythm that moves in two ways. It identifies characteristics, practices, and philosophies that inspire teaching. It also highlights teaching that inspires valuable characteristics, practices, and philosophies. Individually, every essay could plausibly fit within any of the book's major categories, but each has its particular place because some authors emphasize one of the book's three dimensions more than others.

"Teaching Teachers," the book's briefer and concluding fourth part, contains two postscripts that sum up how the Carnegie professors may teach other teachers, including themselves. Generously sharing research he has done on the Carnegie professors, John R. Lough wrote one of these postscripts. The other is my attempt to say what one Carnegie Professor of the Year has learned from studying what his colleagues have to say.

When I was offered the chance to edit this book, I wanted to do so because it seemed a fitting way to express gratitude for the recognition I received almost a decade ago. As the project developed, however, I found that I owed more thanks than my work could give. At every point in the book's development, it has been immensely instructive and satisfying to work with Susan Anker. With the help of Jim Anker, she especially is the inspired publisher who made *Inspiring Teaching* possible. Everyone who benefits from this book is indebted to the two of them as well as to the writers—each and all— who labored long and hard to write their clear and helpful essays. From The Carnegie Foundation for the Advancement of Teaching, we owe much to Ernest L. Boyer and Bob Hochstein. At the Council for Advancement and Support of Education, Peter Buchanan, who was instrumental in the growth of the award program and wrote the informative introduction, and Sarah Hardesty Bray and Kim Hughes provided important support and advice.

During the summer of 1995, while I was still making plans for the book, I traveled from Claremont, California, to Oslo, Norway, where I spent my sabbatical year as a Fulbright scholar. International work on the book proceeded without many hitches, thanks to fax messages, e-mail, and phone calls that were often handled by Connie Bartling and her staff in the Faculty Support Center at Claremont McKenna College and by Barbara Lysholt Petersen, executive director of the U.S.-Norway Fulbright Foundation, and her staff in Oslo, Norway. To facilitate the book's production, the various essays had to be organized in a common computerized format. Lyn Roth efficiently handled the necessary word processing. All of these good people deserve and get my heartfelt thanks.

Few persons, if any, have done more to encourage excellent teaching than Ernest L. Boyer, who for many years led The Carnegie Foundation for the Advancement of Teaching. He died while this book was in the making. In many ways its contents bear witness to his vision. With gratitude for his life and work, *Inspiring Teaching* is dedicated to his memory.

John K. Roth
Claremont McKenna College

Introduction

Great professors profoundly affect those they teach way beyond their college years; their contributions often resonate throughout the entire course of their students' lives. The Professors of the Year program celebrates the lifelong impact an excellent teacher can have. Indeed, the program's genesis was a direct reflection of that fact.

It all began in 1981 as a response to the comments of an outstanding alumni volunteer and supporter of education, Thomas B. McCabe, former CEO of Scott Paper. He challenged the Council for Advancement and Support of Education (CASE) and its member educational institutions to recognize teachers like those at his *alma mater*, Swarthmore College, who had inspired him to become an active volunteer and donor. CASE took up the challenge and organized the first annual Professor of the Year competition, with 119 nominees representing 26 disciplines competing to be the top national professor.

The initial goals of the program have remained the same throughout the past 15 years: to recognize outstanding undergraduate instructors for their commitment to teaching, and to acknowledge the role of faculty in helping students reach their dreams. In an era when professors' achievements in research have been more easily measured, and therefore often more easily acknowledged and rewarded, the award has broken new ground by recognizing college and university teaching. That aim is even more important today as the need to encourage good teaching becomes more widely recognized at institutions all across the country. By highlighting excellent instructors, the program identifies models that others everywhere can emulate.

In 1985, CASE also began organizing competitions in various states. And the following year, CASE established an award for faculty at Canadian institutions. This enabled more excellent professors throughout North America to receive recognition.

The Carnegie Foundation for the Advancement of Teaching has contributed to the program's growth since its inception. Carnegie began hosting the final round of judging in 1981, and in 1982 became the sponsor of the cash award given to the U.S. national winner. Through 1993, CASE and Carnegie named only one winner at the national level in the United States.

However, in 1994, the program was restructured to include four award categories based on the Carnegie classification of institutions of higher education: 1) Research and doctoral university; 2) Master's university/college; 3) Baccalaureate college; and 4) Community college. This expansion encouraged wider participation by reinforcing the fact that great teaching occurs at all types of colleges and universities, and by establishing a means to evaluate teaching within the context of various institutional missions. Also in 1994, CASE renamed the award after the Carnegie Foundation because of its historic involvement with the practice and the scholarship of teaching.

Numerous other higher education associations also have supported the program financially or have encouraged the participation of their members. The sponsors of the program include: American Association of Colleges of Nursing; American Association of Community Colleges; American Association of University Professors; American College Testing; American Council on Education; Association of Governing Boards of Universities and Colleges; Council of Independent Colleges; National Association of Independent Colleges and Universities; National Association of State Universities and Land-Grant Colleges; and National University Continuing Education Association.

Today, almost 600 professors are nominated annually, and dozens receive recognition in virtually every state. Institutions acknowledge their winners in a variety of ways, including special receptions, invitations to serve as convocation speakers, award ceremonies during football games, and other honorary campus events. Local communities also honor these outstanding professors, inviting them to be guests on local radio shows and to speak before numerous business, civic, and professional groups. Additionally, local, state, and national media celebrate the accomplishments of the winning professors by featuring them in print and broadcast outlets. These acknowledgements represent the enormous impact the professors have on their immediate and extended environments.

Each year, CASE and Carnegie assemble teams of distinguished experts and opinion leaders in education to serve as judges, including academic deans, faculty members, education reporters, students, government officials, and foundation and association representatives. Several rounds of judging determine the state winners and national finalists; then a grand jury organized by Carnegie selects the final U.S. winners. The primary characteristic the judges consider is an extraordinary dedication to undergraduate teaching, which is demonstrated by excellence in the following areas: impact on and involvement with students; scholarly approach to teaching; service to students, institution, community, and profession; and support from colleagues and current and former undergraduate students.

What specific characteristics make a great professor great? Over the years, the judges have found some common skills, talents, and approaches that most, if not all, excellent teachers bring to their work. The best teachers have a contagious enthusiasm and are "crazy" about the subjects they teach. They motivate students and boost students' self-esteem. The top professors also use participatory or active learning and apply technology creatively in their instruction. They think creatively, are accessible, and engage students in their work.

Great professors usually have a unique and major impact on each of their students. In students' own words:

> The impact of the professor as an educator, motivator, mentor, and friend grows through time . . . no one person has had nearly the magnitude of impact on my career as she has.

> Through his inspiration and encouragement, I have learned to be confident in my abilities, and I plan to pursue further education. I believe that the joy of learning will stay with me throughout my life and career and will challenge me to always be my best.

> By his example, each of us learned how much positive influence one sincere and dedicated individual can have on another. We will not forget.

CASE is extremely proud of its role in creating and administering the Professors of the Year awards program. It is a great honor to be associated with the exceptional individuals who annually receive the award. It is even more gratifying to know that they represent only a fraction of the wonderful teachers throughout the U.S. and Canada—those who bring respect and admiration to the scholarship of teaching by striving daily to make an immeasurable difference in the lives of so many students. We salute them all.

Peter Buchanan, President
Council for Advancement and Support of Education (CASE)

1

What Makes a Good Teacher?

PETER G. BEIDLER

The Lucy G. Moses Professor of English at Lehigh University, Peter Beidler was named the 1983 U.S. Professor of the Year by the Council for Advancement and Support of Education (CASE) and the Carnegie Foundation for the Advancement of Teaching. He teaches and publishes widely in several fields, particularly Chaucer and Native American literature. In 1987–1988, Beidler was a Fulbright professor at Sichuan University in China. He was named the Robert Foster Cherry Distinguished Teaching Professor at Baylor University for 1995–1996.

On September 22, 1995, the *Chronicle of Higher Education* published an acerbic letter to the editor by an assistant professor of history named Antonia Levi, who teaches at Whitman College in Walla Walla, Washington. Professor Levi wrote a bitter renunciation of the whole tenure process in American universities. She wrote, for example: "The sad fact is that by creating lifelong communities and institutionalizing a five- to seven-year apprenticeship in toadyism, tenure is building an academic culture of corruption and cowardice" (p. B3). I do not wish to take issue with her statement about what getting and granting tenure does to the professoriate, but I was interested in her statement that part of the trouble with the system is that "No one has ever defined what . . . makes a good teacher." Actually, of course, thoughtful people have been defining what makes a good teacher ever since they started noticing that there were so many bad teachers in the world. What Professor Levi seemed to mean is that no four people would probably agree on any one definition.

It seems only logical that in a book called *Inspiring Teaching* someone ought to attempt a definition of what a good teacher is. I tried and failed. A good teacher is fair to students, cares about them, and models the life of the mind. No, too sappy. A good teacher loves her students, loves her subject, and loves the society she prepares her students to serve. No, too saccharine. A good teacher always dresses well and maintains good discipline in class. No, too restrictive. Good teachers don't sexually harass their students. No, too controversial. A good teacher motivates students, sets realistic goals for them, and prepares them for an occupation that will prevent them, on their deathbed, from having to look back on a wasted life. No, too career-oriented. Maybe Professor Levi was right. I can't even agree with myself about what makes a good teacher.

I am not a student of the science of pedagogy. I have not read or understood much of the "literature" about what educational psychologists can tell us about the effects of grading, whether lecturing is worse than cooperative learning, or whether "open concept" classrooms work. I can't talk more than thirty seconds about learning styles—and even filling the thirty seconds would mean talking pretty slow. But I have been a student for half of my life. In that half-life, I have had my share of bad teachers and more than my share of good teachers. In my other half-life, I have been a teacher surrounded by other teachers. I have come to develop a sense both of what students expect in responsible teachers and of who among my many colleagues in the professoriate are good teachers. After a lifetime as a student and teacher, I have developed, if not a definition, then a sense of what makes a good teacher.

In this essay I want to talk about ten of the qualities that make a good teacher. My method is absolutely unscientific. Readers who want to know what experts say about good teaching should stop reading right now and open to a different page of *Inspiring Teaching*. Readers who want to know what Pete has noticed about good teaching are welcome to read on. My evidence is personal, memorial, observational, and narrow. I have known teachers in Indiana, Pennsylvania, Arizona, Texas, England, and China. Like Henry David Thoreau, I refuse to apologize for writing so much about myself. There is, simply, no one else I know as well. My hope is that my readers will be inspired to think far less about what I have noticed makes a good teacher than about what they themselves have noticed.

1. GOOD TEACHERS REALLY WANT TO BE GOOD TEACHERS

Good teachers try and try and try, and let students know they try. Just as we respect students who really try, even if they do not succeed in everything they do, so they will respect us, even if we are not as good as we want to be. And

just as we will do almost anything to help a student who really wants to succeed, so they will help us to be good teachers if they sense that we are sincere
in our efforts to succeed at teaching. Some things teachers can fake. Some
things teachers must fake. We have, for example, to act our way into letting
our students know that we can't think of any place we would rather be at 8:10
on a Friday morning than in a class with them talking about the difference
between a comma splice and a run-on sentence. An acting course is a good
preparation for a life in the classroom because it shows us how to pretend.
Our students probably know on some level that we would rather be across
the street sipping a cup of Starbucks coffee than caged up with 24 paste-faced
first years who count on our joyous enthusiasm and enlivening wit to be the
cup of Starbucks that will get them ready for their 9:10 class. But they will
forgive our chicanery, even if they suspect that we are faking our joy. They
will know it by the second day, however, if we don't really want to be good
teachers, and they will have trouble forgiving us for that. Wanting—really,
truly, honestly wanting—to be a good teacher is being already more than
halfway home.

2. GOOD TEACHERS TAKE RISKS

They set themselves impossible goals, and then scramble to achieve them. If
what they want to do is not quite the way it is usually done, they will risk
doing it anyhow. Students like it when we take risks. One of my own favorite
courses was a first-year writing course in which I ordered no writing textbook
for the course. On the first day I announced, instead, that my students and I
were going to spend a semester writing a short textbook on writing. It was, I
said, to be an entirely upside-down course in which the students would write
lots of essays, decide as a group which ones were best, and then try to determine in discussion what qualities the good ones had in common. Whenever
we hit upon a principle that the good essays seemed to embody and that the
weak papers did not, we would write it down. Then we eventually worked
our discovered principles into a little textbook that the students could take
home with them. It was a risky course. It was built on a crazy notion that
first-year college students in a required writing course could, first of all, tell
good writing from less-good writing, and, second, that they could articulate
the principles that made the good essays better. My students knew I was taking a risk in setting the course up that way, but because they knew that my
risk was based on my own faith and trust in them, they wanted me—they
wanted us—to succeed.

We teachers have something called academic freedom. Too many of us
interpret that to mean the freedom from firing. I suggest that we should

interpret it rather as the freedom to take chances in the classroom. I love taking risks. It keeps some excitement in what is, after all, a pretty placid profession. I like to try things that can fail. If there is no chance of failure, then success is meaningless. It is usually easy enough to get permission to take risks, because administrators usually like it when teachers organize interesting and unusual activities. For some risky activities it may be best *not* to ask permission, partly because the risks that good teachers take are not really all *that* risky, and partly because it is, after all, easier to get forgiveness than to get permission. Teachers who regularly take risks usually succeed, and the more they succeed the more they are permitted—even expected—to take risks the next time. Taking risks gives teachers a high that is healthy for them and their students. It makes good teaching, good learning.

3. GOOD TEACHERS HAVE A POSITIVE ATTITUDE
I don't much like being around people who are cynical about their work, who complain about students or student writing or student-athletes or fellow teachers or administrators or trustees or teaching loads or salaries. I occasionally succumb to cynicism myself, but I find that I don't much like *myself* when I am waxing cynical, and I try to unwax myself. I like humor, but not when it is directed against others. I distrust whiners who put themselves into the role of victims. "How can we do anything with the students the admissions office is sending us these days?" "My goodness, I've never had such a hopeless set of students." "Don't the high schools teach them *anything* anymore?" "How do they expect us to teach these kids at 8 a.m.? All they do is sleep after partying all night." "This profession surely isn't what it used to be. Why, I remember . . ." Casting ourselves in victims' roles gets us off the hook, but we teachers ought to enjoy being *on* the hook. We ought to enjoy, not eternally complain about, the challenges students give us. Why do we think we deserve smart, self-motivated, hard-working, wide-awake students—students who do not really need to be taught? Why do we think we deserve not to be challenged? I do not always succeed in being positive about my students or my job, but when I feel the need to scratch my cynical itch, I remind myself that the teachers I admire the most are sometimes frustrated, usually underpaid, always overworked, but rarely cynical or negative, and then almost never about students.

4. GOOD TEACHERS NEVER HAVE ENOUGH TIME
Just about all of the good teachers I have known are eternally busy. They work 80–100 hour weeks, including both Saturdays and Sundays. Their spouses and families complain, with good reason, that they rarely see them.

The reward for all this busy-ness is more busy-ness. The good teachers draw the most students, get the most requests for letters of recommendation, work most diligently at grading papers, give the most office hours and are most frequently visited during those office hours, are most in demand for committee work, work hardest at class preparations, work hardest at learning their students' names, take the time to give students counsel in areas that have nothing to do with specific courses, are most involved in professional activities off campus.

For good teachers the day is never done. While it does not follow that any teacher who keeps busy is a good teacher, the good teachers I know rarely have time to relax. The good teachers I know find that they are as busy teaching two courses as teaching three. They know that they do a much better job with the two courses than the three because they give more time to the individual students, but they also know that for a responsible teacher the work of good teaching expands to fill every moment they can give to it. They might well complain about how busy they are, but they rarely complain, partly because they don't want to take the time to, partly because they don't like whining. Actually, they seem rather to like being busy. To put it more accurately, they like helping students—singular and plural—and have not found many workable shortcuts to doing so.

5. GOOD TEACHERS THINK OF TEACHING AS A FORM OF PARENTING

No one likes to think of college teaching as *in loco parentis*, but the best teachers I know seem to find that their best teaching feels a lot like parenting. By that they do not mean that as teachers they set curfews or lock the dorms up at 11 p.m. or take away television privileges for students who get below a C or confiscate X-rated videos or Jack Daniels. It does not mean that they offer sex education (though they will, if a student trusts them enough to ask), and it does not mean that they offer spiritual instruction (unless a student asks them to). But good teachers seem to find that the caring that goes into their teaching feels a lot like the caring that goes into parenting. It means knowing when to stand firm on a deadline or a standard of excellence, and when to bend or apologize. It means knowing when to give students someone to talk with, when to be the rock that students can test themselves by trying to move out of the way, when to protect students from the ugly evils of the world, and when to let them face those evils in all of their ugliness. It means knowing the difference between soft caring and tough caring. It means recognizing that students are adults, sort of, but children, sort of.

Looking back, I know that as a student I found several father and mother figures among my teachers. And now, at a time in my life when all four of my own children are in graduate school, I know that they are finding replacement parents out there, teachers who are continuing and in some ways correcting the job my wife and I did as parents. But mostly I know that I feel especially comfortable with college students these days. Having just come away from years of parenting young people very much like the ones I see in my class-rooms, I feel that I know them, their insecurities, their problems, their capaci-ties. I feel that I have a reasonably sure instinct about when to stand firm and when to bend, when to be someone to talk with and when to say "Well, see you in class tomorrow" and when to say "Got time for a coffee?" Actually, it feels a lot like love.

6. GOOD TEACHERS TRY TO GIVE STUDENTS CONFIDENCE

I have come to the conclusion that the specific subject matter I teach is less important for itself than for what students learn by learning it. My Chaucer students can for the most part get along in life just fine without knowing much about Chaucer's language or the *Canterbury Tales* or why the low-class Miller feels free enough to tell a raunchy tale in reply to the tale of the high-class Knight. My Chaucer students cannot get along, however, without the confidence they gain by mastering a new language, learning to understand what social classes were in Chaucer's time, and why a miller would, in the car-nival atmosphere of pilgrimage, feel enough courage to joust verbally with a knight. When students write papers, it is far less important that they say something worth reading about the Wife of Bath's fifth husband than that they develop the confidence to know that, when they really do have some-thing important to say, they will be able to say it clearly, forcefully, and with a proper marshaling of evidence.

Allen, one of my best students in 1995, did well on tests and papers, but refused to speak in class. In a conference I asked him why, since he was doing so well, he would not contribute to the classroom discussion. "I guess it kind of scares me," he replied, "with all of those really smart students in there say-ing such intelligent things. I learn more if I just listen." I understood, of course, because I gave similar excuses when I was an undergraduate. Like Allen, I counted on hard work and good test and paper grades to pull me through, but I never talked in class. I told Allen he was as smart and as artic-ulate as anyone in the class, and I hoped he would feel comfortable sharing his ideas with the rest of us. I told him that most of those other students looked and sounded smart in part because I tried always to find something in what they said to praise, because I had tried to develop a knack for creatively rephrasing what they said so they sounded smart, and that if necessary I would do the same for his comments. Shortly after that, he did, once, offer a comment in class, and I said something encouraging about it. But then he clammed up again for the rest of the semester.

About a week after the last class, Allen came in and asked if I would write letters of recommendation for him for his applications to law school. I said I would, of course, but when I found out about his desire to be a lawyer, I knew I should have pressed him even harder to be more aggressive in class. How much of a future is there, after all, for a smart lawyer who does well on tests but is afraid to speak his mind in front of others? Allen will do all right, of course, and he will gain the confidence he needs to succeed in his profession, but I wish I had pushed him harder while I had the chance to force him to feel the confidence he has every right to feel. I think I should have tried harder to knock him off balance.

7. GOOD TEACHERS TRY TO KEEP STUDENTS— AND THEMSELVES—OFF BALANCE

I have learned that when I am comfortable, complacent, and sure of myself I am not learning anything. The only time I learn something is when my comfort, my complacence, and my self-assurance are threatened. Part of my own strategy for getting though life, then, has been to keep myself, as much as possible, off balance. I loved being a student, but being a student meant walking into jungles where I was not sure my compass worked and didn't know where the trails might lead or where the tigers lurked. I grew to like that temporary danger. I try to inject some danger into my own courses, if only to keep myself off balance. When I feel comfortable with a course and can predict how it will come out, I get bored; and when I get bored, I am boring. I try, then, to do all I can to keep myself learning more. I do that in part by putting myself in threatening situations.

A couple of decades ago, I developed a new teaching area—an area I had never had a course in when I was a student: Native American literature. It would have been more comfortable for me to continue with the old stuff I knew, but part of what I knew is that I detest stagnation. I rashly offered the department's curriculum committee a new course. When they rashly accepted it, I was off balance, challenged by a new task in a new area. I now teach and publish in Native American literature regularly.

In 1988 I began to feel that I was growing complacent teaching the privileged students I have always taught at Lehigh University—mostly the children of upper middle class white families. It was getting too comfortable, too predictable. I applied for a Fulbright grant to teach for a year in the People's Republic of China. When the appointment came through, I was scared, but I signed the papers and not long after went with my wife and four teenaged children to Chengdu in Sichuan Province to take up the teaching of writing and American literature to Chinese graduate students. I have never felt so unbalanced in my life—teaching students who could just barely understand me, even when I was not talking "too fast." It was a challenge to teach such students to read the literature of a nation most of them had been taught to hate and to write papers in a language that was alien to them. And that was only part of the unbalance. The rest was riding my bicycle through streets the names of which I could not read, eating with chopsticks food that was almost always unrecognizable and often untranslatable because nothing quite like it grew in my native land. Never have I felt so unbalanced for so long a time, but never have I learned so much in so short a time.

I have noticed that good teachers try to keep their students off balance, forcing them to step into challenges that they are not at all sure they can handle. Good teachers push and challenge their students, jerking them into places where they feel uncomfortable, where they don't know enough, where they cannot slide by on past knowledge or techniques. Good teachers, as soon as their students have mastered something, push their best students well past the edge of their comfort zone, striving to make them uncomfortable, to challenge their confidence so they can earn a new confidence.

8. GOOD TEACHERS TRY TO MOTIVATE STUDENTS BY WORKING WITHIN THEIR INCENTIVE SYSTEM

Most undergraduate students of my generation—at least the ones at Earlham College, where I took my bachelor's degree—were eager to serve their fellow humans. Most of the undergraduates I encounter these days, on the other hand, are eager to make a lot of money. Some humanities teachers complain about the crassness of these students. Others try to figure out ways to use their students' desire for financial security to motivate them. They point out that many business executives were liberal arts majors in college, and that while a good liberal arts background does not always help college graduates get their first jobs in business and industry, once they have that first job they tend to advance more rapidly than graduates with more narrowly technical degrees. They point out that liberal arts graduates know how to synthesize things, how to explain things to others, how to persuade others to their point of view, how to understand the people who make any business work. In English departments, I sometimes point out, we teach students all sorts of money-making skills, like reading and analysis, speaking and writing, picking up ideas quickly, critical thinking, psychology, pedagogy, pattern-finding, drawing conclusions from evidence, persuasion, and so on. We also encourage students to think about why they are on earth, about where they are going, about what some of the greatest thinkers and most creative writers in the past have said about the meaning of human existence, about what is most worth doing in life, and about how wealthy people might best spend their hard-earned money. Good teachers do not complain about how crass the students are these days. They try to understand what makes students tick these days, and then they build on that knowledge to make them tock.

9. GOOD TEACHERS DO NOT TRUST STUDENT EVALUATIONS

Neither do bad teachers. But there is a difference in their reasons for distrusting them. I have noticed that good teachers, when they get really good evaluations, don't quite believe them. They focus instead on the one or two erratic evaluations that say something bad about them. The good teachers tend to trust only the negative evaluations: "I wonder what I did wrong. I suppose I went too fast, or perhaps I should have scheduled in another required conference after that second test. I wish I could apologize to them, or at least find out more about what I did wrong." The not-so-good teachers also do not trust student evaluations, but they distrust them for difference reasons. They tend to trust the positive evaluations but not the negative ones: "Those good evaluations are proof that I succeeded, that my methods and pace were just about right for these students. The others just fell behind because they were lazy, because they never bothered to read the book or study for the exams. Naturally they did not like my course because they put nothing into it. Besides, how can students judge good teaching, and anyhow, what do they know? Anyone can get good student evaluations by lowering their standards, being popular, and by pandering to the masses." Good teachers tend to discount the positive evaluations, however numerous they may be; less-good teachers tend to discount the negative evaluations, however numerous they may be.

10. GOOD TEACHERS LISTEN TO THEIR STUDENTS

Shortly after I read Professor Levi's statement that no one has ever defined what makes a good teacher, I asked the students in my undergraduate Chaucer course at Baylor University (where I was a visiting professor during 1995–96), to write a sentence or two about what, in their own experience, makes a good teacher. The responses ranged widely, but I sorted through the pieces of paper on which they wrote them and put them in different piles. Then I combined the piles into ones that seemed to be generically related. Three quarters of their responses fell into two piles. The first of those I call the "A" pile, the second I call the "E" pile.

In the "A" pile I found words like "accessible," "available," and "approachable." Here are some of the sentences they wrote in response to my question,

"What makes a good teacher?" I have edited them slightly, mostly to put them into more parallel constructions:

Good teachers...

... are available to assist students with questions on the subject, and they show concern.

... do not have a lofty, standoffish attitude.

... can interact with a student on an individual basis.

... want to know each individual student.

... give time, effort, and attention to their students.

... are personable, on your side.

... are willing to be a friend to students.

... are actually interested in the students.

... are actively involved with their students.

... are first friends, then educators. The friend encourages, supports, and understands; the educator teaches, challenges, and spurs the student on.

In the "E" pile I found words like "enthusiastic," "energetic," "excited":

Good teachers...

... love what they teach and convey that love to the class.

... have both an enthusiasm for and an encyclopedic knowledge of the subject.

... have such an obvious enthusiasm for what they do that it is contagious and their students pick up on it.

... have a desire to learn, and for others to learn, all of the exciting things they have learned.

... are obviously excited about teaching. When a teacher enjoys teaching, it is usually obvious, and that enjoyment is passed on to the students. The classes I've had with teachers who loved the subject they were teaching are the ones I've enjoyed the most, and the ones I've been the most eager to learn in. A teacher who isn't enthusiastic can ruin even the most fascinating of subjects.

These students are English majors at a Christian university in Texas. Their answers might well not ring as true for computer science majors at MIT in Massachusetts. The point is not that all good teachers must be available to their students and enthusiastic about what they teach—though that is surely not bad advice for anyone aspiring to be a good teacher. The point is that good teachers listen to what their students try to tell them about what makes a good teacher.

Hey, I've done it! Good teachers are those who want to be good teachers, who take risks, who have a positive attitude, who never have enough time, who think of teaching as a form of parenting, who try to give students confidence at the same time that they push them off balance, who motivate by working within the students' incentive systems, who do not trust student evaluations, and who listen to students. Who says no one has ever defined what makes a good teacher?

But wait. The trouble with good teachers is that, finally, they won't be contained in a corral labeled "good teachers." The trouble with exciting teachers is that they are almost always mavericks, trotting blithely off into some distant sunset where no one can brand them. The trouble with inspiring teachers is that they won't stay put long enough to be measured, perhaps because they know that if they did they would be expiring teachers.

Damn.

2

Stretching Minds: Personal and Academic Aspects of Teaching

JAMES W. VARGO

Since 1975, James Vargo has taught courses in the psychological aspects of illness and disability and in rehabilitation counseling at the University of Alberta, where he is associate dean of undergraduate studies in the faculty of rehabilitation medicine. Co-founder of the Canadian Journal of Rehabilitation, *which he edited from 1987 to 1994, Vargo focuses his research on the psychological factors that affect adjustments to disability and attitudes toward people with disabilities. In 1994, he received the Jack Sarney Award from the Canadian Rehabilitation Council for the Disabled for his lifetime contributions to rehabilitation. The Council for Advancement and Support of Education (CASE) and the Carnegie Foundation for the Advancement of Teaching named Vargo the 1994 Canadian Professor of the Year.*

This essay is an account of one professor's views of teaching—what teaching is and how to practice it well. These views have evolved as a result of twenty-five years of teaching at the college and university levels. I shall discuss both the personal and the academic aspects of teaching, but I want to make clear from the outset that I do not believe that these two facets of teaching and learning can be separated.

The major premise underlying everything that follows is this: What we *are* speaks to students much more loudly than what we *say*. Effective teachers need to present themselves as "real people" to the students. This effort does not mean revealing intimate details about one's life, but it does mean demonstrating to students through various means that the professor has a life outside of the classroom as well. Similarly, I think it is impossible to teach well if the instructor is not enthusiastic about the subject matter. This also means that an effective instructor must be a "real person."

PERSONAL ASPECTS OF TEACHING
Help students view you as a "real person"

I make a conscious effort to get my students to view me first as a person, not just as a professor, administrator, researcher, or psychologist. In my very first class meeting, I mention that I use a wheelchair because, at the age of twelve, I fell from a tree and broke my neck. As a result, I am a quadriplegic with an incomplete lesion between vertebrae C3 and 4. I tell the students these things for three reasons: 1) I believe, especially given their field of study (rehabilitation medicine), that most, if not all, of the students are curious about my disability; 2) my openness shows them that I am not sensitive about talking about my disability; and 3) I know the minute that they entered the room most of the students have diagnosed me anyway, so they might as well find out whether they are right!

Long ago, the psychologist Carl Rogers (1957) stressed the importance of genuineness in the therapeutic relationship. Sociologist Erving Goffman (1959) made complementary observations on what he called "communication out of character" and "the arts of impression management." In both instances, he was alluding to the ways in which many of us feel pressured to hide our "real selves" from others, to play roles, and to present ourselves to certain people in a manner calculated to make a good impression. These masks we all wear from time to time are the antithesis of Rogers's notion of genuineness. I mention these things because I believe that genuineness is one of the necessary conditions of teaching effectiveness.

In this respect, good teaching may be more of an art than a science. Some people seem inherently to possess a natural aptitude for becoming good teachers. Of course, there are also a great many skills required to teach well, but these skills can be learned. In addition, although many may disagree, I believe a sense of humor is crucial to effective teaching. A sense of humor helps add perspective; it's a prism that refracts what may otherwise be invisible into an understandable, sometimes even obvious insight. And other times, it's just funny! (But even this is beneficial because every good belly laugh releases endorphins into the body.)

Another benefit of humor is that it can help to put people at ease. Because any humor I use is totally spontaneous, never scripted, it is difficult for me to recall many specific instances of using humor in the class. One I do remember, though, occurred in a course in which, in my very first class meeting with the students, I start by randomly selecting three students from the class to interview me for approximately ten minutes each on what it is like to live with a spinal cord injury. Understandably, the students are usually nervous. There they are in front of their classmates, having never conducted a clinical interview before, in a situation where they are now interviewing a real person with a disability. Often they are fearful that they might ask or say the wrong thing, hurt my feelings, embarrass themselves, or look incompetent. From my perspective, the purpose of this exercise is to demonstrate that, for the most part, a clinical interview is little more than a conversation structured in a particular way for a particular purpose. I also want the students to realize that an interview need not be intimidating. So one of my goals is to help put the interviewers at ease. One student—she later stated that she was extremely nervous about interviewing me and (to her credit) did not want to dwell only on the negative aspects of disability—asked me, "So what are some of the advantages of having a disability like yours?" My immediate response was, "Well, no one asks me to help with the dishes!" She and the rest of the class broke into laughter. The result was that she became much more relaxed and proceeded with the interview in a way that was more productive for all of us.

Treat students with respect
Everyone, including students, wants respect just as much as you and I do. The American psychiatrist William Glasser (1965, 1972) postulated two psychological needs that each of us has: the need to love and be loved, and the need to feel respected. I attempt to show respect for every student I encounter, and even though I occasionally rail against what I term an "exaggerated sense of entitlement" exhibited by a few of our students, overall I have found that students are rarely disrespectful towards me.

Any instructor who does not show respect for students probably will not receive respect in return. So how can respect be conveyed? First, I attempt to provide a safe learning environment for everyone in the class. This goal is often difficult to achieve in large classes because I don't get to know the students individually. I don't even learn their names. These classes vary in size from 70 students to my all-time high of 104. I also hope that students soon come to recognize that I believe there is no such thing as a stupid question. I attempt to be open to all points of view, even though I do not agree with some of them. (My students also quickly come to terms with my view that not all opinions are of equal value. Uninformed opinion is not given the same consideration as that based on data or grounded in a solid theoretical foundation.)

I also make a point of making myself available to students outside of class. Meeting with them privately goes a long way toward manifesting my interest in them as individuals. Both in and out of class, I attempt to highlight the intrinsic worth of all human beings, including each of them. Some of our students have survived horrendous experiences in their short lives and come to us with high grades and low self-esteem. I (and many other professors) try to impart to them the fact that they are valuable as individuals, as learners, and as citizens. If we can help to underscore that fact and to assist them in believing it, I believe we provide an important service. Rogers (1957) also expressed the essentialness of what he termed "unconditional positive regard." Such regard means valuing people just because they are human and communicating that value to them in our interactions. When this valuing and communicating are done, the students recognize it, feel it, and, if we teach well, live it themselves.

I teach in a facility that has extremely high admission standards. In the physical therapy program, for example, there are typically ten applicants for every person admitted. We are what is called a "quota program," and the quota for physical therapy is 66. That means that we have space for only 66 students, no more. Yet, well over 600 individuals apply every year. As a result, the students in my classes are intelligent and, for the most part, very highly motivated.

Nevertheless, difficulties occasionally arise. Inevitably, some classes contain at least one student who seems to be the human embodiment of a hemorrhoid. In such cases, I have learned that the verbal "Preparation H" is best administered outside the classroom. Despite overwhelming urges to confront a student in the classroom ("Boy, I'll show him!"), I believe that it is rarely, if ever, advisable to confront a student in the presence of classmates. It is much more productive to meet with the "offender" in the privacy of my office. That way the student is more likely to receive the message I want to convey, and it is delivered in an atmosphere where we both save face.

I remember one student who spent nearly all of the first two class meetings reading the campus newspaper and computer magazines. During and after the first class, I did nothing about his behavior. During the second class I also did nothing, but at the end of the second class I asked him to accompany me to my office. With the two of us alone, I told him that I found his behavior distracting, that I had a difficult time concentrating on what I wanted to say when I could clearly see that he was reading something unrelated to class. I asked him if he was aware that I noticed him reading newspapers and magazines in class. "No," he replied, apparently thinking that he was invisible to the professors in his classes because he always sat in the back row. I then asked if he could understand how his behavior might be distracting to me. "Yeah," he said, "I guess so." So I asked him to describe to me in his own words what the difficulty was for me. He did a reasonable job of paraphrasing my concern. Then we made a pact: if he wanted to read other material instead of attending my class, that was OK (although he was still responsible for obtaining that day's notes from a classmate); but it was not OK to read other material while attending my class. He agreed, and the problem was resolved without my having to ask him in front of his classmates to put the campus paper and computer materials away until class was over.

Pay attention to "little things"

The "little things" in life can make a big difference (Lazarus, 1981). As the French philosopher/mathematician Blaise Pascal said: "Little things console us because little things afflict us." I believe this statement is true and that, as a result, the smallest act or word of kindness is seldom given in vain. I have experienced many occasions where former students have thanked me for something that I have long forgotten—little things like bending the rules by backdating a course withdrawal form so the student receives a full refund for the course fee; or lending my building master key to a student who left her purse in a now-locked teaching lab; or requesting special consideration from a departmental admission committee to accept a late application from an out-of-town applicant who gave her application to her parents to submit personally when they were in town (so it wouldn't get lost in the mail), but the parents forgot! Or, to cite one final example, spending up to four hours per student (a limit I impose) counseling them, at their request, about personal issues in their lives. Some crisis intervention may be all they need to help them over the rough spots. Those who need more extensive help I refer to Student Counseling Services.

None of these examples are major favors or interventions. They're just little things. But I have discovered that little things mean a lot to the recipients of our actions, and so it is probably best if we try to make those little things positive ones. What I may consider to be a small favor may be a large favor indeed to the recipient. Sometimes a small act of kindness makes a big difference, but for it to do so, we must take the time to perform the act. Even the smallest deeds always outperform the grandest intentions. That is where I, too, often fail. I *intend* to make that call, send that note, or drop by to say hello. But in the hustle-bustle world of academic life, I sometimes don't follow through. It's unfortunate when this happens, because it means that I am allowing myself to be a prisoner of my own busyness. Inertia takes hold instead of the vigilance that is required.

ACADEMIC ASPECTS OF TEACHING

View students as candles to be lit, not as reservoirs to be filled

Seeing students not as receptacles to be filled but as candles to be lit means that I don't consider students to be human vats to be crammed with as much information as classroom times permits. Rather, I hope to provide a spark to ignite a candle or kindle a desire to learn just for the intrinsic value of learning. Of course, the only evidence that I have regarding my success in this respect is anecdotal. Recently a student who was in one of my classes approached me to say how much he enjoyed the course and that he was certain that he learned much more from the class meetings than his final grade in the course reflected. He was not saying his grade was unfair—just that he believed that he had benefited more from the course than any examination could measure. This type of informal feedback is heartwarming and relatively common.

Nonetheless, all courses contain information that must be imparted. How can we convey concepts that are abstract and difficult for many students to learn? The principle is simple: Relate unfamiliar concepts to what learners already know. My teaching style is one in which I make great use of quotations, analogies, examples, and anecdotes. I have been told a number of times that I have a rare ability to make abstract concepts real. I believe this simply means that I am able to translate these concepts into concrete, applicable terms. I don't believe that there is any magic in this or any secret to doing it. It simply is a result of discussing theoretical constructs in practical terms that are down-to-earth. The philosopher Benedict Spinoza knew this long ago: "The more intelligible a thing is, the more easily it is retained in the memory, and contrariwise, the less intelligible it is, the more easily we forget it" (Lorayne, 1986, p.10). And a mind once stretched by a new idea never returns to its original dimensions.

To vary a statement attributed to Gail Godwin, good teaching is probably about 40 percent content and 60 percent theater (Byrne, 1988, p. 159). What I mean, first, is that, regardless of what subject matter we teach, the content changes quickly. The information I teach in class today will not be the knowledge of tomorrow. According to Janice Moyer, president of the Information Technology Association of Canada, the cumulative total of all knowledge that was acquired up until the end of 1991 was just one percent of what will be available approximately fifty years from now (*Globe & Mail,* 1992). Similarly, Richard Warch, president of Lawrence University in Wisconsin, estimated that about 100,000 scholarly journals currently exist, with nearly 1,000 new ones appearing each year (Warch, 1991, p. 8). He calculated that, just for professional journals of science alone, researchers are pumping out published manuscripts at the rate of one every 30 seconds, 24 hours a day, 365 days a year! (When I make this point to students in reference to the information explosion, I gently reassure them that they won't be assigned *all* these readings—even though some days it may seem to them that they have been.)

The point is that the students I teach in 1996 will need to possess much different knowledge to be state-of-the-art clinicians in their disciplines in the year 2006. If they still use 1996 technology, they will be dismally out of date. As a result, I attempt to emphasize to all students—at both the undergraduate and graduate levels—that professionals in all disciplines must keep reading the current research in their fields and continue learning throughout their lives or they will soon become obsolete. What I can do as a professor if I am doing my job well is to instill in students a passion for lifelong learning. That is what I mean by theater—turning students on to learning so that they don't believe that once they have graduated they know all there is to know and will never have to learn more. I have failed any student who lives by that fallacy. As Will Rogers said, "It's not what we don't know that hurts, it's what we know that ain't so" (Byrne, 1988, p. 578).

For me, the theater aspect of my teaching involves many things. First and foremost, it means demonstrating enthusiasm for what I'm teaching and showing that it's important to me that the students learn it. It means speaking from notes, not reading them. My class notes consist of little more than an outline to keep me on track, with a few key points under each so that I won't forget to mention them. The purpose of my notes is to ensure that I am providing today's learners with sufficient content for them to comprehend the basics of the subject matter at hand. Elaboration comes via free-flow. I rely on the appropriate synaptic connections to be there because, other than what's contained in my notes, what I say is largely a result of wherever my free association takes me. And where it takes me depends on whatever related experiences, quotes, anecdotes, books, movies, research papers, or news items come to mind. I like this style of teaching because it keeps me fresh, involved, and interested, which, in turn, I believe, keeps the class interested as well.

I started teaching this way when I first taught college courses. One of my teaching assignments was three sections of an introductory psychology course. The sections met back-to-back three times a week. If I had taught every section in exactly the same way, by the time I got to the third class, I would have been asleep! There is a downside to this style of teaching, however. Because so much of what I say is *ad lib*, there are some days when I'm not "on" quite as well as on others. Nonetheless, I do believe that I have many more classes in which I am "on" than in which I am not. And it is so much fun to teach this way.

Help students to develop a passion for reading
In my classes, I often mention in passing the reading I have done or am doing at the time. I do so because I try to infuse in students a passion for reading, both for pleasure and for professional development. It astonishes me that,

according to Alvin Kernana in his book *The Death of Literature,* approximately 60 percent of adult Americans who have finished school claim they have not read a single book since that time, and most of the rest say they read about one book a year (cited in Kesterton, 1992).

I consider books to be the gentlest and most patient of teachers. I hope to encourage my students to love reading as well. Sometimes I do this by talking about what I have read in the past (both fiction and nonfiction) that is salient to the topic at hand. I do have some perennial favorites, fictional and real characters who assist me in clarifying or illustrating certain points. A sample of my fictional "friends" includes George and Lenny, "Doc," the Joad family (Steinbeck); a number of characters from Shakespeare; crusty Joe Alton (Wallace Stegner); Tom Sawyer and Huck Finn (Mark Twain); and Grandpa E. Rucker Blakeslee and Will Tweedy (Olive Ann Burns). Nonfictional characters who often enter my classes are too numerous to mention, but favorites include Socrates, Plato, Aristotle, Confucius, Lao Tsu, the Buddha, Catherine the Great, Albert Einstein, Winston Churchill, Marie Curie, Will Rogers, Bertrand Russell, Franklin Delano Roosevelt, Eleanor Roosevelt, and a host of novelists, psychologists, and psychiatrists.

Occasionally, I also find opportunities to insert into a lecture a brief comment about what I'm reading now (again, fiction and nonfiction). I view books as friends, consultants, and sources of inspiration. I bring books and articles to class. I lend them to interested students. (Yes, some are never returned, which brings to mind a quote by Anatole France: "Never lend books, for no one ever returns them; the only books I have in my library are books that other folk have lent me.") But what is most reassuring to me is that sometimes students recommend and/or lend books to me as well. Maybe they're getting it!

As mentioned earlier, one of my most basic goals in teaching is attempting to get learners interested in the subject matter I am teaching. In addition, if I can help to teach them how to learn and instill an interest in or even a passion for learning, then I believe I have done my job. Students need to realize that there are many ways of learning and that many of the great thinkers in history were not "typical" students. Many of them had their own idiosyncratic ways of learning, and the world is a better place as a result. Einstein correctly said, "Imagination is more important than information" (Fulghum, 1988, p. 135). In my view, however, that thought has to be balanced by one from Confucius: "Learning without thought is labor lost."

One of the most difficult things for me to accomplish, especially with students who are in a field such as physical therapy (where many of them want "the answer"), is to impress upon them that there are many questions in life that have no answers, or that perhaps the answers are different for different people or even different for the same people at different times in their lives. In my experience, students who enter professions in the sciences have a low tolerance for ambiguity. But the major questions, issues, and concerns of life are often ambiguous, and thus, I believe, we need to develop a much higher tolerance for ambiguity or we will be discouraged, disappointed, and depressed much of the time. Reading provides one way to learn that lesson without having to experience the pain of living through it first-hand. Despite his melancholy manner, perhaps Franz Kafka had the right idea when he said, "A book ought to be an ice pick to break up the frozen sea within us" (Winokur, 1990, p. 46).

Differentiate between making a living and learning how to live
Probably everyone needs two different types of education: one to teach us how to make a living, and one to teach us how to live. Most of my teaching emphasizes the former, but, whenever I have the opportunity and in whatever way I can, I like to help students with the latter as well. I attempt to convey the message that, in this highly competitive world where most of us are our own worst critics, it probably behooves each of us to measure ourselves by our best moments, not by our worst. In addition, I pepper my lectures with some of my favorite aphorisms about life. Here are a few that I use:

"The more a man knows, the more he forgives." (Catherine the Great)

"You are no bigger than the things that annoy you." (Jerry Bundsen)

"There are no people living who aren't capable of doing more than they think they can do." (Henry Ford)

"We make a living by what we get. We make a life by what we give." (Author unknown)

"There is more to life than increasing its speed." (Mahatma Gandhi)

"For fast-acting relief, try slowing down." (Lily Tomlin)

"Life itself still remains a very effective therapist." (Karen Horney)

The quotation above from psychotherapist Karen Horney reflects the truth that real learning does not come just from experience. It comes from what you do as a result of your experience. This sentiment has been expressed by many people throughout history, including Emerson, who said, "The things taught in schools and colleges are not education, but the means of education." In other words, just knowing what to do is not sufficient; one must actually do it. The same notion was conveyed in a business magazine called

Bits and Pieces: "It is not so much what we know as how well we use what we know" (July 20, 1995, p. 3).

Of course, one of the hazards of attempting to impart this message is that the reaction is often that what is being said is only common sense. I used to cringe inwardly when a student responded in such a manner, but now I relish that response because it provides me with the opportunity to talk about what our collective notion of common sense is. The fascinating thing about common sense is that it is extremely uncommon. This is clearly delineated by L. E. Joseph (1994), who provides evidence that the practice of common sense in all societies is probably quite rare.

Many people believe that common sense involves knowing the right thing to do; I attempt to stress that common sense is doing the right thing. Knowing that smoking is injurious to your health is no advantage if you continue to smoke. The same principle pertains to all knowledge that is potentially applicable. To know something but not to do it is just as disadvantageous as not knowing it. Many people in the world seem not yet to have learned this lesson. The last word on common sense goes to Joseph who wrote: "To say that someone has good common sense is to pay no small compliment; it implies a sharp eye for the significant, a grasp of the obvious—like seeing the emperor's new clothes—that at times makes everyone else seem colorblind" (1994, p. 1).

CONCLUSION

In conclusion, let me reiterate that although I have distinguished the personal from the academic aspects of teaching for the purposes of this discussion, in reality I believe them to constitute the yin and yang of practice. Both aspects are necessary for effective classroom teaching; neither one alone is sufficient.

There are few activities I would rather engage in than teaching. I am fortunate that my university position allows me to participate in a variety of activities including research, service, and administration as well as teaching. But to date there is no doubt that the greatest satisfaction I receive is from teaching. I practice in a profession that allows me to enter the lives of others and perhaps to influence them for the better. I look forward to almost every class. I hope the students feel the same.

AUTHOR'S NOTE

I would like to express my appreciation to Al Cook, dean of the faculty of rehabilitation medicine, for his many helpful suggestions on how to improve previous drafts of this essay. Al has a rare ability to provide feedback that makes me feel supported, not criticized. Thanks, too, go to John Roth, this book's editor. His encouragement and patience were just what I needed during a time when other events in my life made it seem that the words you read here would never appear on paper.

REFERENCES

Byrne, R. (1988). *1,911 best things anybody ever said.* New York, NY: Fawcett Columbine.

Fulghum, R. L. (1988). *All I really need to know I learned in kindergarten: Uncommon thoughts on common things.* New York, NY: Ivey Books.

Glasser, W. (1965). *Reality therapy: A new approach to psychiatry.* New York, NY: Harper & Row.

Glasser, W. (1972). *The identity society.* New York, NY: Harper & Row.

Goffman, E. (1959). *The presentation of the self in everyday life.* New York, NY: Anchor.

Joseph, L. E. (1994). *Common sense: Why it's no longer common.* Reading, MA: Addison-Wesley.

Kesterton, M. (1992). Social studies column. *Globe & Mail.* February 26.

Lazarus, R. S. (1981). Little hassles can be hazardous to your health. *Psychology Today.* July 1981.

Lorayne, H. (1986). *Harry Lorayne's page-a-minute memory book.* New York, NY: Ballantine.

Rogers, C. R. (1957). The necessary and sufficient conditions of therapeutic personality change. *Journal of Consulting Psychology 22,* 95–103.

Warch, R. (1991). Communities of mind and spirit. *The Teaching Professor 5* (8), 6.

Winokur, J. (Ed.). (1990). *Writers on writing.* Philadelphia, PA: Running Press.

3

Classroom Atmosphere: A Personal Inventory

HARVEY D. BLANKESPOOR

 *The Frederich Garrett and Helen Floor Dekker Professor of Biology at Hope College, Harvey Blankespoor was named the 1991 U.S. Professor of the Year by the Council for Advancement and Support of Education (CASE) and the Carnegie Foundation for the Advancement of Teaching. His earlier awards for teaching and scholarship include the Class of 1923 Literature, Science, and Arts Award for Outstanding Teaching of Undergraduates, which he received at the University of Michigan in 1976, and the Outstanding Professor-Educator Award, as voted by the senior class, which he received at Hope College in 1980.*

My interest in becoming a teacher did not begin until I was a junior in college. Little encouragement to become a teacher was given by my parents because they did not have an opportunity to receive a formal education themselves. In fact, neither my father nor my mother was able to attend high school because they were members of large rural families. Each was expected to contribute significantly on the family farm. So there was no time for much formal education.

My parents set stringent restrictions on my older brother, but they were less restrictive with my younger brother. As for me, I was allowed to play sports and to sing in the choir, but with the understanding that I had to spend a lot of time preparing the fields for planting or harvesting the crops. After high school, my two brothers and I continued our education. All three of us graduated with Ph.D.s in science within one year of each other.

By the end of my junior year in college, I had decided to enter the teaching profession. Enthusiastically, I enrolled in the necessary education courses to obtain a teaching certificate for secondary education in Iowa. The last course was student teaching, which took place in the small town of Hull, Iowa. This experience played a very important role in shaping my interests and my drive to become a good teacher.

Student teaching was a very fulfilling experience for me. Upon its completion, I was sure that I had made the correct decision—to become an educator. Unfortunately, my teaching supervisor thought otherwise. I was shocked, disappointed, and somewhat bitter when I received a low grade for my student teaching. I made an appointment to see my instructor. Candidly, he gave me his criteria for the grade and at the conclusion of our brief conversation, he suggested that it might be in my best interest to decide on another career. After some deliberation, however, I decided to continue in education. My decision was validated when the school where I had done my student teaching offered me a job. From that point on, I looked at myself as a teacher, and I have always tried to find better ways of educating.

Since receiving the Carnegie award as Professor of the Year in 1991, I have often been asked, "What is the secret of being an outstanding teacher?" A similar question was asked by President George Bush while we discussed education in the Oval Office of the White House.

I feel very strongly that a teacher must continue to evaluate his or her classroom performance to see if the job of teaching can be done better or to find other ways to become more effective. This essay will not deal with the latest theories about learning and teaching. Instead, it will deal informally and personally with my ways of teaching in the classroom and in the laboratory. Although my readers may not be teaching biology, I will try to include practical applications that will apply to any specialty or discipline. My hope is that my readers and their students may benefit from what I present. Finally, understand that the way an individual teaches needs to be molded by interests and style of teaching. I have my style because of the type of person I am and because of my interests and background.

WHAT ARE MY BIASES?

Professors often take certain biases with them into their classrooms, and those biases may be barriers to good learning. When I first began teaching, my focus was on the class as a whole and not on individual students. For example, those enrolled in Biology 372 (Biology of Animal Parasites) at Hope College were my parasitology class. I did not attempt to treat each student as an individual—with his or her unique abilities, background, and interests. But as I started taking a personal inventory, I found that I had to overcome certain biases that made me less effective as an educator. It should be noted, however, that students need to make reciprocal adjustments because they, too, have biases about their classmates, teachers, and often about learning as well. Some of the prejudicial baggage that we may carry with us in the classroom may include the following elements.

Favoring the best students

Most educators are more generous with their time for students who are highly motivated and who perform well. Often lengthy discussion or discourse in our field of interest is not possible because our students do not have the drive and background of graduate students. Perhaps at the expense of lower achievers, most of us like to interact with those who are doing well in our class.

Gender

Some professors spend much more of their time with members of one gender. They seem to identify and relate better with male or female students. This tendency can be frustrating for those students who do not get the attention they deserve.

Athletic ability

As an active participant in sports—intercollegiate and nonintercollegiate—I find it very easy and natural to initiate conversation with student athletes. Unfortunately, I have not always spent as much time becoming informed about students who actively participate in nonathletic activities on campus. I became much better informed about campuswide activities, however, when my wife and I moved on campus several years ago. As a result, my rapport with students in general has improved.

Race

I was reared in a farming community in the Midwest, where I was exposed to very few people of non-Caucasian backgrounds. It was not that I had innate biases. Rather, I felt reluctant to approach minority students, partly because I was afraid that I would say the wrong thing. Not until I conducted research in other continents (Africa and South America) did I feel comfortable being around students of ethnic backgrounds different from my own. On one occasion, I was in Sudan for more than two months before I saw another Caucasian.

Level of student

Many professors prefer to teach students in upper-level courses. They find more fulfillment through interaction with students who have more extensive backgrounds, who are critical thinkers, and who have better oral and written skills. Such teachers may focus their efforts on these students at the expense of those in freshman-level courses. In many institutions, teaching first-year students is work done by new faculty or by those who have the lowest seniority in the department. I strongly feel that we must take a personal interest in developing students at all levels. In my opinion, it is necessary to have some of the best teachers involved in the introductory courses.

Student appearance

Many of us would not admit that we have biases toward people based on their appearance. But we professors ought to ask ourselves: Based on the way students style their hair, the type of clothes they wear, or their economic status, are we influenced negatively or positively? If so, how does that influence affect our interaction with and evaluation of our students?

Cultural background

One of the benefits of our shrinking world is that students in our courses often have different cultural backgrounds. This means that we have new resources in our courses. Do we take advantage of the fact that these students can add a lot to our classes? Do we make those students feel comfortable in our classroom or laboratory settings? Some students may not write while you are talking, because that seems impolite to them. Others prefer that you don't point at them or look them in the eye.

A good way to monitor whether some or all of these biases are present or absent from our classrooms is to do an assessment. Such assessment can be done, for example, by asking students specific questions at the time of the course evaluation. These questions might include: Did you feel accepted in the course? Why or why not? Were you at any time offended?

The key to reducing or eliminating biases about students is to take a personal interest in every student. This can best be achieved by maximizing the opportunities for interaction with them, both inside and outside the classroom, laboratory, or studio. Group activities such as discussions, projects, and hands-on experiments are some of the ways to provide natural settings for student-faculty interaction.

My wife and I take advantage of the fact that we live on campus. We are with or around students every day and night, including weekends. One unique activity that we use to meet students, especially those from abroad, involves our bread machine. On Tuesday nights, we hold a bread raffle in one of the dorms. Students sign up by room for the raffle. The winners are invited to come at 10:00 p.m. for hot bread, butter, honey, and jelly preserves. They come to our apartment for the prize and usually stay for about half an hour. This event gives them a study break while it give us a chance to meet the students. On another evening, usually Thursday, we reserve a loaf of fresh bread for invited students, often those who come from foreign countries.

WHAT KIND OF LEARNING ENVIRONMENT DO I PROVIDE?
When I began teaching, most of my time and effort were spent on passing subject information to my students. Although I believe that the subject material is still important, I now place more emphasis on teaching attitudes and intrinsic values as well. I am very concerned about the learning climate or atmosphere in the classroom and laboratory. For example, I tell my students that our class is "family" for the semester, and that I expect them to make contributions to our class "family" in the same way they do in their own families. I want them to be positive, sensitive, considerate, polite, and tolerant. I want every one of my students to find their experiences to be very positive and rewarding. I try to make my classroom one where students and professor are happy and helpful.

The classroom's physical setting
Several years ago, a friend entered my classroom and asked, "What is taught in this room?" This question slammed me because my area of science is biology, the study of life. I realized that I was teaching about life, but my students were getting a very limited exposure to living organisms. So three major changes occurred in my classroom: 1) I placed plants throughout my classroom; 2) A portable aviary was constructed for tropical finches; and 3) I installed modern audiovisual equipment. This equipment allows me to play music at specific times. Most of the music includes animal sounds as part of the background. As a result of these changes, other faculty members want access to the room, and students find it a favorite place to study during evenings and on weekends. The students have a positive impression of the room and of the activities they have done there.

Interaction
The key to having a good learning environment in the classroom is to work with small groups or on a one-to-one basis. We learn about each other as individuals in the context of such a classroom setting and its hands-on activities. We discuss science, family, the students' future, their careers, hobbies, sports, and politics. I find that the students respond very favorably to this style of teaching. With this approach to teaching, I spend a lot more time in preparation for my classes because I am continually seeking different activities that allow me to work with the students in an informal setting.

During the summer of 1992, I taught a field course in parasitology at the University of Michigan biological station. The previous academic year had been a very difficult one for me, because I gave more than forty lectures and seminars around the country, served as chairperson of my biology department, and had a heavy teaching load. During the summer, I also tried to keep an active research program going, one that involved a lot of students. When the course began, I was physically tired and emotionally and intellectually drained. Do you know the feeling?

On the first day of class, I told my students—comprising undergraduates and graduates—that I was physically tired and emotionally drained, and that for those reasons I was not ready to teach. I told them that I needed their help and patience to make the course a meaningful experience. I knew that they expected a lot because they had heard about my Carnegie award, and in the past the students had liked my Ecology of Animal Parasites course very much. The students responded by making that 1992 class one of the best I have had during my nearly thirty years of teaching.

My needs at that particular time appeared to be the glue that cemented those students together, irrespective of their interests and backgrounds. Many of them offered to assist me with mundane tasks such as mixing chemicals, driving vans, washing glassware, replenishing empty flasks, and sweeping the laboratory floors. In addition, they made a special effort to work together on course assignments such as lab reports, observing microscope slides, and collecting field materials. During leisure time, they would invite me to play sports, attend movies, and accompany them on hikes.

One event that I will never forget was a weekend trip to the Osborne Tract, a property that had been donated to the University of Michigan. The parcel consists of approximately forty acres located near the southern tip of Sugar Island, just south of Sault Ste. Marie, Michigan, on the banks of the St. Mary's River. Typically, we trap small mammals and "mist net" birds to give students the opportunity to handle animals, draw blood, stain for parasites, and identify pathogens. The students have some time to hike trails, play cards, read, or refine their photographic techniques. On this particular Saturday afternoon, members of the class decided to play capture the flag. We played until dark.

Everyone enjoyed being together, whether it was working or playing, and we formed a close bond. On the last day of class, most of us had tears in our eyes, knowing that our "family" would never be together again.

Personal relationships and professional expectations
During the semester, students from all of my classes are invited to my home to meet my family, to eat, to participate in games, and to talk about upcoming exams. In addition, we meet to play Frisbee, or go get ice cream, or take in a

movie. Because we get to know each other very well, I find out about some of the crises the students have in their lives: family deaths, broken relationships, sicknesses. I have a chance to be sensitive to their needs.

I want to emphasize, however, that I do not let the students take advantage of me. In fact, some of my practices are quite rigid. For example, I rarely give make-up exams. During the semester, I give three or four regular exams, plus a cumulative final. Students are allowed to drop their lowest hourly test, but they must take the final. If they miss an exam because of problems such as those mentioned above, that missed exam is the one they drop, irrespective of their performance on the others.

DO I PRACTICE THE POSITIVE ATTRIBUTES OF A GOOD TEACHER?

An important component of any classroom is the teacher. There are several attributes of a good teacher that make the classroom atmosphere conducive to quality learning. Some of them include the following.

Concern

I want every student in my classroom to know that I am interested in them as individuals and that I care about their performance. My goal is to make this concern permeate all aspects of my teaching. The students will know that I care by the way I teach and by my interaction with them outside of class. On the first exam, for example, I tell them that I hope they all do well. This does not mean that my courses are easy or that I "spoon feed" the students; quite the contrary.

It is my experience that students need affirmation a lot more than they need reprimands. One way to give positive strokes is to comment on exams, especially on the essay questions.

Enthusiasm

A professor's enthusiasm can be contagious. Every course should be a fresh start with new students to motivate and to educate. As one gains experience, however, it is easy to lose vigor and enthusiasm. We professors need to ask ourselves: If we are excited about teaching, do our students get the same excitement? Is each year a unique experience, or are we teaching the same year ten times?

Creativity

Another key component of excellent teaching is creativity, which breaks routines and makes communication much more effective. In science, I work constantly to find better ways of presenting the subject material. Using investigative approaches in biology usually motivates students.

Many students resist memorizing factual information, but in biology mastery of such information is important. By the end of the course, I expect my students in Biology 251 (Biology of Insects) to recognize approximately 100 families of insects. If I gave the students the whole list of families at one time and then tested them, many would not do well on the exam. However, if I spend the first five or ten minutes of each lab reviewing some of the insect families, the memorization becomes easier and much more palatable. I repeat this procedure each day of class for a week, and then I select another set of insect families to review in the next week.

Special vocabulary words are important components in many science classes. Students often misspell such words on exams and in laboratory reports. When I first began teaching, I was very stringent about penalizing those mistakes. It would usually cost students a point for each typing error or misspelling. Because students complained bitterly, and because they often made few attempts to correct their errors, I decided on a compromise. For each exam or report, I record a list of misspellings for the whole class. This list is given to the students. If they subsequently misspell any words on the list, I subtract a point for each misspelled word.

High expectations

Essay questions make up 25–30 percent of my exams. Thus, I stress the importance of writing, and I expect students to improve their writing skills throughout the semester. An important component of this improvement involves proofreading their own writing and mine. On exams, I give students bonus points for spotting typing errors, poor grammar, and misspellings. I usually plant a few errors of this kind in the tests to give students added incentive to examine critically everything they read. If they circle a word that is incorrectly spelled, I add a couple of points to their test scores.

As I mentioned earlier in this essay, I strongly emphasize "doing science" in the laboratory. This "doing" means that students learn a lot of techniques—for instance, staining whole mounts, pinning insects, preparing material for microscopy, and taking pictures. In my teaching I often discover that students bring inadequate techniques into the laboratory. For example, they may use microscopes improperly, leave bottles uncapped, label lids rather than containers, and use ballpoint pens for labeling. In addition, they may leave dirty glassware, dissection tools, and containers on the laboratory benches. It can be a continual battle to keep the laboratory from looking like a disaster area. But the conditions greatly improved once I began assigning two students to weekly laboratory duties. Among other things, this responsibility makes them aware of how much work is required to keep the laboratory tidy.

Role modeling

Students want to know their teachers as individuals. I feel so strongly about this that my wife and I sold our five-bedroom home so we could live on campus in a dormitory as faculty in residence. Because many of our students come from single-parent families, it is important for us professors to teach them intrinsic values both inside and outside of the classroom. For example, students need to be taught to work diligently in their courses. Students often say that my courses require an unusual amount of work and time, but they also know that nobody spends more time in the course than I do.

DO I REINVENT MY TEACHING PERIODICALLY?

Some professors are reluctant to make changes because they find it difficult to cope with the possibility that the changes may not work. Nevertheless, as one pursues the important task of taking a personal inventory of one's teaching, it is also essential to set new goals, implement new ideas, and reassess the outcomes. This effort requires a teacher to become vulnerable, because new methods are not always successful. I had such an experience a few years ago.

Because my students usually give oral reports, I decided that it would be a good idea to have them critique and evaluate each other. Eight criteria that served as the basis of the evaluation were placed on a sheet, and each student had an evaluation form for each presenter. Specific points were assigned for each criterion. If a student gave an outstanding report, he or she would receive 90–100 points. Points for an average oral presentation would be between 80–90, and a below average score would be between 70–80. After twenty-six students presented their papers, I tallied the scores and found that the average score for the class was 99. While discussing the evaluation process with the students, it became obvious that they did not like to evaluate their peers. This particular experiment did not work, and I had to try another approach.

As we professors evaluate our teaching and look for good innovations, an excellent resource is the expertise of colleagues. Within a department, division, or discipline, the sharing of new ideas and insights about teaching styles and methods is one hallmark of an institution that provides quality education. Through this sharing process, individual professors can continually take inventory of their own courses. Such evaluation usually leads to changes and rewards.

When students begin a new course, they do not always have a positive feeling toward the subject material or the professor. On some campuses, students from one division may shy away from courses taught in another. These prejudices often exist among students in the humanities and the sciences. In my opinion, the cardinal sin of teaching is to have students feel less positive toward me or toward the subject areas that I teach at the end of the course than they did at the beginning.

Revamping teaching styles and techniques requires much time, energy, and creativity. But the rewards for outstanding teaching cannot be paralleled by any other profession.

4

Connecting with Literature: The Art of Involvement

BARBARA PAUL-EMILE

Professor of English at Bentley College, Barbara Paul-Emile teaches nineteenth-century English literature, Caribbean literature, and African American literature. This breadth of focus allows her to combine her interests in myth and in Third World literature with her knowledge of European colonial literary influences. In addition to her many scholarly articles, Paul-Emile publishes fiction, including a novel titled DreamWalker. *She is working on a collection of stories set in the Caribbean. Frequently honored for her outstanding teaching, Paul-Emile has received the Adamian Award for Teaching Excellence and the Teaching Innovation Award from Bentley College as well as the Distinguished Scholar Award from the University of Massachusetts, which honors black scholars in New England. She was also named the 1994 Massachusetts Professor of the Year by the Council for Advancement and Support of Education (CASE) and the Carnegie Foundation for the Advancement of Teaching.*

Teachers are drawn to their profession by their love for their subjects and by their willingness to join with others in the enterprise of creating a community of learners. Education is, in its essence, a communal endeavor. It involves enlarging the parameters of our world by making connections between the known and the unknown, the finite and the infinite. All genuine learning serves to awaken us to the nature of our contributions to the dance of life.

The telling, reading, and dramatization of tales or poetry is literature and as such is essential to the human experience. Humans have lived without many conveniences, but society has not survived well without literature, whether in its spoken or written form. In the classroom, among my objectives is the brave intent to share my love of literature with my students, to increase their knowledge and understanding of the subject, and to stimulate personal involvement and response.

I seek to enliven and enrich my literature classes by developing a variety of methods to connect students with assigned material. First, I have learned over the years that the level of enthusiasm and dynamism the instructor brings to the class plays a crucial role in determining student response. Second, students' involvement and interest are immeasurably increased if their personal investment is sought and texts are approached with fresh eyes and ears and a sense of discovery. It is also important that the class bonds to form a vigorous learning community that sets out with the instructor to discover what the material has to offer. Third, students must be encouraged to integrate their new knowledge and their own lives in holistic ways.

Learning need not remain an intellectual exercise alone. It can become a living and transforming agent if, as a learning community, both students and teachers take the journey to understanding together. This essay presents my approach to teaching and learning and the methods I have developed to bring classroom material to life.

SPARKS AND FIRES

At the beginning of each semester, like so many of my colleagues, I go forward with courage and much good intention to fulfill worthy goals, unmindful of the many challenges that lie ahead. Along with the tasks and multiple roles that teachers undertake is the expectation that they will, somehow, generate the spark that energizes the classroom, provide vital life-shaping information, and immortalize texts in the minds of students. No doubt all of these ideals are lofty; nevertheless, effort must be made to attain them. The first step requires that the spark of interest and enthusiasm be lit within the consciousness of the teacher. Then the larger issue follows of transferring that spark to students individually and as a group, for it is from our inner fires that students light their candles. They look to us for nourishment, not only of the intellect but of the spirit.

There are times when busy faculty members feel that presenting information to their classes with thoroughness and diligence is enough. In the same way, there are students who feel that listening carefully in class, taking notes, and doing well on the examinations are sufficient. Information gathered and stored in this way, however, seems to slip away quietly over time. Learning becomes an intellectual exercise removed from our psychological and feeling centers. If education is to have an impact that lasts beyond the final examination, we must engage our students' interest and find ways to keep alive the flame that helps them to see and interpret their lives in a larger context.

The goal is challenging: How do we get our students to connect with class material? How can we show them that the material studied does connect with their lives? I think that the answers are bound up with the words "questing" and "sharing," concepts that are at the heart of good teaching. As a part of the quest, we must seek to expand the boundaries of academic discourse and traditional approaches and venture out together with our students to discover those issues and ideas that impact living and shape lives. We must be daring and creative, searching for that kernel of truth that will explode the paradigm of the commonplace.

Literature is as great a source of intellectual and psychological nourishment today as it was in the past: behold our love for the movies and our interest in three or four basic plots. We seem never to tire of the endless twists and turns of the unfolding developments. Disguised and costumed though the presentations may be, the themes are essentially ageless. In any of a variety of forms, literature presents us with aspects of human potential and poses questions that deal with who we are and who we might become. It opens windows to the world, brings into sharper focus those issues and choices that influence our decisions, and allows us to connect with others who are grappling with their own dilemmas.

As teachers, we are explorers, and therefore we go on quests. But we do not go alone, for we honor reciprocity. We share with others and are open to finding new truths, willing to swim away from the shores of the traditional and to discover what the text has in store for us. In finding ways to nourish the intellectual and emotional lives of our students, we nourish ourselves. In the prologue to the *Canterbury Tales*, Chaucer says of the Oxford scholar, "And gladly wolde he lerne and gladly teche" (Robinson, 1957, p. 20). This phrase still rings true today. Teaching involves sharing; it means "going the distance" with others.

Committed teachers are expected to provide the spark and to be the catalyst, the magnet that draws students into the world of the text. In most instances, students will not become engaged if we are not. As Robert Sardello says in *Facing the World with Soul*, "those who more fully allow themselves to be inhabited by their daemon, who no longer seek to control and keep it repressed but take on the vocation of developing it, are true teachers" (1994, p. 52). In our multifaceted roles as mentors, counselors, and guides, we encourage students to push the boundaries of their knowledge, to search for answers, to discover universal and personal truths, and, ultimately, to take the journey to understanding.

FIRST CLASSES

During the first session, I divide the class into small groups and encourage the students to talk with each other to discover shared interests and experiences relevant to the course. I usually offer a list of possible questions: What is the present focus of your studies? What career do you wish to pursue? Where did you go to high school? How would you describe yourself? What are your leisure activities?

After about ten minutes of conversation, each student introduces another to the class. I also participate by introducing myself, making reference to my own interests and projects. This exercise encourages students to gain better knowledge of each other as individuals and increases feelings of safety and community in the classroom.

In the teaching of literature, I employ both subjective and objective approaches. I begin by requiring that students do close reading of the assigned texts and offer group or individual responses. This exercise is of great importance since it encourages students to become involved and to bring forward, without intimidation, their own insights and personal assessments. It has been said that "the precritical response employing primarily the senses and the emotions is an indispensable one if pleasure or delight is the aim of art. Without it the critic might as well be merely proofreading for factual accuracy or correct mechanical form" (Guerin, 1992, p. 8). Precritical response is necessary and important for the fullest appreciation of literature.

To guide the response process in ways that go beyond spontaneous personal feedback, I ask my students to respond to a list of study questions that are intended to encourage depth and mindfulness in their reading. Individuals or groups of three or four students may then make presentations to the class on selected topics to stimulate comprehension and spark class discussion. These presentations are of great importance because they encourage participants to invest something of themselves in the work. The level of involvement required will pay off later by enlivening discussion and providing the impetus for spirited debates when traditional critical methods offering differing interpretations and approaches are applied to the text. I find that going directly to literary criticism, which dissects and splinters the work before the class has had an opportunity to form honest responses to the material, impoverishes the art of reading and prevents students from entering fully into the work as a whole.

Reading with attention is an art. Close reading, as Robert Sardello emphasizes, "is a form of work, of soul work. . . . Every time we read, a secondary making occurs; reading constitutes a part of the creation of the book itself. A book needs a reader to be a book" (1994, p. 56). Reading is a creative act. It allows us to weave the spell of an enchanter conjuring up worlds, listening and looking for the insights that reveal themselves to us.

When we read closely, we invest something of ourselves in the process. We open ourselves up to the images, visions, and insights offered by the text. We let the words speak to us and wash over us, and we make discoveries about the characters and about ourselves. Close reading is more than mere technical competence. It involves inner work. Like dreams, stories use symbols and symbolic language that speak to us directly, connecting us with universal themes that play themselves out in the sphere of imagination as well as in physical life.

Students should be encouraged to keep a response journal in which they record their commentary on or dialogue with the text. These reaction pieces can relate to any aspect of the material being studied and to class discussions or group exercises. Conference meetings should be scheduled at least twice during the semester, at which time the instructor meets with students singly or in groups to discuss the content of their journals.

Time should also be spent examining the technical aspects of the text. Students are expected to become familiar with key literary terms and devices and with the traditional vocabulary of literary studies (irony, setting, structure, etc.), which allows for clearer communication.

It is also important that the text be placed in an historical and cultural context. To this end, I offer appropriate information to the class on social, cultural, and political developments and movements. Class members are assigned relevant topics that serve—when the research is done and shared with others—to broaden the framework in which the text will be reviewed. As a result of their work, student researchers are able to participate in and appreciate the spirit and mood of an age. Besides promoting the joy of discovery, this exercise gives students a feeling of competence. It offers a knowledge base from which they can formulate questions, hypotheses, and arguments to be discussed in class or developed in papers.

MIXING METHODS
After satisfactory close reading of the text and examination of its technical aspects have been accomplished, the class moves to the discussion of the work from various critical standpoints. I use a mix of methods.

The psychological approach
The psychological approach—where students are encouraged to read between the lines, examine the workings of the unconscious, and discover symbolic meanings—can be quite useful. Discussants are by turn delighted or frustrated by readings or interpretations they do or do not readily see. I tend to proceed

with caution here, so as not to become carried away by theories that interpret texts as psychological allegories where every action has a deep and obscure meaning. Students must be persuaded that the interpretations suggested are not superfluous and tenuous, but real and well-anchored in the text.

The mythological approach

The mythological and archetypal method, integrative and holistic in approach, also has a ready appeal. It lends itself easily to the interpretation of texts of various lengths because of the richness of its possibilities. This approach focuses on the inner spirit of things and can be used to demonstrate the timelessness and universality of themes that spring from the collective psyche. Contemporary methods, such as feminist criticism, are useful for the illumination of particular texts that deal with power imbalances in society, the entrenchment of stereotypical social roles, and the marginalization of women.

Important though these interpretive analyses may be, they are sometimes seen as theoretical constructs applied mostly for the satisfaction of the instructor. We need to honor these approaches, but at the same time we need to find additional methods to reach our undergraduates and to connect them to the essence of the material we teach.

AVOIDING SHUT-DOWN

If students enter into the state of shut-down, the class dies. Each member of the class should be encouraged to make a personal connection with the ideas offered by the text. I realize that this is a tall order, but it is from this connectedness that learning springs. As instructors, we must shoot for high stakes. Our love and enthusiasm for our material must be so catching, so compelling, that more and more of our students will respond. We must encourage our students not to stop at merely studying for the test, but to anchor within themselves the ideas generated by the material so that they are led to raise the kind of personal questions that will ultimately affect their world view and their life choices. To this end, I have found it useful to develop assignments that encourage imaginative and creative responses to class materials.

The sample exercises that follow were developed with a view to drawing students into the drama of the text by having them act as if they faced some of the issues with which the characters wrestle. Such approaches, I believe, can be useful in courses other than the specific ones for which they were designed.

Exercise 1. Group dynamics: Building awareness and increasing perception

In my courses on Literature of American Minorities and African American Literature, I encourage students to see the world through the eyes of members of groups other than their own. This broadening of perception leads to increased awareness and understanding of the text from a more informed perspective. The experience of bigotry is one of the central concerns of the minority experience. In order to awaken students to its impact, I create exercises that move them out of their comfortable identities into the world of the "other."

I divide the class into ethnically mixed groups of four or five students. Each team is expected to do research and present a ten or fifteen minute dramatization that reveals bigotry in one of its many forms, whether based on age, race, religion, gender, or national origin. Students who are shy or uncomfortable about performing in front of the class can have their presentations videotaped. The effectiveness with which the skit is presented is evaluated by the audience.

Dramatizations must employ all members of the team and can be subtle or strident in tone. The group should feel free to present whatever point of view it wishes. One member of the team will present a prologue to the class members so as to orient them to the nature of the presentation.

Students enter wholeheartedly into the simulation, bringing a depth of understanding many did not believe they had. Using humor, satire, or pathos, students create dramatizations that carry considerable power. In their papers, they speak to the impact that this participation had on their outlooks both in and outside of class.

In other class presentations, students wear masks and can elect to speak with the voices of members of ethnic groups other than their own. Majority group students who are members of teams that identify as minorities will be expected to speak with the "voice" of such persons and vice versa. In one instance, a black student speaking as a member of a majority team began her remarks with the comment: "What do they really want? We have given them so much already. We must not let them get any further." The white student behind the black mask answered: "We wish to be seen for who we are—not as stereotypical paste-board characters cut from pre-set molds." The question-and-answer dramatizations, the poetic monologues on the search for respect and place in the society, not only explore personal thoughts and feelings, but also bring literature to life as little else can. Students learn to co-create with the text. Stepping into the experience of others can shake us out of our complacency and show us that bigotry in any form diminishes us all.

Exercise 2. Time jumpers: Reinventing the past

In my class on Caribbean Literature, students read a variety of textual materials from a number of islands. To interpret and analyze the literature better, class members must become aware of the cultural patterns that shape and make up the mosaic that is West Indian society. They must examine the role played by Africans, European colonials, and Asian émigrés in creating the cultural fabrics that are presented so evocatively in such works as Jean Rhys's *Wide Sargasso Sea,* Sybil Seaforth's *Growing Up with Miss Milly,* or Jacques Roumain's *Masters of the Dew.*

In this exercise, the class is divided into groups to reflect the hierarchical structure and racial stratification of many Caribbean islands in the eighteenth century: for example, 1) the governor and his administrators, who ruled in the name of the king; 2) the rich European landowners, who held slaves and controlled profitable plantations; 3) the mulattoes, who were connected by family ties to both the whites and the blacks and who lived in poverty or on inherited wealth; 4) the artisans and professionals—poor whites and mulattoes, for the most part, with a sprinkling of free blacks—who held on tenuously to their places; and 5) slaves, who made up the majority of the population and gave of their sustenance to create a wealth in which they could not share.

Each team identifies with one segment of the society, and the team members must learn all they can about the group they elect to represent. The students spend time researching behavior patterns, interests, and general island experience to prepare themselves for their panel appearance before the class. Groups are free to decide how they wish to be perceived. Most groups present themselves as "time jumpers" and speak in the first person when they tell us about the eighteenth century. Others prefer to speak about the characters from a distance, commenting on values, behavior, and manners. During the presentation, each person offers his or her findings supported by textual material in order to recreate the experience of their particular group. Questions are then directed to the panel from the class or from select groups of interviewers. Presenters must be careful to focus on conflicts between groups or on intra-group contradictions and dilemmas that impact group behavior. To complete this exercise, students write a paper in which they further explain their selected group's existence.

Exercise 3. The hero and the dragon
Students in the course on Myth and Folklore study the nature of myth and its expression in international literature. The class is reminded that myth deals with the ways in which our lives fit into a spiritual and psychological framework larger than ourselves. Study of its patterns suggests that life is not merely a series of blind repetitive motions but a rich tapestry of events layered with meaning. The students come to see that they, too, take journeys, overcome dragons, and seek their own treasures.

In their assigned work, students are asked to discuss the assumptions on which the heroic ideal rests and to show how the protagonist attempts to achieve his or her goals. They are asked to look for similar patterns—for example, the call, obstacles, and trials—in the context of their own journeys. Class members are encouraged to access the courage, endurance, and resourcefulness of the protagonist and to become the hero of their own stories.

In addition to analysis of the epics, students are assigned the task of creating a mythical tale set either in the distant past or in the present. The writers may construct tales where persons from mythical times visit our world or vice versa. The tale should show complexity and ingenuity; it should make use of symbols, metaphors, and other literary devices that lend themselves to analysis. Students should feel free to draw on mythical themes such as the call, the journey, wholeness and separation, shape-shifting, the conflict of opposites, and on such archetypal figures as the orphan, the warrior, the martyr, the trickster, the maiden, and the seer.

In some instances, students assume the roles of reporters and set up situations where they find themselves face to face with mythical figures they wish to interview. The characters could be Agamemnon after the fall of Troy and before he returned home to meet his wife Clytemnestra, Gilgamesh after the death of Enkidu and before he sets out on his quest, or Beowulf before he meets the dragon for the last time. Papers chronicling the interview must show knowledge and ingenuity.

Other assignments direct students to view films or television dramas and find the mythical pattern within these forms. They can also be asked to create an imaginary biography and identify the mythical and archetypal patterns to be found there. The nature of the hero is also to be examined: What qualities and actions give nobility and significance to life? What demeans humans and destroys the fabric of society? What are the gates that lead the hero to a larger sense of self and community? What causes him or her to grow? After the journey is completed, does he or she show increased awareness? In their papers, students are expected to identify figures such as the antagonist, the helper, and the guide; explain their roles; and determine the value of the treasure. In short, students are asked to look beneath surface activities and identify the mythical elements and themes that are to be found in all literature and which seem to connect all cultures.

LEARNING FOR LIFE

At its best, the study of literature should enlarge our world and that of our students, while nourishing and improving our lives. Setting, plot, structure, literary devices, and critical approaches should serve a larger purpose: the re-imaging of the world and of our place in it. Literature is a gateway to more viable self-concepts and to broader senses of possibility. Literature can open us up to life.

Our students seek this kind of connection. With few exceptions, the shallow resistance they offer, their shyness and reluctance to try are quickly washed away when they realize that we are together with them in the quest. Initial diffidence is replaced by a sense of freedom and inventiveness. They soon come to know that literature enriches their lives and increases their options as to who they can become. It shows them that they are part of a larger community: the human family. Through exercises that bring them closer to the cultural energy from which the texts spring, students participate in the recreating of the literary work. In one way or another, all learning is the search for self-knowledge, whether as an individual, a community, or as a species. When we tap the imagination and share in active exploration with our students, we learn more about ourselves and about each other. We become a community of learners.

When learning is successful and students have integrated new concepts and ideas into their thought systems, the intellect, the imagination, and the feelings come into play. All cognitive centers serve to anchor the new knowledge, resulting in a shift in the students' general interpretation of reality and hence of their world view. Such changes in comprehension last beyond tests and examinations. They become part of the psyche.

In the teaching of literature, we must find ways to stimulate, interest, and engage the imagination, to reveal how the reader's private worlds connect with that of the text. From the rich matrix of textual material, we must be able to identify issues, ideas, characters, and relationships that speak to us and to our audience. Finding the means to do this is not always easy; but when those discoveries are made, the result is rewarding. Learning that engages all cognitive centers remains with students beyond the final examination. It stays with them for life.

REFERENCES

Guerin, W. L., et al. (1992). *A handbook of critical approaches*, 3rd ed. New York, NY: Oxford University Press.

Robinson, F. N. (Ed.). (1957). *The works of Chaucer*, 2nd ed. Boston, MA: Houghton-Mifflin.

Sardello, R. (1994). *Facing the world with soul.* New York, NY: HarperCollins.

5

Relations of Mutual Trust and Objects of Common Interest

JOHN DAVID DAWSON

John David Dawson teaches at Haverford College, where he is associate professor of religion. With a focus on the theory and practice of interpretation, his teaching and research integrate the fields of ancient Christianity and modern religious thought. Dawson is the author of Allegorical Readers and Cultural Revision in Ancient Alexandria *(1992) and* Literary Theory *(1995). His research and writing have been supported by grants from the National Endowment for the Humanities, and he has been a member of the Center of Theological Inquiry, Princeton, New Jersey. He was named the 1994 Pennsylvania Professor of the Year by the Council for Advancement and Support of Education (CASE) and the Carnegie Foundation for the Advancement of Teaching.*

"Do you think people are basically good?" asked the supervisor of the study skills center at the large state university where I was just starting my sophomore year. We had all been gathered together for a few sessions of orientation before beginning work as part-time English tutors for our fellow undergraduates. What an odd question, I thought. Shouldn't she be asking whether we could recognize a split infinitive when we saw one? "Or do you think," she continued, "that people are basically bad?" A lengthy discussion ensued, all of which I have forgotten, except that both positions were defended and, in the end, we all agreed that people were basically good. Or so we said.

But our supervisor suspected that many of us did not really believe it. A social psychologist by training, she was convinced that, as the products of a residually religious and triumphantly capitalist culture, we had all been led to devalue ourselves (unconsciously) and those around us (often explicitly). She worried that some of us would turn our tutoring positions into occasions for compensating for our own dim self-assessments by devaluing those who came to us for help. Perhaps she had read Nietzsche's *On the Genealogy of Morals*, where he explored how the categories of good and evil get invented and deployed by those who become teachers (Nietzsche said "priests," not "teachers," but in our post-religious age, what is a teacher but a priest manqué?). At any rate, she would have understood the dark implication behind a poster I saw recently, one designed to entice students into the profession: A teacher stands before a blackboard wielding a piece of chalk while the text below exults, "Seize the Power!"

What, if anything, keeps the power of teaching from becoming one person's power over another? Can such a worry be addressed with new teaching strategies or techniques? Does it require some new theoretical reflections on education? Or is the issue finally rooted much more deeply—beyond the reach of either technique or theory—in the more subterranean wellsprings of individual character? The very form of these questions—the way in which, together, they divorce practice from theory, theory and practice from individuals, and individuals from the relationships in which they find themselves—often stems from just those circumstances in which the pernicious exercise of power between students and teachers most readily flourishes. We must, I think, learn to overcome this habitual way of thinking, riddled as it is with a host of oppositions that I suspect strike many of us as increasingly alien to what we hope education can become. Only by once again reintegrating these features of teaching and learning can we begin to discern more generous and productive possibilities for our power. Generated by power's self-abdication, generous and productive possibilities emerge when hierarchy gives way to mutuality, teachers learn and students teach, and objects of shared interest foster relationships of mutual trust.

MUTUALITY, NOT HIERARCHY

In his *Philosophical Fragments*, Søren Kierkegaard contrasts two sorts of relationships between teacher and learner. In the first relationship, a teacher (Christ) brings to the learner a truth that the learner does not possess and could never possess on her own. Such a teacher is most appropriately regarded as a revealer. In the second relationship, the teacher (Socrates) asks the learner questions that enable the learner to recognize a truth that the learner already possesses. Plato has Socrates refer to this sort of teacher as a midwife. Kierkegaard's contrast between revealer and midwife is invidious, designed to defend classical Christianity against what Kierkegaard saw as its Hegelian perversion. That agenda does not concern us here, except in the most indirect of ways. But in the course of his polemic against the Hegelian-Socratic relationship, Kierkegaard nonetheless insists that between human beings, the Socratic relationship alone is the highest relation. The notion of the teacher as revealer applies only to the relation between human beings and the god, but when teacher and learner are mere human beings, the teacher can only be an occasion for the learner's act of self-knowledge, a midwife who helps the learner give birth to himself or herself and who quietly disappears when his or her role is finished.

Kierkegaard and my supervisor challenge the hierarchies that destroy the teacher-learner relationship. Kierkegaard challenges the notion that the teacher knows something that the learner does not know and can obtain only from the teacher. My supervisor challenges the notion that a teacher is better than the learner just by virtue of being the knowledgeable teacher. The two assumptions are mutually reinforcing. If I have what you need but lack, why do you lack it? Perhaps you are slothful, or have some other character defect. If I think you are basically inferior, perhaps you need my teaching to improve yourself as a human being. Both Kierkegaard and my study skills supervisor had it right, I think: The heart of teaching and learning is found in the relationship of trust between teacher and learner and nowhere else. Together, they help us pinpoint the single greatest impediment to true teaching and learning: the suspicion that teachers possess knowledge that learners cannot possess without them, and that therefore teachers are superior to their students.

But wait just a minute, you may insist. Surely most of this is nonsense. After all, let's face it—we teachers really do know more than our students, do we not? And surely none of us actually believes that our possession of more knowledge makes us superior to our students, do we? Well, let's see. Have we ever written an exam—or made a remark—designed to show students what they don't know (but we do), to "put them in their place" (which is not our place)? When we cross out "mankind" in a student paper and write "humanity" or "humankind" in the margin, do we do so without even a little self-satisfaction at our superior moral knowledge? What do we say to one another in private about our most "disappointing" students? Together, Nietzsche and Foucault have taught us all something about the seemingly inescapable relations among morality, knowledge, and power. The old saw, "those who can, do, and those who can't do, teach," when combined with a bit of *ressentiment*, begins to look ominous rather than amusing: "Those who teach, seize the power."

The many really good teachers recognize this temptation for the subterranean, insidious, and wholly human thing that it is and work constantly to resist it. Of course, teachers know some different things than do their students, but who is to say they know more? Philosophers have had ideas that students have not had; physicists know things about the cosmos that students do not. But if one recognizes that knowledge includes values as well as facts, interpretation as well as observation, and application as well as recitation, then it is clear that the richness, complexity, and nuance of knowledge have infinite reaches at every moment, simply by being a matter of a fully human concern. Our relative degrees of knowledge in highly limited spheres (protected, at least until recently, by tight disciplinary boundaries) collapse into common perplexity when we stand before the basic mystery of the meaning, purpose, constraints, and obligations of our existence.

TEACHING AS LEARNING, LEARNING AS TEACHING

I believe that superior teaching and learning are rooted in a fundamental commitment to the absolutely equal value but utterly unique contribution of oneself and others in every situation, including the teacher-learner relationship. Nothing about that relationship alters this equality of value and uniqueness of vision. And teaching and learning do not just acknowledge that equality and uniqueness; rather, they discover in equality and uniqueness the conditions of their very possibility. There is no distinction to be made between teachers and learners—we are all, at every moment of our lives—both. Furthermore, teaching and learning are not two separate processes but rather two points of view on a single event. We call that event "learning" as it emerges in the student as the realization of the student's potentialities. We call that event "teaching" as it emerges from the teacher as the realization of the teacher's potentialities. Teacher and learner help one another actualize their potentialities in their relationship with one another. All teaching is collaborative learning; all learning is collaborative teaching. But collaboration is really a bit misleading; it sounds a bit too strategic: There are not two persons putting their heads together, but two persons engaged in an ongoing relation with one another.

To regard teaching and learning as separate events is already to have abandoned the more fundamental reality of relationship. In his *Treatise on Teaching the Uninstructed*, Augustine of Hippo observes that in that single event called either teaching or learning, teacher and learner dwell in each other: Learners speak from the teacher what they hear the teachers say, while teachers learn from their students what they teach. Think of friends who come to visit and ask to be shown the sights. You see your town day in and day out, to the point when, beset by the lethargy of custom, you can no longer see it at all. When your friends come to visit, you find yourself pointing out your town's features, and suddenly you begin to see them—and appreciate them—once again, as though for the first time. We might say that you have come to see the world through your visitors' eyes: They see through your eyes what you have pointed out for their eyes, and you see through your eyes what you point out for their eyes, and you see through their eyes what you have seen with your own eyes.

A recent seminar was probably my most rewarding effort at this style of teaching. I presented the seminar to students as an opportunity for common reading and discussion of texts designed to stimulate independent research projects—both mine and theirs. I decided early on that I was not about to mask the legitimate distinctiveness of the roles of teacher and student. Instead, I sought to define those roles more sharply, but also to distinguish them from a more fundamental human equality that we were all going to respect: Everyone was going to play both roles in this class because we all "had what it takes," just by virtue of our unique existences, to be teachers and students.

So, on the one hand, I set the initial agenda for the seminar, basing it on readings explicitly related to my own research project, which was concerned with the intersections of theology and literary theory. The explicitness of this agenda-setting matters here; this was not going to be one of those all-too-common undergraduate seminars marketed under some trendy topic (as though designed solely for students), but consisting in fact of an unacknowledged, self-serving vehicle for the professor's own research. On the other hand, as the seminar proceeded, the students were going to be able to reshape that explicit agenda in light of their own individual projects. If such an opportunity to reshape was going to be real, it would have to mean at least three things: 1) Students would need to be able to take over the discussions on the assigned texts as they saw fit, through presentations, responses, and largely self-guided conversation (the available "air time" of the two-and-one-half-hour seminar needed to be largely in their hands); 2) they would need the chance to offer presentations based on their own developing research; and 3) they would need to feel free to insert into the original syllabus additional texts for general discussion, ones that they felt were important—either to my research agenda, to theirs, or to any unanticipated lines of reflection that might develop.

Just as it was vital to the seminar that my agenda reflected a real intellectual project of my own, so it was vital that students understood that their emerging projects needed to owe no allegiance to mine: Students were to be free to write their seminar papers on any topic at all—the only restriction being that the topic had to have something to do with theology, literary theory, or both together (partly to justify why we had all gathered together under the rubric of the seminar topic in the first place, and, more profoundly, to offer the possibility of finding new common interests amidst the multiple and divergent interests that were brought to the class).

In retrospect, the most remarkable feature of this class was that the students really did seize the power to shape, to construct—indeed, to constitute—the work of the seminar. My trust in their capacity to do so was, on the whole, richly rewarded. Conversations throughout the semester with individual students, as well as subsequent written student assessments, also convinced me that, on the whole, the students' initial trust that their freedom and opportunity would be neither illusory nor trivial had been honored as well.

I say "on the whole," twice, because I and the students certainly managed, from time to time, to let one another down. Nothing I've said here about the success of this particular class as a consequence of mutual trust should suggest that I or my students somehow miraculously escaped what I will shortly describe as the inevitability (though not the necessity) of betrayal.

I learned a lot through reading student essays addressing all sorts of things unrelated to my own particular interests of the moment (and, in reading them, I also learned as well why I should start taking an interest in them, and how doing so could alter the view I was currently taking of my own project). Likewise, I saw ways in which students had come to think in new ways about their own topics simply by virtue of having formulated them in dialogue with, in opposition to, or along with the dismissal of, my own agenda.

This classroom experience also led me directly to my own writing—and back again to the classroom. I committed myself to writing at least ten pages of close analytical prose on the texts for each week. (In preparation for the seminar meeting, on an alternating basis, the students were doing just the same thing, presenting their results to the group and responding to one another's presentations.) More importantly, I also committed myself to going back to those ten pages the morning after class and revising them on the basis of insights that had emerged in discussion. This commitment sounds easier than it was. I've found that there is nothing more exhilarating than to be in an evening seminar in which lots of new insights emerge, and nothing more difficult than to get up the next morning, with that groggy feeling that always seems to accompany late-night classes, and turn those insights into something productive for my own scholarly work before they fade away. Lots of insights did emerge (and eventually a book manuscript), mainly because the students pushed me really hard. I pushed them hard, too, and together, we didn't let one another escape too many difficult passages without thinking to the point of mutual bafflement!

I do not want to paint too rosy a picture, however. This way of teaching was exhausting, and the students found the seminar an exhausting class to take. I was fortunate to have gathered together a small group of especially talented and self-motivated students. Indeed, one major challenge was keeping those few who were less prepared or motivated engaged in the discussions, while not slowing everyone else down. The key to managing this common problem was twofold: I needed to look hard (sometimes very hard) for the more subtle nuance or implication of confused remarks, and I needed to lead the strongest students to put their observations into less jargon-ridden or obscure terms, and to take on the role of being teachers of their peers. Much of my effort throughout the semester consisted of such acts of translation. Would I do it all again? Yes—but not right away, and not with the same material. I would want to wait until my own engagement with new material was at the point of maximum freshness and intensity, since teaching this way is like making myself take one of my own courses. We should all imagine ourselves doing this as we plan our courses; we would teach differently, and more effectively, if we did so.

MUTUAL TRUST AND COMMON INTERESTS

What would it mean in practice to resist the temptations of hierarchy and to embrace the equality and uniqueness of teacher and learner as the very presupposition of one's teaching? Practice must, I think, be rooted above all in a basic disposition of trust: One must trust one's students. What does this mean? Trust them in what way? Trust them to do what? Trusting is not the same as expecting. One often hears it said that the best teachers have high expectations for their students, that they expect the best from them. But expectation remains too wedded to hierarchy: Kings expect their subjects to obey, but parents come to trust their children with the family car. Behind failed expectation is condemnation; behind failed trust is betrayal and hurt.

In its authentic moments, my teaching is based on the trust I have in students as learners and teachers—as persons who want to learn from me and from one another and who, simply by virtue of their unique visions, have something new to teach me and other students about the objects of our mutual inquiry. My teaching is equally based on the trust students have in me, as one who is eager—in reality and not in carefully cultivated classroom posturing—to learn from them. What does this translate into in practice?

I try to enable students to become independent and original thinkers. I try to help them think of themselves not as passive consumers of information but as active producers of knowledge. To help my students do these things, I must first try to do them myself. I have found that only when I go into a classroom ready to think genuinely new thoughts am I really able to lead students to think new thoughts of their own. It is hard to prepare for this kind of teaching. Although one can foster an environment for innovative reflection, one cannot simply contrive such reflection or make it happen on demand.

The key for me seems to be thinking hard about the material before the class meets, but then being prepared to abandon in an instant previously considered lines of thought in order to pursue the new ideas that inevitably emerge in any intellectually free discussion with intelligent students. While I do need to guide discussion, I also need to avoid manipulating it: What never works is pretending to think "on the spot" while attempting to force discussion in directions one has decided on before the discussion begins. Students are often reluctant to embrace the hesitancy, confusion, and sheer stumbling character of trying to arrive at a genuinely new point of view. Like all of us, they generally prefer what's safe and comfortable to what's risky and unsettling. I have discovered that my students often begin to gain the courage to embark on their own truly uncharted adventures of thought only when they can see firsthand the difficulties and uncertainties I face when trying to do the same thing. And I, in turn, cannot model for them the character of independent and original reflection unless I have confidence in their own willingness to respond.

None of these practices will strike effective teachers as novel. All of my colleagues who are exceptional teachers do such things—and many other things that are considerably more exciting and creative. For me, once a relationship of basic trust is in place, various strategies and techniques tend to suggest themselves in response to different classes and different times—different subject matters, different mixes of personalities, different cultural norms and subversions. Without the relationship of trust, no set of strategies is likely to do more than help one continue to hide from the difficult entanglements that all authentic teaching and learning entail. Teachers like to fancy themselves cultural radicals—always ready to drink the hemlock as they lead their students into uncommon, and therefore dangerous, knowledge. But teachers know that the real danger lies in not letting themselves be subject to, and affected by, the complicated lives of those they seek to serve. A great deal of professional pedagogical instruction is designed to ward off such a possibility.

One can fail to live up to an expectation, but one *betrays* a trust. Betrayal is the painful and disenchanting cost of assuming the stance I have described in this essay. Students will betray your trust in them. And you will betray their trust in you. They will, on occasion, not seek knowledge but self-advancement, and so will you—in the paper written to curry favor for an upcoming letter of recommendation, in a syllabus designed to strike the fancy of the multicultural or anti-multicultural administrator before an upcoming promotion evaluation. On occasion, students will plagiarize a paper, and teachers will deliver a lecture lifted straight from their graduate student notes. But it is vital that teachers and learners not allow such betrayals to define the teacher-learner relationship or set the agenda for its future possibilities. For these betrayals are mere human deformations of a more basic humanity that underlies them, endures them, and can resist them, if given sufficient trust.

A "more basic humanity": Here we encounter a third thing, something beyond teacher and learner as individuals, something that forms the basis for their common trust. In ordinary language use, we tend to say we trust those who are closest to us—either because we have come to know their stability of character over time ("they have proved themselves trustworthy"), or because family ties lead one to put confidence in one's kin ("I trust him; after all, he's part of the family"). Our students don't fall into either group: We meet them for the first time in September, and they are not members of our families. They seem eminently unworthy of our immediate trust (and we of theirs—though teachers get an initial benefit of the doubt thanks to the combined clout of professional rank, institutional prestige, and the psychological consequences of being *in loco parentis*).

Fortunately, the basis for trust does not lie either within ourselves as teachers or within our students as individuals, in the sense of some possession each of us must bring to the table of an educational transaction. Instead, the basis for trust is found in what we regard as the object of our common interest. The relationship between teacher and learner is not polar but triadic: Teacher and learner come together as a consequence of the relationship that each, through the other, has formed with the object of their common interest. What interests us is what "is between" *(inter esse)* us, that which draws our mutual attention. The teaching role as such can be distinguished from the student role by the ability of the teacher, through a cultivated self-discipline, to keep the object of common interest in the forefront of attention. As I have already suggested, students and teachers play both roles in the course of their common inquiry. When the object of common interest, the third thing that makes the educational relationship a triad, loses focus and dissolves, the teacher-learner relationship can easily become a debased polar relationship, a banal reciprocity of mutual stroking and self-satisfaction.

WHOM DO WE SERVE?

When Augustine wrote about teachers and learners dwelling each in the other, he spoke of the "bond of love" as the basis of that relationship. Could we ever conceive of the trust that is the basis for the effectiveness of our teaching and learning as grounded in mutual love? What could this mean? In our pluralistic, secular environment, the love that is the basis for public education cannot, and perhaps should not, be all of what Augustine had in mind when he invoked the term (for him, teacher and learner were human beings united in love because of their common relation of love to a deity who loved human beings). But if we are to teach and learn authentically, I think we must be able to enact love's most central feature, however secularly interpreted, in our own particular ways. The love at the heart of the relationship of teacher and learner is a disposition to give oneself to others for the sake of that more basic humanity that is the common interest of us all. For the purpose of secular education, Ludwig Feuerbach puts the matter the right way: Truth, as the object of common interest, is our common humanity—that ideal form of life from which we customarily find ourselves alienated but toward which, through a pedagogy that alienates us from the customary, we seek to return. For Feuerbach, our conception of objective truth is the way we project "out there" our deepest fears and aspirations for ourselves and for those we love. In our moments of greatest extremity, the truth of his judgment seems to bear itself out. Military commanders, I am told, know that they cannot motivate their soldiers for battle by exhorting them to die for country, but only for one another. Likewise, teachers and learners teach and learn for—or against—one another.

Yet, while our relationships with one another are, in some ultimate sense, the point of it all, when they are based solely on what we possess as individuals, they founder. Why is this? Is Nietzsche right? Is it because our professed commitment to seeking a truth other than ourselves necessarily masks the individual exercise of power that is the all-too-human truth of our relationships? Or is Augustine right? Is it because we have not yet encountered any truth genuinely other than ourselves because what we presently are is finally more satisfying to us than what we might become? In our day, the first question is too easily answered, the second too readily dismissed. Teachers who want to teach rather than oil the machinery of culture must make both of them genuine questions once again.

6

Motivating and Mentoring: Teaching the Developmental Student

VASHTI U. MUSE

 *Born and educated in Mississippi, Vashti Muse specializes in developmental education at Hinds Community College. A former president of the Mississippi Association for Developmental Education and the National Association for Developmental Education, she has spent her professional life motivating and mentoring "at-risk" students, especially those who are deficient in basic reading skills. Muse's many honors include: Outstanding and Distinguished Instructor awards at Hinds Community College; a Joint Resolution of the Mississippi Legislature Commendation for Service to Developmental Education; an award as the Association of Community College Trustees Southern Region Faculty Member of the Year; and recognition as the William H. Meardy National Faculty Member of the Year. Muse was also named the 1994 Mississippi Professor of the Year by the Council for Advancement and Support of Education (CASE) and the Carnegie Foundation for the Advancement of Teaching.*

STANLEY: THE CHALLENGE

His name was Stanley. He stood just inside the door, a young black man whose anger energized the space around him. He glared, and I suddenly understood the coach's admonition that I might not want this student.

It was certain that Stanley didn't want me. Although we were in close contact for the next few weeks, the scowl would never leave his face. The sullen, short answers—when he deigned to answer at all—were uttered in the same clipped voice. That awful anger pulsated from him at every meeting.

TEACHING THE AT-RISK STUDENT

Stanley is an "at-risk" student: a catch-all phrase that is often used by the profession to identify the underprepared. According to Hunter Boylan of Appalachian State University, statistics from the National Center of Education and the Southern Regional Education Board estimate that one of three incoming students is an at-risk student taking one or more developmental courses. At all locations in the Hinds Community College district, approximately 55 percent of the new academic and technical students enrolled in the fall of 1995 were placed in one or more developmental classes. Teaching and helping such students is what I do.

The following poem—by an author unknown to me—has been an important influence in all of my teaching experiences.

> A builder built a temple;
> He wrought with care and skill;
> Pillars and groins and arches
> Were fashioned to meet his will;
> And men said when they saw its beauty:
> "It shall never know decay.
> Great is thy skill, O Builder,
> Thy fame shall endure for aye."
>
> A teacher built a temple;
> She wrought with skill and care.
> Forming each pillar with patience,
> Laying each stone with prayer.
> None saw the unceasing effort;
> None knew of the marvelous plan;
> For the temple the teacher built
> Was unseen by the eyes of man.
>
> Gone is the builder's temple;
> Crumbled into the dust,
> Pillar and groin and arches
> Food for consuming rust;
> But the temple the teacher built
> Shall endure while the ages roll;
> For that beautiful, unseen temple
> Was a child's immortal soul.

I want the temple—no matter the size, shape, or color—to contain the best material that I am able to help place there.

WHO IS THE AT-RISK STUDENT?

Who is an at-risk or—to use a better term—a developmental student? I like to think that he or she is one who hasn't yet become what he or she wants to be. A developmental student does not have the basic skills to guarantee success in the classroom. Often, the background of such students may include poverty and single-parent homes. Developmental students usually lack skills in reading, and that lack affects all the courses that they take. They may be defensive, ashamed to be labeled not-quite-college-material and to have to take courses for which they do not receive college credit. Their self-esteem is low, although they may hide this with bravado, lack of concern, or, as Stanley did, with a demeanor that says, "I can wipe the smile off your face, lady." Many times they will just give up.

Often the developmental student is older and female, and she comes to the class with little academic preparation. She is divorced or widowed, or simply finds herself alone with a shaky future and children she cannot care for financially. She is afraid and excited, unsure that she can make it but determined to try. Sometimes, like Stanley, she will be angry, positive that the American Dream is for everyone else. And when she is, I know that I can help.

TURNING FAILURE INTO SUCCESS

Most of my developmental students have endured years of failure and have been beaten down either physically or emotionally. They have suffered abuse in different forms. Stanley was one who heard his mother cry at night, worn out from working all day to support her two children after their father deserted them. Others have experienced other traumas: having had hot grease poured on their hands as punishment; living in a school stadium; not having enough money to buy the required books; needing dental work on aching teeth; going home to a shack with a dirt floor; sleeping in a car after being run out of the house by a drunken father; going hungry; raising children alone.

They often feel that school is an alien and uncomfortable place, and they resent being in a reading class and taking a course for which there is no transfer credit. They may think the teacher "gave" them the "F." They can't accept responsibility for test scores and feel no responsibility to attend class or to do the assigned work.

TAKING THE FIRST STEPS

When I began teaching at Hinds Community College, developmental math and English were mandatory. Developmental reading was only encouraged, not required. As I became more involved with my students, I was convinced that reading must also be mandatory. After receiving a scholarship to the

Kellogg Institute for the Training and Certification of Developmental Educators and Leaders at Appalachian State University, I returned home determined to improve my teaching while promoting concern about the at-risk student. At my urging, a District Developmental Study Committee was formed. I served as chair of the reading subcommittee. I made presentations at in-service workshops and gave speeches to educate others about the needs of these students.

Within two years, we had a district developmental study policy. It ensured that any student with an ACT score of 15 or less and/or low placement levels indicated by the Nelson-Denny Reading Exam would be placed in a reading class. In November 1993, my department mandated that an elective study skills course, already in place, be required of any student on probation. In addition, we required one hour per week in the lab for all students in the three developmental reading courses. Our work produced the academic curriculum program that now has districtwide coordination. With the development of comprehensive syllabi and policy sheets used by many in our district, I felt that I was keeping my promise to find ways for my students to achieve success. In addition, I set up the first newsletter of the Mississippi Association for Developmental Education (MADE) as a vehicle for sharing ideas and teaching tips.

Motivating the at-risk student is not an easy task. Although much had been accomplished for our students, the next target was to establish a learning assistance center. Help in designing the center came from nationally known developmental educators whom I had met during the Kellogg program. The Hinds administration, which has supported us in all these endeavors, designated the recently replaced cafeteria as the space where our dream could come true. We have been in the building almost a year, and the learning assistance center is a showcase that visitors envy. With state-of-the-art technology for math, English, and reading, we are kept busy discovering the possibilities available to us.

MENTORING AND MOTIVATING

Even with our special facilities, the question of motivation still remains paramount: How can we motivate students who are defensive, angry, fearful, powerless, and exhausted from dragging along behind them a lifetime of failure in the classroom? Reading William Glasser's *The Quality School* reaffirmed for me the importance of the caring message as the foundation of what we seek to do in the lives of students. Thus, mentoring the student becomes synonymous with motivating the student. Thus, I serve as a mentor for students who come to me. The mentoring may be a phone call to their home or dorm when they are absent from class. It may be listening to their problems and offering what help I can, whether the problem is with other subjects, or with their jobs, or with their friends, or, as often happens, with the loneliness that is rampant on our college campuses.

I have helped out-of-state students get home over a holiday period, paying for their bus or airplane ticket until they are able to repay me. I have purchased textbooks until their financial aid or other money becomes available. I have walked a student to the bookstore to purchase books when he too often "forgets" to buy them. I have assisted in finding jobs. I have gotten free dental work for a student in need.

I now serve as secretary for the Athletic Committee. In that role, I meet prospective athletes and their parents and provide special testing for those students. I attend most extracurricular activities, from athletic events to club activities and theater productions. I buy raffle tickets from my deaf students, sponsor students in walk-a-thons or bike-a-thons, and support the fundraising efforts of our student associations. Participation in these activities is one way I attempt to motivate and mentor my students. They know that I care and that I am involved in their education, both in and outside of the classroom. In much the same way that the developmental students need repetition in mastering learning skills, they need the same positive feedback from caring faculty.

To be a mentor, I must be sensitive to the needs of my students. When I notice that one is unusually quiet, looking tired, depressed, absent more than is good for school success, argumentative with me or classmates, I talk to the student privately. I try to arrange a time outside of class, but if that is not possible, the student and I walk into the hall or sit together in class while work is going on. Perhaps she is a young single mother with a sick child who has kept her up the night before, and who holds two jobs in addition to school. Or perhaps the student has just learned of the death of a friend or a relative from a drug overdose. Personal problems abound in the lives of students who feel that they have no control over what happens to them. Arrangements are made to allow these students to make up a test for which they are not prepared because of their problems. I meet with the excessively absent student to make up missed classes and work, so that I do not have to drop him or her from my roll. Our attendance rule demands attending 80 percent of any class. Our mentoring program slogan, "I Am Here for Students" means just that to me. If students are willing to ask for and receive help, I'll meet them more than halfway.

TEACHING STRATEGIES
Numerous teaching strategies have been especially important and successful with my students.

Learning names

Believing in the importance of knowing my students' names, I prepare a temporary roll before the first class meeting, and, as attendance is called, I ask what name is preferred. When a student replies, "It don't matter; just whatever you want," I impress on him or her that our name is our identity and very important. Without a name, we are only a description, and I want to be called by my name. Next, we begin a phonics lesson with my name, which is unusual, and I have them use their peers' names and mine throughout the semester. To give further identity, we learn a few facts about each other throughout the semester. We practice introducing each other in class and listening to any information the person wants to share. With warmth and caring for each other, the class becomes like a family. We also laugh "together" and not "at."

Pretending

To encourage all students to participate without fear of ridicule, we "pretend" situations. We're permitted to laugh only if the actor laughs. I never hide my mistakes or errors, for I believe this is another teaching and learning experience—everyone makes mistakes, which is all right. What is wrong is the way we may react to our mistakes—often we try to hide them, or we make excuses, or we withdraw into a shell. Some of my mistakes are rather embarrassing, such as giving out a level-one test to my level-three students, or consistently switching names of two students, or making a spelling error on the board, or mispronouncing a word. Learning to laugh frees and delights the students.

Making eye contact

To ensure closeness and eye contact, I seat my students in a circle, a threatening experience to most of them. My classes usually sit this way because I found that my deaf students could feel more a part of the class. Since they cannot hear, they benefit from seeing the person speaking. It also became apparent that the class became closer as they learned more about their classmates, though many never liked the arrangement. I know, however, that a student can learn more quickly in a nonthreatening environment, for shyness remains a problem with the developmental student.

For example, Reggie, like Stanley, was a young football player who came to me the first semester of his freshman year. One of six children, he was raised by a single parent. He could not hold his head up and look at me. After several days of downcast eyes, I said, "Reggie, hold up your head and look me in the eyes when you speak!"

Every day we practiced. He was in obvious pain but determined. Gradually Reggie's downcast eyes began to look up and meet mine. He overcame his shyness and became a leader not only in school work but also on the athletic field. He told his story in Kansas City when he received the 1994 National Association for Developmental Education (NADE) Award as the "Outstanding Alumnus of a Developmental Program." For a number of years now, Reggie has been an employee of Hinds Community College working with Institutional Advancement as a recruiter. He has become a mentor and role model for our athletes and the students in my classes as he regularly schedules visitations. He counsels and shares his personal experiences, relieving the students' fears and encouraging them to realize that they, too, can be successful.

Changing the pace

To keep the class interested, I change the pace often. After introducing the skills and objectives for the lesson, we use activities such as underlining the text, participating in group work, and practicing oral reading. Often we do silent work, class discussion, and physical exercise. No one is allowed to be passive. On some occasions, if interest warrants, we leave the text and react to some current event, national or local.

Accentuating the positive

When the words are positive, nothing builds self-esteem and a sense of importance more than seeing one's name in print. Therefore, I make sure that my class bulletin board and the one in the corridor are filled with positive newspaper accounts about the school and our students. Many of these students are athletes, singers in the choir, or members of the Hinds Hi-Steppers, a precision dance team. Whenever I am able to find favorable printed references to our students, those stories go on the bulletin boards.

Writing and publishing

When I teach vocabulary, I organize groups of three or four students to write stories using the assigned words. A recorder, who writes the story as it is composed, is chosen by the group. At the end of the class period, a copy of the story is made for each "author." The next assignment is to proofread the story, either individually or collectively, and to make the necessary corrections. The final version is read at the next class meeting and critiqued by the class. For the students, this assignment is ominous in the beginning but generally appreciated as it is experienced.

Using humor

Because we learn faster when learning is fun, I use comic strips: "Peanuts," "Garfield," and "Wizard of Id," to mention only a few—to develop main ideas, inference, and vocabulary.

"B.C.," "Hagar," "For Better or Worse," and "Beetle Bailey" are among my favorites for vocabulary development. For instance, Sarge says, "Zero, I've explained it every way I can. I just can't get through to you." Zero responds, "Perhaps it's advisable to succumb to the inevitable and capitulate." As Sarge's hat shoots straight up and his eyes bug out, Zero continues, "Whatever that means."

I have a framed "Nancy" comic strip on my office wall. During an interview for a college publication, I had used the then unframed strip while explaining my teaching outlook, behavior, and personality. Sluggo asks, "Nancy, what makes some people naturally bossy? Is it the weather? Parents? Hormones?" She answers, "Brains!" As Sluggo walks away disgustedly, she yells, "Sorry, but we bossy people have to call 'em as we see 'em!" The interviewer had the strip framed and gave it to me.

Using technology

Not only does technology reinforce learning skills, but also it provides the students with skills for the world of work. The computer lab makes drill work fun, and the lab is available for extra practice when the students choose. We are able to diagnose and prescribe work through our learning assistance center, which houses an English writing lab and a math lab in addition to our reading lab. Many of our students are in at least two developmental classes; some are in three. The convenience and close proximity of these labs encourage the students to take advantage of all three.

Encouraging personal responsibility

All graded work is filed in an individual folder that is available to the student whenever he or she wishes to see it. The folders are handed out after each test. Every test is graded the day the test is taken and made available the next class period. I mark and explain each error on the test. I go over the test in class and/or when a student comes to me privately. I assign or suggest activities to improve skills. I give the students a summary sheet exactly like the one I keep, and I encourage them to record test and lab grades. This procedure gives them responsibility for keeping track of their grades and for noting missed tests that must be made up. Again, this process gives the student control, since they must make a conscious decision to arrange the make-up test or to accept a zero.

DEVELOPING A GOOD ATTITUDE

Treating students with respect is essential. It is especially important when conflicts occur. If there is discourteous classroom behavior between students or between a student and me, I use the same methods that have worked with my own children and grandchildren: In the privacy of my office, or in the classroom, I emphasize the ground rules given at the beginning of the semester, the behaviors that will not be tolerated, and the ways we will attempt to settle differences. Usually this counseling succeeds, and the conflict ends with a hug or a handshake. If there is no resolution, however, I have the students choose different seats, away from each other, and get them to agree to eliminate contact or conversation.

If the conflict is between a student and me, I reassure the student that my disapproval is not of him or her but of the behavior. I recently had occasion to put a young lady out of my class—only the second time this has happened in my thirty-two teaching years. She was given the choice of changing her behavior or leaving the class, and she chose the latter despite my efforts to avoid that solution. When she attempted to get back into the class, we discussed her choice and the behavior, but she could not see that she had any responsibility for the result of her actions. I gave her a copy of my report to the Dean of Students and, because she had only one absence, I allowed her to withdraw from the class with a "W" instead of an "F." A week later, she came to talk to me. Again, I attempted to help her see that she was responsible for her predicament. She could only "wish she could take that day back." When we met for the disciplinary hearing in the Dean's office, she finally asked, "If I can change my attitude, would you let me come back into your class next semester?" I answered that I would be glad to have her back, that I could forget the events of this semester, and that I would welcome the opportunity for us to start over. She was assigned a paper on "Attitude Adjustment," which included a discussion about choosing positive behavior. This proud young woman subsequently chose positive behavior that reinforced her power needs.

What we think we can achieve affects the degree of our success. Very often students who have not had success think nothing they do will alter their failure. I work diligently to show students ways they can be successful when they choose positive rather than negative behavior.

No one—not even a teacher—likes to fail. Nevertheless, I have lost too many students who drop out or who just give up. The dropouts may drop in again—but not always. I am not able to help all students. Sometimes I, too, have negative thoughts. There are even days when I feel it's time to quit. I'm discouraged. I'm a failure. I don't teach as well as someone else might. There's not enough time in the day to fulfill the demands on me. I'm tired. But then I straighten up and refuse to quit. I seek help. I share and learn from professional conventions, seminars, and workshops with kindred spirits. I am energized and share tears and laughter with my family. I look with pride at the success of a student and realize that I played a part in his or her achievements. That student might not have achieved if I had given up, and I think of what I might have missed.

In all that I do, I acknowledge my students' humanity first. I try to nurture their spirit and to show them the possibilities for their lives. I urge them to let their hearts take courage. But as I watched angry Stanley during that long semester, I feared he would be lost, for his needs seemed as great every day as the first day I saw him. And I continued to feel his anger. Throughout his angry semester, my faith wavered every time I saw him.

I could not imagine what his life had been, but I felt the awful injustice of not being given a chance. Yet, at times I did not even care, for it seemed that nothing I did worked with Stanley. I had learned—though not from him—that he was homeless and that he slept under a stadium. I knew that he distrusted people, and this distrust was the barrier that separated us. But his negative energy drained me of joy. I dreaded meeting his class, for his sullenness and anger darkened my days. I just could not reach him. He was a glaring giant whose anger and hurt went too deep to reach. When the semester was over, I gave thanks and went home to nurse my wounds over the Christmas holidays.

Early on the opening day of the spring semester, before the students arrived, I walked past my classroom. A lone student sat with his book opened. Stanley looked up and smiled.

The Stanleys are my motivation. They keep my hopes alive.

7

The Student Who Felt Ugly and How She Played Richard III

MARTHA ANDRESEN

 *The Phebe Estelle Spalding Professor of English at Pomona College, Martha Andresen was named the 1992 California Professor of the Year by the Council for Advancement and Support of Education (CASE) and the Carnegie Foundation for the Advancement of Teaching. A five-time winner of the R. J. Wig Award for Distinguished Teaching at Pomona, she was also named a co-recipient of the Robert Foster Cherry Award for Great Teachers at Baylor University in 1992, and has served on the National Selection Committee for the Bingham Awards for Teaching Excellence at Transylvania University. Andresen's specialty is teaching Shakespeare to undergraduates, but she has also engaged general, professional, and corporate audiences through her lectures, seminars, and media presentations. She is the creator of* WordPlay, *a solo lecture series seeking to connect Shakespeare's art to what matters in our private and public lives.*

P*ay attention.* That imperative is the teacher's classic line, a command surely evocative of a stern or gentle voice from our own student days when we were called back from doodling or dreaminess to the lesson at hand. When we became teachers, such an imperative was now an earned prerogative, a signal of authority, a call to distracted students with our own proffered awakening.

But teachers get distracted, too, defended by seeming mastery or practiced professionalism from our own vulnerabilities to the mysteries of deep discovery and felt connection at the heart of true learning. What follows is a true story about a student who caught me dozing, so to speak, and awakened me to a lesson at hand.

The story develops in new ways the old imperative for teachers and students alike: that we *pay attention* to the subject matter and to the subjectivity that matters, the complex, unfolding humanity of our students and ourselves in relation to one another and what we teach. My subject is Shakespeare, a specialized field. But the subjectivity I seek to explore here is that of the great and urgent human themes and conditions, captured and particularized in a Shakespearean character but also richly imagined, deeply felt, freshly experienced and embodied by a troubled, talented young woman who many years ago taught me about teaching.

I offer this story not as prescription but as parable. Shakespeare is but a vehicle for what every teacher, in distinctly personal, highly subjective ways, needs to discover about connections between self and subject and student. I practice this connection by using many kinds of performance exercises in my classroom, but any classroom activity that encourages students in independent, creative, collaborative, and active use of subject matter fosters such connection and brings joy. Within a disciplined structure and defined analytic context, then, we all can search for ways to set students afire and free. Attention gets paid and the effort is extravagantly rewarding.

A Teaching Story

I had just come back from my first sabbatical leave in England—some twenty years ago—and so I first noticed her teeth. This student had perfect teeth: white, straight, even; beautifully set, proportioned, gleaming. A dentist's fine art, I speculated, and the efforts of proud parents who made her drink calcium-fortified milk and invested in her braces.

How unlike this young woman's perfection were the marred smiles that had shocked me in London, especially one flashed by a pale waitress her age who cheerily poured steaming tea for me in a shop near the British Museum one dismal, bone-chilling November afternoon. Too many sweeties, and too little orthodontia, I sadly mused then, newly aware of the privilege of proper diet and dentistry back home. On a break from my shivering labors in the drafty main reading room, I smiled back gratefully but felt a stab of homesickness. I was cold and lonely, and missed California warmth and smiles.

And so months later, now back in Southern California and in the presence of a Pomona College student again, I noticed her teeth. But where was her smile? I was smiling. Nothing felt better to me, after that dreadful London autumn chill, than February in California and a warm spring day. Why didn't this young woman thrill to the sun that had bronzed her skin and bleached her long hair? Why didn't she rejoice in her privilege to be a student, in her willowy natural beauty? She was very tall and thin, and wore no make-up or frou-frou of any kind. Dressed in an oversized white Jockey T-shirt and frayed azure jeans, her light hair, tan skin, and perfect teeth enhanced a bony beauty that some women would kill for.

But she didn't smile. Her pinched face, clenched teeth, and melancholy eyes signaled some winter of deep discontent. About what?

"I don't like this class," she exploded, tossing contemptuously her mane of hair. "I don't like *Macbeth*. Or *Hamlet*. Or *King Lear*." She paused. "Shakespeare doesn't do anything for me. Your class doesn't do anything for me."

Startled, I feigned in reply the cool of an experienced teacher for whom nothing comes as surprise or hurt. "Well then," I said. "I guess I can't do anything for you."

"Yes, you can," she said. "You can give me an extension on my paper. And I need you to write for me a letter of recommendation for medical school."

It was a moment, not uncommon on a bad teaching day, when I wished I had gone to medical school. Then I could do something useful for someone, and get better paid. What, I asked myself, does Shakespeare do for a student like this? Fix teeth? Set bones? Raise the GNP and redistribute the world's income? This young woman had perfect teeth, lovely bones, plenty of resources, and happy prospects. Not just privileged, I thought to myself spitefully, injured in my sense of usefulness. She's spoiled. Let her lose a few teeth, wait tables in a dreary little London teashop for a few years, get soaked in the cold November rain to her long, straight, strong bones. Then she can tell me what this class doesn't do for her.

Get a life, this student's reproach had said. "But Shakespeare *is* my life," I said aloud, a strange reply to her requests and a sure signal that I had lost my cool. "He's not *my* life," she shot back. "He doesn't even touch my life. That's what's wrong with your class."

Then her voice dropped, and her slender hands trembled. She was clutching *The Complete Works*. "I just can't take him in."

The direction of her reproach had changed. Her self-blame, her real pain stifled my own self-doubt and called me back to my rightful responsibilities. "Come by my office sometime this afternoon," I offered. "We'll talk."

She came by early that afternoon, breathless and eager. I had brought back from England an electric plug-in kettle adapted to American voltage, and glad to try it out and to observe English civility, I brewed for us a pot of Celestial Seasonings herb tea. Sipping it would soothe us both, I hoped. No need for a jolt of caffeine or English sweeties on this balmy February afternoon; no need to invite damage to those dental wonders. "Thanks for the chance to talk to you," she said. "I've wanted to come by all term."

I wondered why she hadn't. I always announce my office hours and advertise my accessibility. Many students come. Some do not. What had kept this young woman away?

"I didn't come before," she said, "because I didn't want to be rude. Sorry I was rude today." She hung her head, her face shrouded by her long hair. She had curled up in the chair across from mine and clasped her knees, her posture accentuating a girlish frailty. "Thanks for not tempting me with food," she said abruptly, eying the English biscuits on my shelf. "I have an eating disorder. Once I start, I can't stop. I binge. I obsess. So I don't eat."

It's food, then, I realized. Her bony beauty is not the triumph of fashionable workouts, her bored bravado not the cultivated insolence of skinny women who model designer jeans. But she is not empty, she is telling me. She's filled—with something, pain or rage. Filled and starved. Maybe for English sweeties and real tea. Or acceptance and autonomy. Maybe Shakespeare's art, too.

"I guess it's rude to say that your lectures are perfect," she said strangely. "Perfect. I've never heard anything like them. None of us have. They're celestial," she smiled wanly. "Just like this tea." She had put down her cup without sipping a drop. "That's how you shut us up."

It was my turn to put down my cup. The afternoon was balmy, but I felt chilled, too astonished by this revelation to be offended. A moment of truth uttered by a diffident student with perfect teeth had punctured my pride in years of effort to achieve perfection of sorts: studied mastery of Shakespeare's art, eloquent delivery, seamless, incontrovertible arguments, intricate, ingenious analysis, rehearsed dramatic effects. I was in love with Shakespeare and sought, I guess, to seduce others to his art. I never dreamed I was silencing.

But then as a student I had sat silently in classrooms for years, listening for hours to my masters' voices. Silently, patiently, I had awaited my turn behind the podium, my chance to find a voice. As a newly appointed assistant professor, I deemed myself the master now, and talked with passion and a vengeance. But on this spring morning an impatient young woman was telling me that she wanted a turn, that she didn't want to wait. Where was her chance to take in Shakespeare's art, to make him her own?

So little was her own, she said. "Maybe only my bare bones!" She was, she then revealed, the "chosen" child of a well-meaning, ambitious, but troubled family, bearing her parents' anguish as well as their mission for her stellar, unblotted academic achievement. She carried most painfully her mother's thwarted dream of medical school and practice. Her unwell mother had willed that her daughter would make others well and heal her in the bargain.

This young woman bore as well a commercial culture's cruel prototype for Barbie-doll female beauty, malnourished and plastic, constructed and reconstructed out of mass-produced molds. Hair color and costumes change over the years, I reflected then, but Barbie's shape remains the same, imprinted on the minds of adolescent girls who by that unreal standard judge the burgeoning bodies they see in their mirrors, reflected back to them as painfully ill-shaped.

The years of strenuous orthodontia, I soon understood, had disciplined her teeth into gleaming perfection and were a generous parental gift for her well-being. But they indicated as well years of psychic and social wires and retainers that had pulled into line her spirit, stifled her appetite, robbed her of her own sense of self and direction. She had colluded in this wiring, she knew, imposing her own will to power on her marvelous genetic gifts of brains and beauty. She had achieved perfection indeed: She had a perfect academic record, nearly perfect SAT scores, and everyone marveled that she had such looks to boot.

But the family who had driven her and the teachers and friends who had marveled seemed in the long haul to retreat in envy, resentment, and indifference, or—more painfully—to turn to ordinary lives and pleasures that to this extraordinary young woman seemed inaccessible. "I'm a real freak," she told me matter-of-factly as she described a life increasingly isolated, despondent, and self-controlled. She could sit at a table loaded with French fries, she could sit silently during my lectures, and not take in a thing. No weight gain, no mind gain. "I don't take in," she told me ruefully, "and I don't act out."

The sugar-free, decaffeinated jolt of this revelatory teatime encounter now awakened my sense of adventure. "Maybe in my class you can act out in order to take in," I suggested. She unclasped her knees and stared at me with a flicker of curiosity. "Shakespeare invites acting," I ventured, bravely noting this most obvious truth. "Instead of taking an extension to write your essay, why don't you choose a passage from a play—any play—and act it out? I'll give the same option to everyone in class. That will spare me the work of creating another perfect lecture. You do the preparing. And have the fun."

"Thanks for the tea!" she called as she left my office. "Thanks for the chance."

What happened next surprised me. It surprised us all. At the next class meeting I announced my new assignment as an option only, a chance to try a dramatic reading or enactment instead of writing another essay on "The Meaning of *Hamlet*." Several students, none of them English or drama majors, jumped at it. And during the next few weeks they worked hard to prepare. They would be joined on performance day, I knew, by the student with perfect teeth. She was waiting in the wings. I wondered what she would do.

Performance day arrived and our revels began. An anthropology major did Hamlet in the graveyard, draped in a black traveler's cloak and crooning to a beetle-browed plastic Australopithecus skull, "Alas, poor Yorick! I knew him, Horatio." A diminutive economics major played a sleepless Lady Macbeth who carried a small candle stocked from her dorm kitchen, to be used in case of power failure. "Yet here's a spot," she said. "Hell is murky. Fie, my lord, fie, a soldier and afeard?...Who would have thought the old man had so much blood in him?" A muscular tennis player with his stubble whitened with baby powder played King Lear. "Howl, howl, howl," he cried to the heavens.

It was awful, you could say. But to us it was wonderful. Our amateur theatricals and flamboyant clichés newly liberated us from my controlling perfectionism and the students' inhibitions. Visible to each other and vocal for the first time, they clapped wildly after each performance. From my front row seat, I joined them in applause.

There was a pause. Then she came forward, the student with perfect teeth, from where she was sitting in the back of the room. She was simply dressed, as always, this time wearing a black turtleneck sweater and black tights. She was barefoot, and she had plaited her long hair in a face-revealing French braid. She carried only a cardboard-backed full-length mirror.

She put the mirror against the south wall of the classroom where through the tall windows the morning sun streamed in. She signaled to us to sit on the floor in front of the windows, leaving sufficient space on the shining linoleum to do her thing. So positioned, we at once faced the blinding dazzle of the sun and the mirror where some of us could see our own reflections. She has worked all this out precisely, I marveled. She has checked out the time of day and the position of the late February sun. But why?

"Now is the winter of our discontent/ Made glorious summer by this son of York," a steely voice suddenly boomed out, "And all the clouds that lower'd upon our house/ In the deep bosom of the ocean buried."

Richard III! I was astonished by the young woman who now stepped out. She had chosen a play I hadn't lectured on, and she had worked it up on her own, a part startlingly incongruous to the image of loveliness who stood poised before us on slender, high-arched bare feet like a dancer in the blazing sun.

The breathtaking power of her opening lines came from her delivery and positioning: She stood between us and the mirror, stalking toward us with the rhythm of the lines, the sun blinding us to her face but creating an aura of light around her brow and hair. "Now are our brows bound with victorious wreaths," she continued, now pacing slowly back and forth parallel to us, her face only visible when her full presence stood between us and the sun:

> Our bruised arms hung up for monuments,
> Our stern alarums chang'd to merry meetings,
> Our dreadful marches to delightful measures.

Her rhythmic pacing had quickened and changed into the measure of a two-step; she now paused and repeated the pattern of march and then measure:

> Grim-visaged war hath smooth'd his wrinkled front;
> And now, instead of mounting barbed steeds
> To fright the souls of fearful adversaries,
> He capers nimbly in a lady's chamber
> To the lascivious pleasing of a lute.

The mock-caper of her long legs she accented with a sensuous verbal hiss and roll: With relish she slowly lengthened and emphasized the consonants: "The lascivious pleasing of a lute!"

She paused, momentarily motionless, then crouched down to whisper to us in conspiratorial confidence:

> But I, that am not shap'd for sportive tricks,
> Nor made to court an amorous looking glass—

She had spun toward the mirror. Her face, now visible in it to those of us sitting at the proper angle, was bleached white in the full sun and lit up with a smirk of contempt and despair. Her perfect teeth gleamed in a chilling half-smile as she made a deep bow to her own reflection in the mirror:

> But I, that am rudely stamped, and want love's majesty
> To strut before a wanton ambling nymph—

She now spun around again to face us, echoing again the first person singular that drums through this opening soliloquy in a bitter litany of self-lament and self-laughter:

> But I, that am curtail'd of this fair proportion,
> Cheated of feature by dissembling nature,
> Deform'd, unfinish'd, sent before my time
> Into this breathing world, scarce half made up,
> And that so lamely and unfashionable
> That dogs do bark at me as I halt by them—

That line of halting monosyllables—*that dogs do bark at me as I halt by them*—she mimed with the hint of a halting gait which now exploded into a bone-dance of demonic puppetry. This is no Richard Crookback, I mused in awe. She has wisely avoided the incomparable Sir Lawrence Olivier's stooped Richard with raised and padded shoulder. She has created instead with her elegant elongated frame her own Richard Crookjoint, her beautiful bones strutting at odd angles and rhythms to mirror a crooked mind and soul:

> Why I, in this weak, piping time of peace,
> Have no delight to pass away the time,
> Unless to see my shadow in the sun
> And descant on my own deformity.

Unless to see my shadow in the sun. A line I had read and heard performed so often I now saw and felt as if for the first time. Here, I understood, was her performance concept, her central metaphor. Her bone-dance was a shadow-dance. We watched it in semi-silhouette as she stood between us and the blinding sun; we watched it in the patterns her angular and halting shadow cast on the shining floor. The shadow side of Richard—the dark deformity of spirit mirrored by a deformed body—she like Richard had projected outward onto the world and others, at once a dark shape of Richard's ugliness *and* the spellbinding object of his playfulness. That's when I saw it: Her Richard Crookjoint had the effect of a brilliant and warped child at play. The shadow-dance was *fun* to him—and to her; a perverse but real delight to pass away the time.

Just then I saw another image of the lonely actor-dancer before us. I imagined her as a child in her bed at night, reading for hours by flashlight while everyone else was asleep, then putting down her book and turning her flashlight to the ceiling. By holding her fingers in certain positions and then moving the flashlight nearer or farther from them, she had learned as all kids do to make shadow-shapes on the ceiling of different patterns and sizes—flapping butterflies or quacking ducks or rabbits with twitching ears. Or monsters maybe, or maybe freaks. Strange and lonely creatures, things unfinished and rudely stamped.

In her childhood game and in this latter-day amateur acting exercise, I could see that this child-woman with perfect teeth was projecting and playing out the shadow-side of ugliness she felt within, those dark and secret regions of loneliness, pain, and anger she felt lurking behind her mask of beauty and perfectionism. She is using all she has to create this Richard, I saw: her past and her present, her head, heart, and bones.

Yet there was more to this student's shadow-dance than pathos and playfulness; there was a thrust to power, Richard's and her own. The opening soliloquy, I knew, now takes a concluding turn from pain and play to power-play and *ploy*. He will convert private posturing before a glass into public politics on a stage—the stage of the play before us, and the stage of history as the next to the last act in the brutal War of the Roses. Through shadow-tactics of deception, seduction, and control, this shadow-man, a son of York, becomes the last York sun-king, each role dark and deformed, his language of "plots have I laid, inductions dangerous" applying at once to theatrical and political villainy.

Richard's opening soliloquy, I reflected then, is prologue to his bravura performance as actor-destroyer. Brother Clarence is dispatched first, then brother King Edward dies in grief and disgrace, then Lady Anne, widow of Richard's victim Edward, is seduced, discarded, and later poisoned, and then the little princes are smothered in the tower at Richard's orders. Not to mention other enemies and friends who are destroyed, including his co-conspirator Buckingham. This villain who wants love's majesty will stop at nothing to gain majesty's crown. But all that, at the play's beginning, is to come. He has to start somewhere, he says: Why not with Clarence?

Had my student worked all this out on her own, I wondered—without the benefit of my usual fall term lectures? Had she discovered on her own that Richard's conversion of pain and play into power oddly mirrored her own? Not in her case to exercise villainy but to achieve the outer image that seduced the world and kept her inner pain at bay? In her own life had she experienced the split between her sense of hidden ugliness and her visible aspect of beauty? Did this enable her to enact the opposite in Richard, an aspect of outer ugliness that masks what is, to him, his beautifully superior mind and will? Whatever her insight, I saw that such splitting had made her, through playing Richard, an exuberant ironist, a master-manipulator, a jaunty wit whose dark humor draws from incongruity between surface and reality a seductive energy, bravado, even glee.

All this, to my mind, was in the performance before us as the young actress now stood motionless and uttered with compelling simplicity the close of Richard's soliloquy. The capering measure, halting gait, sardonic posing, and twitching puppetry of the earlier lines ceased as she now confidently drove pain and play into ploy:

> And therefore, since I cannot prove a lover
> To entertain these fair well-spoken days,
> I am determined to prove a villain
> And hate the idle pleasures of these days.
> Plots have I laid, inductions dangerous—

She paused, almost done, still motionless. Now while she spoke half her final line, "Dive, thoughts, down to my soul," she made her last gesture. She did a slow, deep plié, her hands on her thighs, her knees and her elbows now starkly akimbo, her silhouette before us and her shadow on the floor one of bony angles compressed in a posture of fearsome energy, a folded geometric coil poised to spring into terrible action. She now turned her head sideways toward the classroom door and said simply, flashing those perfect teeth in a smile of triumphant expectation: "Here Clarence comes!"

We looked toward that door too, all of us, expecting her first victim to enter. The power of her illusion had captivated us, and we willingly suspended our disbelief, now drawn into that magic circle of theater where anything seems possible. This unhappy student's Richard had wooed and won us as surely as Shakespeare's Richard woos and wins Lady Anne in the play. I wondered if any professional actor has captured better the use and abuse of women's beauty than this beautiful young woman had done. How would her ironic self-understanding of not only beauty and power but isolation and defeat shape her performance of Richard's last soliloquy before his death at the Battle of Bosworth Field?

> I shall despair; there is no creature loves me,
> And if I die no soul will pity me.
> And wherefore should they, since that I myself
> Find in myself no pity to myself?

She had masterfully rendered Richard as shadow-puppeteer, gleefully twitching his own strings while he dangled and strangled others. How would this lend pathos to the man who at the end has become himself a mere puppet, an unwitting instrument of Providential power that uses him to scourge and punish a guilty king-killing England? How would she play the Richard who falls mortally wounded in Bosworth Field, now a pitiful heap of broken strings and broken bones, who calls at the end for only "a horse! a horse! my kingdom for a horse!"

My speculations about what this young woman might do with the remainder of the part were interrupted by wild applause for what she had achieved with just the opening soliloquy. She had created a complex illusionism whereby beauty before our eyes played an ugliness that had its own beauty, that despite its dark promise of tragedy in plots laid and inductions dangerous sparkled as well with its own comic joy. She had been true to her own complexity, and to Shakespeare's art.

Such was the triumph achieved by this young woman. I jumped up to tell her so amidst the press of admiring students, including the tennis player who had also rushed forward to pay tribute. "We all should celebrate," I exclaimed. "Celestial Seasonings tea in my office?" "No," she grinned broadly, "French fries at the dining hall. I'm *starving*." Led by the tennis player, who had a lean and hungry look himself, we gathered a group of exultant students and headed north across the campus to the feast.

AN EPILOGUE

The day ended. The term ended; my student graduated. Ten years passed. I went about my life; she went about hers. In due course, I had another sabbatical leave. This time, instead of shivering in the main reading room of the British Museum, I went joyfully to theaters in London and at Stratford. I read and re-read Shakespeare's plays in light of acting and performance history and criticism. I watched and I learned from actors on the stage. I spent a summer at the Shakespeare Festival in Ashland, Oregon, where I talked to actors and directors about how they worked the transformation from page to stage. I returned home to Pomona College with a better understanding of performance and its transforming effect on scholarship and teaching, knowing in my bones now that the play's the thing.

My teaching changed. I lectured less, watched and listened more, found ways to activate my students' imaginations and my own. I jettisoned a final exam and created instead a full-blown performance project for all my students whereby in five separate groups they perform at term's end five very different acts of an entire play. It was as effective and recreative as my first foray had been several years before, and so I began to use this expanded exercise every term. Over the years it has become a tradition of sorts at Pomona and has acquired, through my students' good will and work, a life of its own.

For a decade I never heard from my student, but I often thought of her. She had transformed my life as surely as Shakespeare's art had touched her own.

Then I heard that she was coming to campus, the student with perfect teeth, to celebrate her tenth Pomona College reunion. I saw her name on a list of alumni who would be gathering in April on a grassy quad to picnic with their families and former classmates and professors. I was invited by her class to join them, and so I inquired after her. I learned that she had gone to medical school after all, had pursued intensive therapy, and had finished medical school with honors. She had just completed a long residency and had married. Now a new mother, she was in the process of setting up a joint practice with her physician husband. Orthopedics, I imagined. Bones like that should beget and set bones.

On a breezy April afternoon, I walked towards the picnickers on the quad, scanning the crowd for some sign of her. Across the lawn I spotted the tennis player first, the one who had played King Lear, now (I learned) a successful stockbroker. He was seated cross-legged on the grass staring at someone.

I saw her before she saw me. She was standing next to her tall husband who carried their blonde baby in a Gerry carrier strapped to his back. She was happily attentive to them both. Her willowy frame had filled out some, helped over the years, no doubt, by a few French fries and recent motherhood. Her long hair, now smartly trimmed and fluffed, was lifted by the breeze and gleamed in the bright sunshine. Thus haloed and healthy, she was radiant. When she saw me, she bounded towards me across the grass, flashing a perfect smile—celestial but real. Heads turned and faces looked startled as she called out on the run: "Professor Andresen! Do you remember? It's me. Richard III!"

Pay attention.

AUTHOR'S NOTE

The author wishes to acknowledge the kind permission of the Robert Foster Cherry Office at Baylor University for use of material originally presented as part of the Robert Foster Cherry Lecture Series, September 1992, © Baylor University, Waco, Texas.

8

Opportunities and Responsibilities: Competence, Creativity, Collaboration, and Caring

SALLY PHILLIPS

 *Professor of Nursing at the University of Colorado Health Science Center School of Nursing, Sally Phillips has been instrumental in the development and implementation of an innovative Doctor of Nursing program. Phillips's numerous publications focus on state regulatory and professional practice issues in her profession as well as on curriculum development. Her expertise in curriculum design and creative teaching strategies makes her much in demand as an educational consultant. A former president of the Colorado State Board of Nursing, Phillips has been a member of the University of Colorado faculty for nearly twenty years. The recipient of many awards for contributions to her profession and for her excellence in teaching, she was named the 1994 Colorado Professor of the Year by the Council for Advancement and Support of Education (CASE) and the Carnegie Foundation for the Advancement of Teaching.*

Increasingly, our society has access to advanced knowledge and technological innovations through television or home computers connected to the Internet. The need for universities and colleges to be information centers is no longer so central to their purpose and function. Journals and books are available on-line. Interactive encyclopedias not only provide written materials, but also replicate voices and images, thus enabling individual scholars to share their emerging knowledge. A Nobel laureate can be "delivered" instantaneously to a student.

What do we professors have to offer to students that they can't have in the convenience of their own homes and with only time and creativity as barriers to learning? Why would or should a student come to a university or college today? What will bring them to our classrooms or to our networked learning organizations? In this rapidly expanding information age, what added essential value will students find to enhance their learning and challenge their intellects?

I believe that certain values and characteristics, opportunities and responsibilities, are essential for professors in this technologically enhanced age. I believe that it is vital that our conduct as teachers be consistent and congruent with a personal value and belief system. As a professor, I hold sacred the trust and responsibility to be a role model, mentor, and colleague, to provide not only a quality education about a substantive body of knowledge, but also to guide people on a journey of lifelong growth and learning. The central beliefs and values that I share in this essay are intended to convey the essence of my teaching and of my self.

The information age affords me the opportunity to free my creativity and to let go of the need to be the primary conveyer of factual knowledge. With the availability of and easy access to information in diverse forms, the focus of my teaching has evolved into modes that emphasize discovery, integration, and application. The examples that I share here are intended both to provide some insights into my teaching and to stimulate my readers to grow and discover ways to synthesize their own values and beliefs in a teaching role. Thus, this essay focuses on four themes that are central to my teaching and personhood: competence, creativity, collaboration, and, most of all, caring.

COMPETENCE

Today's students have the right to expect competence from their teachers, which means more than just keeping current in their fields. Since students can access the premier scholars in a field of study via e-mail or the Internet, they should also expect to find innovation and excitement in the classroom, exemplified by professors who are actively engaged in the subject matter and who can bring into the classroom current events and developments that are unavailable through traditional media or published materials. Today's learners should be able to engage in state-of-the-art learning experiences. The particular colleges and universities the students attend, and especially the professors who teach in them, must strive to make those experiences possible.

Active engagement

Professors who are actively engaged in their fields can share the proceedings of a conference recently attended, relate current information on innovations, or introduce newly released published materials. They can foster and address the learner's needs for "real time" information. The professor who understands and values the availability of Internet information or student discussion bulletin boards will encourage students to incorporate this technology into their learning, thereby enriching the educational environment. This type of learning environment both reaffirms the worth of traditional knowledge and engages the student in expanding knowledge.

Stenhouse (1975) uses the term "expert learner" to describe the competent teacher, who should be a learner along with the students as well as a guide for the students' learning. The teacher, then, is a "senior learner," who offers something of added worth to the "junior learner" (1975, p. 91). Such relationships are implied when Ernest Boyer describes the scholarship of teaching as "the dynamic endeavor involving all the analogies, metaphors, and images that build bridges between the teacher's understanding and the student's learning" (1990, p. 23).

As a teacher, I have the responsibility to be actively involved in learning and to stimulate students' involvement. I have the opportunity to teach courses that address a broad array of ethical, legal, political, policy, and professional concerns that are relevant to my profession, health care, and the consumer. I am most effective in my teaching when I am actively engaged in the issues to be addressed. Therefore, I commit myself to activities outside of the classroom that enhance my ability to be current and to bring state-of-the-art materials to the learning situation.

As an active member or officer in many of the major professional associations in my state, I often bring my students along when I attend the meetings. When I was president of the state regulatory body for nursing, I negotiated, implemented, and regulated policy. My involvement gave me the chance to provide my students with opportunities to become participants in meetings, to bring materials to the classroom that not only were approved rules and laws, but also draft proposals under discussion and debate. My students were able to participate in the deliberation process and, I hope, to continue their involvement after the course ended.

Active learning

My teaching is further augmented by the preparation of concise syllabi that serve as models for the synthesis of literature, computer-mediated learning materials, and other sources of information that can guide "self-discovery" learning. My syllabi and other course materials stimulate an integration of established factual and theoretical knowledge available in print media with currently evolving knowledge—for example, class discussion of emerging legal issues may be augmented by having students use the Internet to access recent

Supreme Court decisions. During the course, I call attention to conference information and proceedings and to new references—from print media, the Internet, or cable television programming—that are relevant to our study.

I include active projects in all of my classes. These activities are negotiated with student groups to incorporate individual interests and with the intent to foster a passion to continue the activities beyond the course's boundaries. When consistent with the learning objectives of the course, I participate with the learners in a service activity that stimulates active learning and also contributes to the larger community. It is a delightful experience to attend meetings months and years later and to find some of my former students playing an active part. Then I know that my teaching and role modeling have helped to inspire another person's contribution to society.

CREATIVITY

Not only must a professor competently and actively engage the learner in synthesizing and generating new knowledge from a deluge of information, but during the engagement process it is also essential to perform these roles within a new community standard of creativity. For example, with the excitement generated by new sound systems, computer-enhanced cartoons, and other new technologies, is it too much to expect comparable qualities of excitement and creativity from a teacher and within learning opportunities? Not only must the professor recognize that the attention spans of most learners have been altered by the media, but he or she must also be a creative user of information and media. Through a recognition of the real-world environment that shapes our lives, professors can begin to tap into the creativity promoted by sophisticated media and thus liberate their own creativity and innovation.

Bevis describes a learning maturity continuum. Moving from lowest to highest learner maturity, it characterizes the relation of student and teacher as 1) charming, 2) anticipatory, 3) resonating, 4) reciprocating, and 5) generating (Bevis & Watson, 1989). Bevis emphasizes reciprocating and generating models of learning that promote creativity, problem solving, and active learning. *Reciprocating* models are characterized by a learning environment that leads students to take personal responsibility for their own learning. Such environments can free students to exchange ideas, challenge the teacher as well as one another, and take the dialogue in directions that meet their learning needs. In this context, the teacher-student relationship is one of adult-to-adult; it emphasizes mutual respect and exciting exchanges. *Generating* models involve creative circumstances where student initiation of inquiry is high and passivity is low or nonexistent. Students initiate topics and introduce problems, content, or issues that explore ideas in relation to learning goals. The teacher becomes a true consultant and an expert learner.

Teaching strategies and learning opportunities that reflect these mature models and integrate enhanced technologies will enable the learner to see the professor as a creative scholar who stimulates thought and involvement and serves as a guide, mentor, or architect to create new ways to approach a field of study. Boyer sums up the point when he suggests that such teachers "stimulate active, not passive, learning and encourage students to be critical, creative thinkers, with the capacity to go on learning" (1990, p. 24).

Recreating courses

I don't teach the same course in the same way twice. I am continually challenged to try new, innovative ways to expand learning opportunities. One strategy that I find extremely effective in moving students and myself away from traditional models is the use of case studies. For instance, I have been responsible for teaching undergraduate students about the care of childbearing women and their families. If I had confined myself to teaching a traditional course that required me only to ensure that students are knowledgeable about the physiological aspects of pregnancy and the related nursing care, many aspects of the care of these women and their families would be superficially addressed—if at all. My own passion and enthusiasm are manifested in case studies that include personal narratives.

Using real life case studies

I have designed the course on childbearing around actual case studies of clients I have cared for. By discussing the experiences of real people, I am able to address concerns that are relevant to all women experiencing childbirth. This case study approach allows the students to reflect on the issues that real people face.

I provide students with guides to the relevant literature and deepen the case studies by examining and integrating ideas that include clinical judgments, ethical dilemmas, cultural aspects, and other dimensions. To extend further my role as guide and mentor, I may invite a new mother and her baby to class for discussion that can explore a particularly complex set of variables. This experience provides an excellent opportunity for students to study the impact of decisions made in patient situations and also to build bridges in learning through the direct exploration of concepts with the patients themselves.

Encouraging breadth of thought

Some of my other creative strategies incorporate the humanities into my highly technical fields. I have long felt uneasy about imposing beliefs and values on others without more fully understanding the other person. So I select, or have the learners select, several modern films or books written by women that deal with pregnancy and family dynamics. We use these materials in small groups with questions that stimulate discussion, dialogue, debate, and criticism. This work encourages students to think beyond the physical aspects of nursing care and to examine the larger human dimensions. I believe that these strategies help students to evaluate popular literature and films, to think through important issues in their professional and personal lives, and to see their teacher as a human being who lives in the same world they do.

COLLABORATION

The professor brings certain requisite expertise to a learning situation and is expected to set the parameters of the learning environment, such as establishing course objectives and defining essential content in its broadest sense. How the course takes shape, however, and how learning happens and is assessed are more open matters. Learners in our colleges and universities today expect to be treated as adults. They expect the banker, grocer, or sales representative to act respectfully and to establish some reciprocal relationship in which to conduct business. Why should a student expect anything different from his or her relations with a professor? The opportunity to conduct a class as a respectful learning engagement between adults can be an exciting and a liberating experience. As learner and teacher enter into a partnership, both can experience reciprocity in the participatory learning environment.

Bevis and Watson define the curriculum as "interactions and transactions that occur between and among students and teachers with the intent that learning occur" (1989, p. 5). In addition, those authors recommend that the "climate must be egalitarian in that all are equal in worth, in rights to interact, and in rights to be treated as equals among equals" (1989, p. 121). Dolence and Morris (1995) concur: The learner today must be an active learner who assumes responsibility for learning outcomes and maintains connections and commitment to learning.

Establishing a learning contract

I have found that establishing a learning contract with students can accomplish many worthwhile outcomes. As adults agree on the terms of the contract, commitment comes from all parties. One way to create such a contract is to allow students to have some input into how a course is conducted, and how they are evaluated. When students share this responsibility, they are generally more excited about the learning process and its outcomes. Learners can often suggest a strategy or content area that has not traditionally been part of the course but may be of great interest to them. In addition, as the creative process of course design takes place, learners often develop a renewed respect for the thought and work that go into course design, and thus they bring a deeper commitment to the final product.

A collaborative teaching/learning style is integrated into all of my classes. My class sizes range from 15 to 100 students, and variations must be considered, but I approach every class with a value system that states that all members of the class should have a stake in determining the development and outcomes of the course. Therefore, the students must be equal participants with me in the learning process. As the teacher, I bring to the course the faculty- and university-approved course description, course objectives, and specific content that must be incorporated into the course to maintain the curriculum design. Drawn from my expertise in teaching a particular course or similar ones in the past, these basic assumptions provide the foundation for my contributions to the course design discussions that follow.

As we begin the process of negotiation, all students are asked to address key questions, such as: What do you expect to learn in this course? What would you like to learn? What content do you feel is essential for us to address? During an open exchange of ideas, a scribe writes down all the comments solicited in the class. I do a content analysis of this material, organize the students' ideas into clusters to form units of content, and draft a course schedule. Student volunteers are invited to participate in the drafting or review prior to the next class.

Other key questions in this collaborative process include the following: What teaching methods enhance or inhibit your learning? Do you have specific suggestions for teaching strategies related to any specific unit of content? These questions usually yield some excellent student suggestions that often I have not considered. For example, students frequently request that a specific faculty expert or community member address a topic. Or some of the technologically inclined students may suggest bulletin board discussion groups between class meetings. Still other students may be aware of a new "Web page" or have other suggestions for learning that goes beyond traditional methods. I have incorporated the use of games such as SimCity or Mathematica not only to emphasize new technology and creative problem solving, but also to model ways to approach games as learning tools.

Brainstorming about evaluation methodologies usually stimulates a healthy dialogue. I use more questions to spark it: How do you best like to demonstrate that you have met the objectives of a course? What evaluation strategies least allow you to demonstrate your attainment of the objectives? How many assignments are reasonable for a course with this number of credits?

Considering that you may have attended most of your other classes already, what dates should we avoid for assignments due in this course? Once I have this feedback, my role—along with any student volunteers—is to draft a document for student review. Then a contract is developed that reflects the entire design of the course.

Content units are set so that times and dates for special events—visits by guest experts, for example—can be arranged. For large classes, a menu of evaluation options is developed; individual students and small groups can select the ones they prefer. The evaluation plans provide a broad range of opportunities. Respecting individual learning styles, this range may include standard tests, essays, formal papers, journals, learning portfolios, bulletin board discussion groups, oral or computer-mediated exams, and artistic interpretations.

Although they are time-intensive, this open discussion and collaborative process facilitate a dialogue that respects each individual's contribution. The resulting evaluation methods are much more satisfying for the students and for me.

At the beginning of the course, we also negotiate a mutual agreement on conduct. To encourage these deliberations, I often use Chinn's principles of unity (1995) to set forth beliefs, values, and ways of working together. Our agreement may take the form of a document signed by teacher and students alike. Underscoring mutual respect, it usually emphasizes not interrupting when another person is speaking, listening to others even if you do not agree with them, coming to class on time, and turning in assignments on time unless different arrangements have been negotiated by the group. These strategies not only promote a safe, respectful learning environment, but also display reciprocity and exchange in the learning process. While large or computer-mediated classes may present special challenges, this type of collaborative process remains possible when all of the participants are committed to it.

CARING

Although filled with exciting possibilities, innovative technologies, and visually stimulating opportunities, the information age can be devoid of caring human contact. An essential part of being human is the need for caring social interaction, and when that interaction is not available, humans will create it. Some students will establish and utilize discussion groups on the Internet to enhance access to human-to-human contacts. Students may not choose to come to our classrooms—even if competence, creativity, and collaboration are present—unless the professor is caring, too.

Developmentalists describe trust as an essential element in human relationships. Learners enter into an educational contract expecting to learn in an environment where ideas can be expressed openly, examined free of ridicule, and valued by all participants. Teachers should expect the same. However, owing to the hierarchical nature of graded authority structures, equality and trust are often difficult to achieve in our traditional learning organizations.

Establishing and maintaining mutuality

Both respect and trust depend intrinsically on mutuality. This relationship stresses that learning is a collaborative process between two or more individuals who agree to decisions that are of mutual concern and benefit. For such a process to work, all parties must be engaged in establishing the learning contract, and they should mutually agree on how to obtain a successful learning experience. All parties are accountable for assuring continued mutuality.

Knowing the "other" is essential not only in establishing respect, but also in deepening human relationships. The learner and the teacher expect to be known and valued. Professors who demonstrate the intent to know and be known by their students take the first step in establishing trust and respect. There needs to be recognition of and appreciation for the knowledge, expertise, and life experiences that both the teacher and the student bring to the learning situation. Professors who share insights about themselves on a personal level also invite the students to share those strengths, weaknesses, issues, and problems that may enhance or inhibit their learning. Failure to recognize these relationships in the learning situation seriously restricts the potential for a positive learning experience. It is our responsibility as teachers not only to convey information, guide, mentor, and model learning but also to prepare lifelong learners who will be caring citizens of the world.

Revealing humanity

Prior to establishing a collaborative process of course development, I begin each course with a brief autobiographical sketch. My remarks include personal and professional details: features of my life that contribute to my expertise and enthusiasm for the course, as well as information that might influence my performance as a teacher and participant in the course.

After mentioning that I received my initial nursing preparation at Ohio State University, I describe the diverse clinical experiences that I had before I moved to Colorado. It is important to me that students understand my great love and passion for nursing. So I spend some time talking about the exciting dynamics that I have experienced in helping individuals and families deal with health and illness, especially in critical life transition times.

I want the students to see me as an individual not unlike many of them. So I mention that I have two children who were very young during my doctoral studies. I share this information because my students are generally young women of childbearing age. Often they are working, going to school, and trying to be good parents, too. If students are interested in knowing more about the difficulties and successes I have experienced as a working, commuting mother, I feel free to talk with them further. The basic information I have shared allows an opening for students to know that they can become further acquainted with my background and family life if they wish to do so. At times it becomes necessary to establish a limit to the level of intimacy I share, but I do not believe in maintaining an aloof distance from my students.

Finally, I describe some of my outside activities. This discussion includes not only the professional associations in which I am active but also the task forces and national consultation bodies on which I serve. My intention is to help the students not only to see that I am competent but also to glimpse what is required to stay current in the field that the course addresses.

The learners also provide similar sketches for the class members. The students are especially encouraged to share any information that may influence their performance in the class. Their remarks are frequently modeled after mine, but they generally include information about factors such as the following: work commitments that may inhibit their ability to participate in out-of-class assignments and group work, or day care problems that may require some latitude on their class arrival and departure times. The students may also talk about engagements, marriages, pregnancies, deaths—family details. A community begins to build, with a foundation of trust and respect. The most challenging part of this process is to ensure that male students in the group, who may have different stories to tell, feel equally respected. But once the community building begins, that difficulty disappears.

Large classes may require modification of this format. I often break up large classes into groups for this activity, or I ask everyone to write a brief statement. With the class's approval, I may summarize and distribute this information. If the group shares this value, some mechanism will be found to create a caring community that respects each member of the group.

Creating networks
Another important way to strengthen the classroom community involves the creation of networking connections outside of class. This step requires respect for each individual's availability, need, and ability level. Distributing e-mail addresses and phone numbers and arranging times and places for small group meetings and bulletin board discussion groups will generally provide access to all members who choose to participate.

One very effective mechanism for small group work or computer e-mail course components is to establish weekly check-in times to allow each class member—including me—to share with the group any circumstances that might influence participation in the class and to bring to the group any concerns, joys, issues, or suggested redirection for the learning. This structure allows for a constant reappraisal and communicates that each individual's learning is important.

A second example involves my use of structured focus groups at midterm, if I or any member of the community feels that there is a need. The group agrees to the structure and format for the focus group, whose work may be facilitated by someone outside of the group, or by a member of the group, or by written statements that the group can review and study. Whatever the strategies, they are all intended to ensure that respect, trust, and freedom are preserved and promoted.

CONCLUSIONS

Students have access to information that, until recently, could primarily be obtained only through institutions of higher learning and through a professor's expertise and knowledge. The information age will continue dramatically to impact the role and conduct of the professoriate. We professors have an imperative to change.

I take very seriously the responsibility to assist and guide students in their personal discovery of knowledge and synthesis of information. But in addition to believing that we professors must bring state-of-the-art knowledge and experience to our learning environments, I also affirm that we are challenged to model caring/learning behavior. We professors have opportunities and responsibilities to promote a way of being in the world that prepares caring learners to understand change and to cope with the uncertainties of a new century.

REFERENCES

Bevis, E. M., & Watson, J. (1989). *Toward a caring curriculum: A new pedagogy for nursing.* New York, NY: National League for Nursing Press.

Boyer, E. L. (1990). *Scholarship reconsidered: Priorities of the professoriate.* Princeton, NJ: Carnegie Foundation for the Advancement of Teaching.

Chinn, P. L. (1995). *Peace and power: Building communities for the future.* New York, NY: National League for Nursing Press.

Dolence, M. G., & Morris, D. M. (1995). *Transforming higher education: A vision for learning in the 21st century.* Ann Arbor, MI: Society for College and University Planning.

Rheingold, H. (1993). *The virtual community: Homesteading on the electronic frontier.* Reading, MA: Addison-Wesley.

Stenhouse, L. (1975). *An introduction to curriculum research and development.* London, England: Heineman.

Watson, J. (1990). Transpersonal caring: A transcendent view of person, health, and healing. In M. Parker (Ed.), *Nursing theories in practice.* New York, NY: National League for Nursing.

9

Teaching Through the Curriculum: The Development of a Comprehensive Honors Program

ANTHONY J. LISSKA

At Denison University, where he has taught since 1969, Anthony Lisska is professor of philosophy and director of the honors program. He has also served as dean and as chairperson of the philosophy department. A medievalist by training and vocation, Lisska is the author of many articles and two books, Aquinas's Theory of Natural Law: An Analytic Reconstruction *and* Philosophy Matters. *He has also written extensively about the regional and religious history of the state of Ohio. Lisska's teaching excellence has been recognized by awards from the American Philosophical Association and the Sears Foundation. He was named the 1994 U.S. Outstanding Baccalaureate Colleges Professor by the Council for Advancement and Support of Education (CASE) and the Carnegie Foundation for the Advancement of Teaching.*

Often we instructors of undergraduate students consider the act of teaching to be rather solitary work, an activity between us and our students within the confines of a class or seminar room. At times, we only think about the "performance" dimension of the act of teaching and don't consider directly the role of the students. Furthermore, we don't immediately see the connections among curriculum, what curriculum structures enable us to do pedagogically, and how these structures assist in the development of the craft of teaching.

By *curriculum* I mean any institutional structure used to organize the academic courses in a college or university. This use of the term *curriculum* does not entail any specific, prescribed content. The structure of the curriculum may be as wide, for example, as a program of general education or as narrow as departmental requirements for a major. Thus, I ask that we reflect on two issues in this essay: 1) the role of curriculum, broadly construed, in effective teaching; and 2) the effect on the student of successful teaching. Both of these issues are central, I suggest, in any discussion of effective teaching.

SETTING THE STAGE: DON'T FORGET THE CURRICULUM

To begin, we might consider the ideas of the great medieval philosopher, Thomas Aquinas, on the concept of teaching. Aquinas is known for his reworking of Aristotelian philosophy within the pluralistic context of the medieval university. Yet Aquinas was, above all, a teacher—a teacher who left as his most impressive monument, the *Summa Theologica*, a book which he expressly notes that he wrote for beginning students in philosophy and theology. Aquinas thought long and hard about the teaching profession. In fact, he considers the fact of teaching to occur only when an appropriate effect occurs in the student. Teaching is not identical with the act of the professor; that act would merely be professing. Rather, teaching depends upon a relation between two actions—the one from the instructor and the other from the learner. Teaching has not occurred, so Aquinas argues, unless the effect of learning something takes place in the learner. Hence, the significant question, as Aquinas sees it, is this: Has the learner indeed learned something?

I suggest that it is to this question as posed by Aquinas that we need to address our attention. One necessary dimension of this question, moreover, concerns the role which curricular structures play in the learning process. Too often we college professors are convinced that the craft of teaching is reducible to the teaching process itself—we dutifully prepare our classes, lectures, and discussions; we read papers and examinations carefully; we prod our students to confront more deeply the issues under discussion; and we praise the progress we believe our students have made while participating in our classes. Yet we don't often consider what effect curriculum as an academic structure may have on our pedagogical successes.

Often curriculum discussions, both broadly and narrowly construed, are initiated by deans or other administrators—sometimes even Boards of Regents—who believe that the present curriculum in a college or department has become obsolete, or that it fails to meet the present concerns of students, or that it is not responsive to contemporary issues. Sometimes change itself is seen as an end to be advanced, so curricular innovations are proposed just to keep things moving. Too often those involved in the principal parts of any curriculum—the faculty—are not part of the driving force for curriculum change. Conversely, it is often the faculty who are blamed when curriculum proposals fail to be enacted. Every academic has heard the old adage:

"Changing a curriculum is like moving a cemetery!" As concerned teachers, however, we faculty should be interested in curricular structure. I suggest that some curricular structures may be necessary conditions for us to practice our craft well. To undertake an activity with care consistently is to reach a state of what Aristotle called "virtue" or *aretē*, the excellence attainable in human activity, and Aristotle and Aquinas both considered the craft of teaching to be a virtue. Curricular structures may be a means for us to perfect our craft and to become virtuous as teachers.

LEARNING: THE *TELOS* OF TEACHING

Let us assume for a moment that one of the principal driving forces behind any curricular structure is to facilitate learning on the part of students. And if learning is, as Aquinas suggests, the terminal point—the end or *telos*—of the teaching process, then learning should produce at least a modicum of satisfaction on the part of the instructor. Successful instruction only occurs if learning takes place. To sound for a moment like a philosopher: If we human agents act for ends, and if the end of teaching is learning, then successful teaching entails learning on the part of the student. The attainment of the desired end—learning—should produce a sense of accomplishment in the agent—the teacher. For the most part, effective teaching—so Aristotle would suggest—produces a sense of satisfaction in the instructor. Similar relationships hold for the successful completion of any craft.

If the above analysis is correct, then we need to ask what are the conditions—maybe even what, if any, are the *necessary* conditions—for learning to occur. I suggest that success in some areas of teaching and learning occurs through and by means of curricular structures. I offer as an example of this claim the development and progress of the undergraduate honors program at Denison University. Modest curriculum innovations offered by the honors program have enhanced the teaching and learning process on the Denison campus. Furthermore, this enhanced teaching and learning environment would not have been attained if the honors program were not functioning as it currently is.

Curricular structures matter. The following account of the honors program at Denison University shows how curricular structure enhances successful teaching and learning on my campus. The Denison experience can be replicated or adapted with equally good results on other campuses.

THE DEVELOPMENT OF A COMPREHENSIVE HONORS PROGRAM

The present honors program at Denison grew out of a faculty committee charged by the president and the dean to consider afresh how an honors program might affect undergraduate intellectual life. In the summer of 1986, four members of the Denison faculty met to determine how a successful honors program might be developed. The honors program then in existence was, by all accounts, moribund. In the fall of 1986, only about forty students matriculated to Denison with honors program invitations. A smattering of seminars were offered but only for freshmen and a few sophomore students. Senior honors projects were completed at the lowest level in some time, with one year witnessing fewer than twenty senior projects submitted to the faculty. Furthermore, students in the then fragmented program claimed that they experienced isolation on the Denison campus. Using the words of John Dewey, institutionally Denison had a "felt need" to resolve a set of problems. Some definite pragmatic action was necessary.

In the summer of 1986, the task we set for ourselves was the development of a comprehensive honors program that would meet specifically the needs of a selective liberal arts college. To meet these needs required, we suggested the accomplishment of several goals as articulated in the following propositions:

1) An honors program must be developed that was thoroughly *integrated* into the curriculum of the college. Since Denison students, like most undergraduate students, do not like to be separated from one another, an isolated honors college model would not be effective.

2) An honors program must be *comprehensive* and offer seminars throughout the four years of a Denison student's undergraduate career.

3) The honors program needed a *structure* that would enable students to become committed to higher intellectual achievement.

4) The honors program needed to be a *vehicle for more systematic advising* for post-Denison awards—the Rhodes, Marshall, Fulbright, and National Science Foundation fellowships, among others.

5) A physical *space* was required that would be devoted to honors students and their work.

6) The honors program director needed to work closely with the admissions office in order to *enroll a more highly talented freshman class.*

SUCCESS IN MEETING THESE GOALS

These goals have been met with astonishing success. Significantly, the teaching and learning situations in the honors program have improved substantially. For example, both terms of the 1995–1996 academic year saw nearly three hundred students enrolled in twenty-three seminars sponsored by the honors program.

The following items relate to the issues mentioned earlier as "felt needs":

1) Offering four credits for a term's work and limited to fifteen students, the honors program seminars for the most part meet general education requirements of the college and often count toward major and minor requirements as well. This arrangement meets the need for integration.

2) Earlier attempts at honors work at Denison focused almost exclusively on the first year. Hence, the honors program was tagged as a freshman-only program. Seminars are now offered in several categories: freshman only, freshman-sophomore, freshman through senior, and junior-senior. This variety enables the program to be comprehensive.

3) In 1994, thirty-nine seniors completed the requirements for graduation in the honors program; in 1995, nearly eighty-five honors projects were submitted to the faculty by graduating seniors. This fourfold increase is evidence of sustained intellectual achievement.

4) In the past five years, Denison students have received five Fulbright awards and three alternate designations; two National Science Foundation fellowships; two Rhodes Scholarship state finalist and three Truman Foundation finalist designations. In addition, four students have been recognized by the *USA Today* Academic All American Selection Committee. In 1995-96 alone, two Rhodes and two Marshall applications, one Truman, and several Fulbright applications were submitted. This fellowship activity is coordinated by the honors program and a faculty committee organized and chaired by the director of the honors program. Better and more effective advising is taking place.

5) Gilpatrick House, a renovated Victorian residence central to campus, became the Honors Center in 1989. This center houses the offices for the director, program secretary, a seminar room (with some hyperbole said to be like a room at Brasenose College, Oxford!), a commons, a kitchen, a small computer room, and an upstairs residence facility for ten students. The commons serves as a meeting place for student activities—study breaks, parties, seminars, student group meetings, and our immensely successful biweekly chowder-hour luncheons, where faculty chefs prepare their favorite dishes for a group of twenty students and faculty. Gilpatrick House meets the need for a designated space.

6) The honors program director works closely with an associate director of admissions. Honors program mailings are sent regularly from the Honors Center—in 1994-95 accounting for about 13,000 pieces of mail. The enrollment results have been astounding. In 1986, forty-two freshman

enrolled with invitations to the honors program. In 1995, two hundred and twelve freshmen enrolled, a fivefold increase. More striking, however, is the fact that the 1995 entering freshman class had nearly ninety secondary school valedictorians and salutatorians. Overall, Denison's 1995 freshman class numbered some seven hundred students. This working arrangement with the admissions office is paying huge dividends.

TEACHING, LEARNING, AND THE CURRICULUM
From the data presented and discussed above, it is evident that the honors program has attained a marked degree of institutional success. One must ask, however, if this program—a curricular structure—has influenced the teaching and learning at Denison? I suggest that it has. The following account provides evidence that curricular structures provide important opportunities and affect the pedagogical successes that we instructors have in the class and seminar room. It is my contention that the honors program as developed at Denison has been a substantive and pedagogically useful vehicle for innovative teaching in both departmental and cross-departmental ways. The honors program has enhanced the ways in which Denison instructors approach their craft of teaching. This program provides the curricular vehicle for teaching and learning to take place in ways unheard of before at Denison.

Teaching-learning opportunities
Team-taught seminars bring together faculty from diverse areas who normally do not have the opportunity to work with one another. A few examples: A team-taught seminar on the issues of human nature brought together an anthropologist and a psychologist; on medieval literature, an art historian and a post-modernist literature professor; on contemporary film, a philosopher of aesthetics and a film critic; on early American life, an American historian and a poet; on the "origins" of things, a physicist and a computer scientist; on writing about the landscape, an essayist and a botanist; on contemporary British theater, the theater department chair working with a visiting playwright in residence. The honors program provided the avenue for these creative seminars to take place. Of course, some of these seminars might have occurred in any case. That so many seminars have been developed so regularly through the creative juices of the Denison faculty, however, can only be attributed to the availability of such teaching opportunities in the honors program. The program provides a curricular structure so that these exciting teaching and learning possibilities can happen.

The norm for the honors program seminars, of course, continues to be one instructor in a seminar room with ten to fifteen students. Nonetheless, the creativity has been phenomenal. A few salient examples: A philosopher developed a cross-disciplinary seminar on the concept of authenticity; a psychologist on cognitive theory; a literature instructor on neglected women writers; an astronomer on cosmic questions; a mathematician on non-Euclidean geometry; a historian on plagues and people; a biologist on doing research through the Internet; a classicist on virtue in the *polis.* The list could go on and on.

For the most part, faculty have raved about their teaching experiences in the honors program. One faculty member recently said that his seminar in French literature was the highlight of his more than twenty-five years of teaching; a psychologist used some innovative discussion techniques with a first-year seminar that she described as one of her favorite courses in nearly fifteen years of teaching.

A community of learners

For students to learn—and especially for them to learn well—an appropriate environment is required so that intellectual life may be approached with gusto and commitment. Seminars in the honors program have contributed to bringing about this environment. Limited to fifteen students, each seminar can utilize different pedagogical devices. They can range, for example, from specialized writing assignments and journal keeping to attendance at professional meetings and taking field trips to places such as Frank Lloyd Wright's "Falling Water." Some exciting student projects have developed from the honors seminars, too. A few examples: Students in biology seminars have produced two issues of a science journal, one featuring the Internet in science research; other students read the texts of neglected women writers and edited their own anthology of these texts and authors; students participating in an ethic dance, jazz, and literature seminar choreographed and produced their own dance show; a senior composed his version of the *Stabat Mater* and then conducted the Denison concert choir in a performance of the work.

In addition, Gilpatrick House—the Honors Center—adds an important outside-the-classroom space for students in the program. Various social events take place there. The chowder hours have contributed to the students' sense of belonging. Denison honors students no longer feel isolated on the campus. Their psychic contentment contributes to an atmosphere in which the craft of their instructors can indeed produce learning—the desired effect of the teacher. Given Aquinas's account, teaching has taken place.

To Engage in Thought and Imagination: The Stuff Dreams Are Made Of

What these results suggest, I believe, is that a curricular structure, open to faculty creativity without the burdens of bureaucracy, provides a wonderful vehicle for substantive teaching and learning opportunities. This prospect, in turn, benefits immensely the learning environment at Denison and assists our students, as one of our honors program publications asks of them, to "engage in thought and imagination." One can almost paraphrase Kevin Costner in the film *Field of Dreams:* "Build an appropriate curriculum, and they will come to learn!"

Why has this program succeeded? I believe an important aspect of this program is that it is a vehicle for faculty to be involved with committed students, conducting seminars in areas about which they earlier only dreamt. Less structure permits the faculty the freedom to engage the students without attending to other superimposed goals. This freedom permits a burst of creativity. The almost libertarian position of the honors program curricular structure views academic management as a means of facilitating, not as a means of micro-managing. This curricular structure is a means—a vehicle—for faculty to teach well. Without this curricular structure, these seminar opportunities more than likely would not be part of the teaching program at Denison. Without these seminars, moreover, there would be less effective learning on this campus.

Composed of faculty and student representatives, the honors committee has never been at a loss for seminar proposals coming from the faculty. In one recent term, sixteen of twenty-three seminars were created freshly for the honors program. I keep reminding the Denison provost that the honors program is the cheapest and most efficient program of faculty development that he has. Our program is characterized by a lack of bureaucracy. Any faculty member may submit a proposal; the honors program committee considers the proposals and attempts to balance a term's offerings. Seminars are run on a temporary basis and thus do not need the sanction of the curriculum committee. The only prescriptive norm coming from the director's office is that the faculty are to engage the students intellectually. Faculty, however, are not simply to "pile on" extra work, a pedagogical method which is often the paradigm for many advanced placement courses in secondary school.

Many evaluations of successful teaching suggest that faculty enthusiasm is a necessary condition for teaching that is well received by students. An honors program fosters enthusiasm by providing an avenue to do serious reading and study of a topic of sustained interest with a committed group of students. If an instructor cannot become excited and enthusiastic in a situation like that, then one wonders what would bring about pedagogical enthusiasm.

The students enroll in the seminars for a variety of reasons. Most enjoy working in a small class setting with an instructor thoroughly excited about a topic. Because most seminars meet general education requirements, students meet their college requirements by participating in the honors program. The seminars foster an active element of learning—full participation is expected and achieved. Sitting in the back of the room with a baseball cap on backwards is not the norm.

A Few Suggestions

The experience of Denison's honors program will not—and probably should not—fit the local conventions of every academic institution. Nonetheless, there are some general principles that should be useful in determining curricular structures to promote teaching and learning.

- Honors program teaching is not a remedial program for burnt-out professors. It may indeed assist a teacher in not becoming burnt-out, but it is not a panacea for instructors having pedagogical problems.

- Very few prescriptive norms need to come from the director's desk. Our experience suggests that faculty work diligently and enthusiastically with their students in the honors seminars.

- Collegewide credit should be given for honors seminars to facilitate students' progress toward their educational goals—especially graduation.

- The seminars should be fully integrated into the general curriculum of the college.

- Some special space for students and faculty is appropriate; this space need not be an honors residence hall, but some space in which to "hang out" is important.

- The honors program and the admissions office need to work closely in the recruitment of students for the honors program; the honors program should insist that academic excellence and not "well-roundedness" is the criterion necessary for honors program acceptance.

Is It Worth It?

What should one say to this question but a resounding "Of course!" Learning occurs in the honors seminars because the faculty are thoroughly committed, intensely involved, and creatively engaged in the construction and teaching of seminars. This claim does not mean that other courses necessarily lack these characteristics. There is strong empirical evidence, however, that learning and engaged instruction do occur in our honors seminars. The curricular structure of the honors program has had an effect in determining effective teaching. Any discussion of effective teaching should not neglect the role that curricular structures might play in assisting effective teaching to occur. Effective teaching is not an solitary undertaking.

AUTHOR'S NOTE

The author wishes to acknowledge editor John Roth's thoughtful reading of an early draft of this essay. Professor Bill Nichols, my friend and successor as Dean of the College at Denison University, also read an earlier draft and offered many probing suggestions. Marianne Lisska, who writes for a major international corporation, generously and thoroughly proofread early and final versions of the essay.

10

Managing Discussion in Large Classes

J. DENNIS HUSTON

Professor of English and the Master of Hanszen College at Rice University, Dennis Huston is the author of Shakespeare's Comedies of Play *and numerous articles on Shakespeare, poetry, and drama. He was named the 1989 U.S. Professor of the Year by the Council for Advancement and Support of Education (CASE) and the Carnegie Foundation for the Advancement of Teaching.*

For over a decade I taught large English classes at Rice University. At least they were large by Rice's standards—between 60 and 100 students each. That I taught them in discussion format made them large classes of their kind for any university; very few undergraduate discussion courses, I suspect, exceed enrollments of thirty students. Mine, however, often do. I teach all of my classes this way because for me the joy in teaching comes from interaction with my students, from the discoveries that we make together. I love teaching, and what I love about it is not only the subject matter—that goes without saying—but also the process itself: the combination of fear and anticipation I feel before every class as I prepare for it; the adrenaline rush I often get in the classroom as we all improvise our way toward understanding; and the "buzz" I feel afterward when things have gone well (for the purposes of this essay I will overlook the depression I feel when they do not).

Teaching a large discussion class is not really very different from teaching a small one; it is much more time-consuming and involves much more work, but the pedagogical principles in both classes are the same. The trick to making large discussion courses work is really no trick at all; it is just doing with a lot more people the same thing one does in a seminar. The successful teacher of a large discussion class still must know the names of all her students; must listen carefully to their answers; and must use their answers to build the arguments she wishes to make that day, even if those answers disrupt the planned order of things. In a large class the teacher must also make everything bigger: She must use a louder voice, larger gestures, and more energy because she has to fill a bigger space. And she must move the action around the room more and faster so that one portion of the class does not feel left out while another portion gets all the attention. But these adjustments are variations upon the techniques of any good seminar teacher, who does the same things in not quite so big a way.

The limit of what I consider a manageable large discussion class is between 60 and 100 students. Numbers larger than that make it almost impossible to learn all the students' names or to meet with them individually in conference, things a teacher must do to establish the personal contact that builds community and trust in a classroom.

I do know of one very successful large chemistry class, of nearly three hundred students, taught in a modified discussion form. To encourage the active involvement of his students, the teacher of this course, my colleague John Hutchinson, not only answers questions in class but also employs strategies that force students to participate actively in the learning process. He poses a problem to them and then has the students talk about that problem with two or three other students around them. Then the groups of students poll their answers and discuss them in class.

Another colleague of mine, Alan Grob, does a similar thing with his Shakespeare class. He asks a question about a problematic moment in the play they are discussing; for example, when, in *Twelfth Night*, does Olivia fall in love with Cesario? He has them write brief arguments supporting their answers to this question, and then he asks students to read their answers. The differences in the students' answers serve as a focus for further discussion.

SHARING THE ENTERPRISE

In large discussion classes I try to meld my educational philosophy with my pedagogical methodology. For me teaching is essentially a human and humanizing activity that brings my students and me together in a shared enterprise of learning, where we all profit from working together, from learning both about and from one another. In the process, we build a community of people who accomplish more together than any of us could accomplish separately. And even though that community dissolves at the end of the semester, its memory may abide for many of us. A class that works, that fosters genuine intellectual excitement and inquiry in an atmosphere of trust, is a class whose effects reach beyond its scheduled time and place to touch—and occasionally change— lives. And that is what I hope every class I teach will do: change lives, by changing the way my students and I think and feel about ourselves, the people around us, and what we value. I realize, of course, that classes rarely do such things. But that fact does not keep me from wanting to do them: I try to prepare and teach every class as if it could have this kind of effect on the students—and on me.

To have such an effect, however, a class needs extraordinary commitment from its students, a fact I emphasize on the first day, when I try to explain my methodology, my style, my aims, and my expectations for the course. Although many of my colleagues think of the first class as focused on bookkeeping activities—handing out a syllabus, talking briefly about the text or texts, and making the first assignment—I think of it as hugely important because it gives me time to explain why I teach by discussion, even in a course of one hundred students. The opening class thus becomes in part an apologia for my whole educational philosophy, a kind of prolegomena for all that will happen in the classes to follow.

I feel I need to offer such an apologia because what I do in class is so different from what most of my students are used to. On the whole, Rice students (and, I suspect, most of their peers in other universities) have been conditioned by their previous educational experience to be passive receivers—consumers—of information. They have gotten where they are by being "good" students, which too often means that they have been rewarded for absorbing and regurgitating information. Such an activity is a necessary part of any learning experience, but it should not be the primary or only skill required of "good" students. Such students should also be able to think for themselves, to trust their own perceptions and feelings, to formulate questions of importance, and to recognize patterns the teacher overlooks.

Many of my students, however, have almost never been asked to do these kinds of things, and almost none of these students has ever been asked to do them *in* a class, in the presence of other students. Rice students have almost no experience thinking on their feet. Even some of my very best students would, if I would let them, remain forever silent in class. But I will not let them, which is what I explain to them on that first day. Because they have been conditioned to play it safe as students, to listen and absorb without actively participating in class discussion, I have to use radical methods to break down this kind of conditioning: I will thus force them to participate in class discussions, I tell them, by calling on them randomly, without prior warning. The questions I will ask them may be general or particular, open-ended or precisely focused, comparative or context-specific. Some-times they may even be questions whose answers I myself do not know because the most interesting questions are often of that kind. I ask such questions, I explain, not because I want to make them feel uncomfortable—though I understand that many of them will feel this way, at least at first—but because I think they have an obligation as educated people to articulate their ideas, to submit them to the judgment of others, to defend them against the challenges posed by conflicting ideas.

EXPLAINING THE AIMS AND EXPECTATIONS

In the process of explaining this methodology, I necessarily must talk also about aims and expectations. Many teachers, I know, choose to include this information in their syllabi, and I include some of it there, but I prefer to talk about it at length in the first class. That way I know for certain that my students understand what I expect of them and why. They also can tell from my tone and from the amount of time and energy I devote to my aims and expectations for the course how important they are to me and should be to them: I count partly, then, on the fact that this first class is different from any they have sat in before, as I intend the classes that follow to be different also, though not quite in the same way as this one. I also explain that this is the only time I plan to lecture in the course, that I am laying down ground rules, not yet practicing what I preach. That world of mutual adventure and discovery lies all before us, in the classes that follow.

When I talk about my aims and expectations, I focus on the aims first, in order to justify the expectations. These aims for my students always include:

1) developing their ability to think more imaginatively, independently, and carefully about the texts they encounter, texts that include not only the reading in the course but also the life they lead outside it

2) broadening and deepening their knowledge of literature

3) learning to trust their own critical instincts and feelings, even when they conflict with other students' or my reading of a text

4) developing their capacity to articulate and defend their ideas in oral discussion and encounters

5) sharpening their writing skills

6) seeing class preparations and discussion as at once both work *and* fun (since most of the students I teach tend to think of work and play as bifurcated rather than as related activities)

THE ROLE OF JOURNALS

To achieve such ends, I explain to my students, they must meet certain expectations I have of them. They must do the reading assignment for every class before that class meets, since they cannot effectively discuss an assignment they have not read. In addition, they must attend class regularly because effective discussion depends upon active participation, which, of course, depends upon students' being there. And finally, I ask all of my students to keep reading journals, notebooks in which they freewrite for approximately ten minutes after they have completed the reading assignment.

In these journals, whose form I borrow from Peter Elbow (1973), I want students to ask—and provide possible answers to—questions raised by the text: What strikes them as surprising, inconsistent, difficult, troubling in the reading assignment? Why? Where have they encountered anything like this before? How does the reading relate to something in their own experience? Did some moment or passage in the text seem to them particularly significant? Why? I also ask students to write their entries fast so that they will not become bogged down in the usual matters of composition: order, logic, precise phrasing. Instead I want them to go where their imaginations and the very act of writing take them; I want their journal writing to be, if possible, an exercise that frees their imaginative and creative energies. I also tell my students that I will read their journals, responding to their ideas with marginal notes, but that I will not grade them. I want them to write primarily for their own satisfaction, not mine.

Because I do not grade the journals, students sometimes have difficulty keeping them up to date. Conditioned to work for good grades, Rice students sometimes cannot bring themselves to work for no grade at all. I therefore collect journals without warning (usually about ten at a time so that I can return them by the next class), which means that students must bring them to class every day. And I warn students that if they do not keep their journals up to date, they will have to drop the course; I may not grade them, but I take them very seriously indeed.

I think journals may be the single most effective way to prepare students for class discussion. To write a journal entry, students must first have thought with some care about the reading assignment: They cannot just skim it quickly, reading words but not really thinking about what the words say. If students are to write intelligently about a text, they must make real intellectual contact with it; they must encounter and perhaps even do battle with it. Only then can they write intelligently and meaningfully about their experience of the text. Students who have written journal entries have at least thought about the assignment with some care. They know what troubles them in it, or what seems to them surprising or important, or what ties this reading assignment to something else they have read in this course or another. As a result, they can talk in class in an informed and intelligent way about the assignment. Having struggled with the text on their own, they often want to share their perceptions.

The worth of journals, however, does not stop with improving class discussion. They have other important effects as well. Often journals provide students with ideas that they can develop into papers. One of my students spent a whole week of journal entries developing, qualifying, and elaborating upon ideas that eventually grew into her first paper for the course. Sometimes, too, journals provide a medium for conversation: Students may raise questions in the journals that they do not ask in class, either because the questions are too personal or because class discussion focuses on different concerns. The journal thus provides me with an opportunity to answer questions, either in marginal notes or in conference, that I would not otherwise know existed. And because students sometimes reveal things about themselves in journals that they would not reveal in class, one or two students a semester may indicate in their journal entries signs of real emotional or academic problems, which gives me an opportunity to talk to them about getting help with these problems. In addition, because some students write more natural-sounding, more humanly voiced prose in their journals than in their essays, journals occasionally provide critical evidence of writing skills I would not otherwise know a student possesses. Having been taught to write essays in sterile, awkward, turgid prose, these students feel empowered when they discover that the prose they write for themselves is also the prose they should write for others. And finally, journals are useful because for some students they become an end in themselves. When I remarked recently in the margin of a student's journal that she was under no obligation to write as much as she was writing, she replied in her next entry: "I write these entries for myself, not for you."

GETTING TO KNOW THE STUDENTS

The final thing I do on the first day of class is to begin to gather information about my students. I pass out 4 x 6 index cards and ask the students to print their names (and the pronunciation of their names), their year, their major, their hometown, and their school telephone number. In addition, I ask them also to write briefly about what they did last summer, about their principal extracurricular activities at Rice (or in high school if they are freshmen), and about what they imagine they will be doing in fifteen years. These cards, which often prove an invaluable resource, serve many purposes. They give me basic information about the students, which helps me to learn their names and, sometimes, to understand reasons why some of them have trouble in the course (lack of experience with the discipline, weak high school education, intense focus on other activities or subjects). To contact such students, who often stop coming regularly to class, I need only refer to the phone numbers on their cards.

In addition to this basic information, the cards also tell me important things about a student's experience outside both the classroom and Rice, information that I can sometimes use during class discussions. If, for instance, I want to draw a parallel or an analogy between something in the assignment and sports, or theater, or movies, or politics, or music, I can call on a student who I know has knowledge of this particular field. In addition, the cards often tell me something about my students' hopes and dreams, which again proves useful when I want to ask content-specific questions. The cards, then, help me to know my students better. And knowing them better enables me to teach them more effectively. For this reason I review the cards nearly every day during the first two weeks of class and with some regularity during the rest of the semester. Even when I begin to know the students pretty well from their class performance, journals, and papers, I often discover something important about them from rereading their cards.

The cards also help me to learn students' names because I add information to them in the first weeks of the semester. After I first call on a student to recite in class, I write notes about his appearance on his card—after class—to help me put names with faces. Some faculty members I know have an even more efficient way of learning names in a large class. On the first day they divide the students into groups of ten, having them make name-tents, and then take Polaroid pictures of each group. The method one selects for learning names does not really matter; what matters is that it works, for perhaps nothing helps build a sense of community and trust in a classroom faster than learning names. In the most basic way, the teacher thus shows her concern for her students: She cares about them; she knows who they are. A teacher who does not learn names in a discussion class—even a large one—sends a signal that undermines the whole discussion process because it implies that she does not care enough about the students (and, by implication, about their ideas) to learn the most basic thing about them. Learning names, then, is an absolutely crucial part of a teacher's responsibility in a discussion class; not to do so is a breach of trust.

THE IMPORTANCE OF CLASSROOM SPACE
I realize that I have said nothing about the classroom space itself, which often profoundly affects the course: A good room definitely helps promote good

discussion, and a bad one is a constant problem to be overcome. Thus, I always make my preferences known early to the person in the university responsible for classroom assignments, because most universities have very few good rooms for large discussions classes; they may, in fact, have none. For me, the ideal room for a large course is a big rectangle, more deep than wide, which enables me to see almost all of the students at once. That way students in one part of the room do not feel left out of the discussions when I am talking to a student or students in another part. The room should also contain moveable chair-desks (so that students do not feel nailed down to the floor), arranged to provide one or two aisles that give me access to the back of the room. That way I can "get in the faces" of the students who often try to hide back there. Sometimes, too, I may find an empty chair next to them, where I can sit and create moments of real physical and emotional closeness, moments that help me to emphasize ideas or exchanges of particular importance. The worst kind of room for a large discussion class is the large lecture hall with a raised stage and auditorium seats secured to the floor. Such a room countermands in almost every way what I am trying to do in the class because it separates me from, and raises me above, the students—as if I am the "true word," and they were there, lined up and nailed down, to receive it. One *can* make discussion classes work in such a room—by sometimes climbing down from the stage, sometimes bringing students up onto it for group work, and sometimes walking along the sides and to the back of the room in order to force a new perspective on the students. But such a room always works against the best interests of the students and teacher; it is a problem to be overcome, not a space that promotes communication and community.

BEGINNING THE DISCUSSION

I think of the second day of class as the real beginning of the course. In it we engage in class discussion for the first time and to it I bring a number of pedagogical objectives. I want the class to be fun and exciting. I want to get a lot of people talking. I want to make something positive out of as many students' answers as I can so that others feel inclined to participate. This I do by writing some of their own words on the board, which enables them to see their ideas valued. Another thing I do in this class is to make sure that students are listening to one another, not just to me. So I may ask one student to elaborate upon an idea suggested by another. During this class, too, I want to help the students move toward at least one really surprising interpretive insight: I want them to feel the excitement of discovering something together that they had not noticed on their own. And finally, I want to dig deeply into a least one student's answer—when it is a good one—following it up with other questions, designed to make the student elaborate upon and qualify his original answer. In this way I can suggest that discussion in the class does not always stop with one answer, that good answers obligate students to think more deeply about their own ideas. I want the first discussion class to set the tone for the class as a whole: I want it to be full of intellectual energy and surprise, involving as many people as possible in an enterprise they feel is interesting and exciting. And I want students to feel that time in this class rushes by because there is so much to say and because everyone is having a good time.

Our first discussion may not affect many students in this way, but I try to make as many of them as I can feel my enthusiasm for what we are doing. I concentrate hard on putting students' names with their faces. And whenever possible, I make references to ideas students have raised earlier in the discussion. I also watch faces very carefully as I teach because they tell me a lot. What students seem most or least interested? Early in the hour, I usually look for faces showing enthusiasm to build my confidence, but as the hour progresses, and I have a better sense of where the discussion is going, I pick out students who look tired or bored, and call on them, trying to draw them into the discussion. I cannot stress too much the importance of really looking at faces during class because they often provide the best evidence of how the discussion is going, not only by signaling enthusiasm or boredom, but also by indicating when students do not understand a concept or argument: It is not hard to tell from students' faces when they are confused. In one of the best essays ever written about teaching, Roland Christensen (1991) talks about the crucial importance of reading students' physical responses—not only their faces but also their body language and their behavior: What does a student's way of slouching in his chair or waving his hand or suddenly growing silent suggest about his response to this subject or this discussion? If we watch our students carefully as we teach, they will show us what is working and what is not. In addition, a student answering a question will often send subtextual signals about what she is thinking or feeling. She may stop talking, for instance, but her face or eyes may indicate that she is not yet really finished. If the teacher then waits a few moments longer, the student may say something really interesting.

LISTENING TO STUDENTS

All of which brings me to what may be the single most important skill a good teacher of discussion classes must possess: the ability to *listen* to students' answers, to hear what the students are really saying, not what the teacher expects them to say. For years I have observed graduate teaching assistants in the classroom, and the most common difficulty they have is really hearing the students' answers to their questions. The teaching assistants have often spent hours preparing a text and designing questions to get at its crucial themes and problems. But they too often know exactly what answer they want to each of their questions, and if they do not get this answer, they feel flustered. Instead of running with the students' ideas, improvising with the material they have been given, they dismiss the student's answer as "interesting" and then ask again the same question they have just asked, hoping the next student who speaks will give them the answer they are looking for. It does not take students long to realize that what they are being asked to do is not to discuss, not to think their own ideas, but to read the teacher's mind. And they quickly lose interest in answering questions.

Sometimes a teacher looking for a particular idea may think she hears it in a student's answer, may misinterpret what the student says because of what she *expects* him to say. This is a mistake I constantly watch for in my classes because my excitement about the interpretation we are constructing together makes me anticipate answers. I may start to develop an idea that I think has been voiced by a student and suddenly see that student's face clouded with confusion. Then I have to backtrack and listen again to what the student has actually said. Listening—really listening—to what students say is crucial to building a successful discussion.

IMPROVISING

Along with listening goes another skill essential to building good discussion in the classroom: improvisation. Lively, interactive discussion develops only when the teacher effectively manages the discussion process by helping students to see beyond the immediate implications of their ideas, to ask questions they did not themselves think to ask, to connect their ideas to those of other students, and to note similarities and differences between different parts of this text or between this text and others. To improvise successfully, the teacher must be prepared to build on ideas as they come from the students, not as he has conceived of them outside of class. In a class built on discussion, organization, which is often the linchpin of a successful lecture, has very little importance. To be sure, the teacher must periodically summarize the important ideas that grow out of the discussion—looking back at where the class has been in order to anticipate where they are going. But the class may get where it is going in a circuitous, disorganized way, often wandering off the beaten path to travel down blind alleys or follow winding detours because the students choose to go that way. Or, suddenly excited by a glimpse of their destination, the students may jump whole sections of the journey and conclude it precipitously. Then the teacher, with the end already attained, must help the students backtrack over the missed parts. When discussion develops naturally, it often does not move forward in a very organized way, but students do not care; they are too busy making discoveries and building arguments to be bothered by a little disorganization. If as teachers we lecture to students, we need to organize our arguments clearly so that the students can follow them, but if instead we build classes on discussions with students, their minds structure and organize the arguments as they develop them. When students actively participate in and shape what they learn, they do not need the same kind of organizational help that they require when they are merely passive receivers of information.

MONITORING THE PROCESS

Although the teacher of a discussion class does not have to concern herself much with organization, she has to think constantly about process. The success of the class depends on controlling both the subject matter and the process of discussion itself. The teacher must constantly monitor and control the dynamics of the group: What does the energy of the class feel like today? Who has prepared the assignment particularly well? Is this material that most of them find interesting or boring? How well have the students understood the reading? How many of them want to participate? Are one or two students carrying the discussion? If so, how can I draw others in? Today who is talking less than usual? Do I need to call on one of my best and most articulate students to give the class a lift? Or is this the kind of subject that might enable one of the quieter, less assertive students to shine? Can I stir them up with some kind of really surprising question? If so, can I think of one? Am I focusing attention too much in one part of the room or on too few students? Am I pushing an interpretation too hard in one direction? Should I come at this topic from a different angle? How? These are the kinds of questions I ask myself during class while I am simultaneously asking questions of students, summarizing what they say, elaborating upon their ideas, and pushing them to think more carefully about the text and the discussion. As Roland Christensen (1991) has argued, the successful teacher of a discussion class is always doing at least two things at once—managing both the process of discussion and the subject being discussed.

PREPARING FOR THE DISCUSSION

To handle this kind of challenge, one must spend substantial preparation time thinking not only about the subject matter but also about how to make that subject matter available to a particular group of students. As I prepare for class, I first go over the material assigned, trying to identify the ideas and passages that seem most important, both for me and for these students. What themes, problems, issues, and questions do the people in this class find most interesting? What important ones are they likely to overlook? Because I tend to see things in clusters and groups rather than in ordered structures, it is relatively easy for me to improvise in class: Student answers tend to bring up information from one cluster or another, and then the students and I begin to build upon the clusters, often crossing from one cluster to another. As I prepare questions designed to provoke discussion, I tend to think only of opening gambits for each cluster of ideas, trusting that other questions will occur to me once we have begun talking about these ideas. I do, however, spend a good deal of time thinking about those opening gambits. Do I want to open with a shocking question, designed to surprise the students into really imaginative thinking? Or should I choose instead a much more predictable kind of beginning: How is this work like _____? What in this work did you find most confusing, important, or notable? Should I perhaps open the discussion in a low-key way by simply asking what issues the students want to talk about, what questions they want answered? Should I focus on a particular moment in the text or use it as a way of discussing crucial themes or problems? Should I begin with a context-specific question that has important subtextual ramifications? Sometimes, even after careful preparation, I cannot make up my mind which of these kinds of questions to ask or what cluster of ideas to explore first. Then I simply trust my instincts: When I arrive in class, I select the one that feels right at the moment. Like an actor, carefully rehearsed, I may feel I have prepared thoroughly enough to live my part moment to moment.

As I prepare, I often think, too, about whom I plan to call on, particularly at the beginning of the class. Who has personal experience that qualifies him to talk in an informed way about these ideas? Who has written perceptively in his journal about the issues we will be discussing? Who has not talked much recently in class? Who in the past has shown real interest in some of the problems I mean to address? Who seemed hostile to, or defensive about, these kinds of themes the last time we discussed them? How can I make positive use of that student's hostility or defensiveness? By asking myself such questions as I prepare class, I sometimes can anticipate the shape that the class discussion will take and who the major players will be. But more often such preparation serves as a source of information to draw on as I improvise my way through a discussion.

When I begin, what questions I ask and whom I call on are often decisions I make on the spur of the moment. Those decisions feel instinctive, and in a way they are, because I improvise them as I go, firing them off of the

11

Suit the Action to the Word: Teaching Minds and Bodies in the College Classroom

MICHAEL FLACHMANN

 *Professor of English at California State University, Bakersfield, Michael Flachmann has published eight books including* Beware the Cat: The First English Novel, Shakespeare's Lovers, *and* Shakespeare's Women—*and over forty articles in such journals as* Shakespeare Quarterly, Studies in English Literature, *and others. He has also worked for many years in professional theater, serving as dramaturg for over fifty Shakespearean productions at the Oregon Shakespeare Festival, the La Jolla Playhouse,* California Institute of the Arts, and the Utah Shakespearean Festival (where he has been the company dramaturg since 1986). An avid tennis player who also teaches courses in self-defense and judo, Flachmann was selected Outstanding Professor for the entire twenty-campus California State University system in 1993. He was also named the 1995 U.S. Professor of the Year for Master's Degree Universities by the Council for Advancement and Support of Education (CASE) and the Carnegie Foundation for the Advancement of Teaching.*

"Why couldn't you just tell me what I wanted to hear? Was that asking so much?" demands King Lear plaintively.

"You know how much I hate these public displays of affection," responds a sobbing Cordelia. "Why do I have to tell you how much I love you? Don't you already know?"

Do you recognize the source of the preceding epigraph? An early rejected draft from one of Shakespeare's tragedies? A television sound bite from a recent exposé on dysfunctional families? The answer is neither of the above.

This dramatic confrontation resulted from two students in one of my college English classes. Performing a theatrical technique called "psychodrama," they impersonated two of the principal characters from *King Lear*. In my Shakespeare courses, I use many improvisational teaching methods that get the students up and moving around and playing different roles in class. I do this not only because the students love these methods and often gain stunning insights into the plays as a result of them, but also because these approaches derive from a sound pedagogical foundation based on 1) a clear understanding of what the phrase "dramatic literature" means, and 2) recent important discoveries, particularly in the field of multiple intelligences, concerning the most efficient ways in which students learn complex educational material. The success I've had with several of these theatrical techniques—not only in my Shakespeare courses but in classes on subjects as diverse as English composition, medieval drama, and judo and self-defense—suggests that many of these methods would work beautifully in other academic areas as well, where professors sometimes neglect the importance of physical learning in their single-minded though well-intentioned emphasis on the intellectual development of their students.

THE TEACHING OF DRAMATIC LITERATURE

The first reason these theatrical techniques are pedagogically sound in the study of Shakespeare has to do with the nature of dramatic literature. As an English teacher, I find comfort and security in understanding clearly what category of literature I am teaching, because I can then tailor my pedagogical approach to a literary type and to the particular class in which I am teaching that material. Most educators would agree, I suspect, that we must fit the method to the matter if we are to reach our students effectively. Adapting our approach to the topic is especially important, of course, in illuminating academic subjects that we believe we understand, but really don't. Plays fall squarely into this category of educational mirages: We think we see them clearly, but they trick us through illusion. As a result, drama is all the more difficult to teach because most English teachers have been conditioned over the years to view plays as strange, mixed-breed creatures suspended precariously between novels and poems. Shakespeare's plays, after all, are composed in verse, which identifies them as extremely long poems; by the same token, they contain characters, speeches, and plots, which means they are somehow akin to novels and other works of fiction.

At this point, the madness degenerates into method. Since few of us are properly trained to teach dramatic literature, we naturally and instinctively gravitate toward the familiar, inherited, and well-worn pedagogical techniques used generation after generation in teaching novels and poems. The problem, however, is that these methods are only partially successful in exploring and illuminating plays because we have essentially had to invent hybrid teaching techniques to help analyze what we incorrectly perceive to be a hybrid literary creation. As a result, we fall back on clumsy, ineffective, and outdated classroom methods that do little justice to the excitement and power of this unique artistic genre.

THE TWO "PLAYS"

Another symptom of this same problem is that most English teachers use the identical word—*play*—to designate both the printed document and its performance on stage. We say "Have you read the play?" and "Have you seen the play?" failing to distinguish between two remarkably different experiences: 1) sitting quietly in the comfort of our own study while reading words on a page, and 2) watching a fully mounted production fleshed out on a stage before us. This semantic confusion is stunningly significant since it implies that reading a play is just as fulfilling as seeing it performed: Neither event is preferable to the other. Ironically, this traditional verbal duplication is actually crucial to our misrepresentation of drama as a genre in the English classroom because we are therefore able to bring Shakespeare's plays into our high schools and colleges without ever having to respond to the clear and patent fact that a play changes dramatically (pun intended) when we export it from the stage into the study or classroom. If we used different words to denote each stage of the process—the play as printed document and the play as performance—we would be forced to admit that we are severely distorting the genre by studying it in virtual isolation from its proper theatrical milieu. Viewed in this fashion, our misuse of the word *play* seems faintly conspiratorial: If we are to have any credibility as teachers of Shakespeare, we *must* argue that reading a play is just as fulfilling as seeing it. Otherwise, why would the world pay any attention to what we do in our classrooms?

If reading a play is an unnatural act, then what is the precise connection between the printed document and its ultimate realization on stage, and how can a clearer understanding of this intimate relationship help transform the way we approach Shakespeare with our students? First, we need to begin using the proper word to indicate what we are studying in our classrooms. When we teach plays, what we are actually teaching is *scripts* intended for performance. The language begs to be spoken by accomplished actors; the characters, dramatic situations, and philosophical significance yearn to be fleshed out with exciting and colorful costumes, evocative sets, vivid lighting, powerful sound and music design, stage movement, audience response, and all the other elements that make watching a play one of the most emotionally and intellectually exhilarating experiences in the world.

TURNING SCRIPTS INTO PRODUCTIONS

This relationship between a script and a play (that is, between the textual document and its theatrical realization on stage) will seem much clearer if we compare it to similar parallels between other sets of objects. For example, a script wants to be a production in the same way a printed recipe wants to be a steaming hot plate of *coq au vin*. No sane person would ever attempt to rip a page out of a book of recipes and eat it, yet we routinely imply to our students that reading a script will be just as tasty and nourishing as actually seeing a production of that script complete with all the magic of live theater. Imagine, if you will, a cooking class in which the participants read and discuss recipes for hours at a time, yet never actually make or taste any meals! Perhaps such classes do exist somewhere, but I cannot believe they are intended for anyone other than highly accomplished chefs who are so adept at their art that they can taste in their minds the delicate blend of ingredients displayed on the pages before them.

Similarly, only a very talented and learned musician could look at a musical score and hear in her inner ear the subtle melodies on the page. Yet we habitually ask our students to respond in the same sophisticated fashion to a playscript by imagining what that script might look like in a fully staged production—all despite the painful fact that over 98 percent of high school students and 92 percent of college students have never seen a live professional production of any of Shakespeare's plays. How can they possibly imagine what this script, this unfinished play, will look and feel like if they have never had a single experience in which they enjoyed watching a script develop into a magnificent and thrilling performance?

In truth, the ability to envision a potential production from simply reading a script is an incredibly complex and highly refined way of reacting to the words on the page. Good directors and designers, who are trained to do this and are adept at working with the process, can use their creative imaginations as naturally as breathing. But for the rest of us mere mortals, the task is nearly impossible. What if, in comparison, our students had only read Mozart's scores and had never actually listened to his sublime, inspiring music? How could they conceivably imagine what one of his concertos sounds like? Would we not consider them horribly deprived in this important artistic area? And how would we feel about a music teacher who spent weeks and weeks in his introductory classes having his students read sheet music without ever permitting them to listen to it? We would, no doubt, find him guilty of gross educational malpractice and railroad him out of the profession.

Yet we continue to tolerate and disseminate such confusion in our English classrooms despite the fact that by doing so we cripple the genre and bore our students—and all because we are apparently more comfortable teaching drama in the same way we teach poetry and fiction. In reality, however, this process of distorting Shakespeare is not comfortable at all: We must work extremely hard in our struggle to reduce plays from the magnificence of theatrical performance to the shallow and barren confines of our classrooms. To do so, we have to steal away almost every shred of excitement by reading the scripts in isolation from the actors, directors, designers, and other stage technicians who create living, breathing worlds on stage out of these bare-bone blueprints for action.

USING THEATRICAL TECHNIQUES

Theatrical teaching techniques can be extremely helpful in returning much of this excitement to the study of Shakespeare by recreating in our courses many of the production aspects that make his plays so interesting and enjoyable on stage. In particular, providing our students with a taste of such important dramatic concepts as blocking, characterization, music, lighting, sets, costumes, and other design elements will allow them to experience some of the exquisite theatricality of Shakespeare's plays, even in an English classroom. These methods can also help supplement and support the use of more traditionally literary approaches that are effective in helping students appreciate the value of reading Shakespeare, as opposed to seeing it performed. In other words, why should we limit the study of Shakespeare to either the page or the stage when we can easily combine both approaches in our classrooms?

In my own English courses, for example, I've had considerable success not only with the techniques of psychodrama (illustrated in the opening lines of this essay), but with many similar methods that work splendidly because they encourage students to respond to dramatic literature as a unique literary genre that begs to be taught in unique ways. Specifically, I teach meter and versification—often difficult subjects to master—by asking ten students to impersonate a line of iambic pentameter. Using Hamlet's famous "To be or not to be, that is the question" speech, for instance, I will ask the students to stand in a straight line and recite the words, each person saying only a single syllable. Their first discovery is that the line has eleven syllables, so they have to recruit another student to be the "tion" at the end of the line. Next, I ask the students playing unaccented syllables to kneel down, while the accented syllables remain standing. Before long, as they continue to recite the line with different inflections, the class will begin to internalize the way in which poetic meter shapes meaning through rising and falling intonations, hard and soft consonants, word repetitions, internal pauses, and all the other glorious mechanics of Shakespeare's verse.

In an interesting variation on psychodrama, I'll ask three students to come up to the front of the room and act out a speech from one of the plays. The first student will read one or two lines of the speech; then the second, standing behind him, will paraphrase those lines to the class; and the third, speaking from behind the second, will tell us what he thinks the character's subtext is in the lines (that is, what the character is actually thinking while he is reciting his speech). An example from Goneril's false praise of her father in *King Lear* (l.i.55–61) might go something like this:

First Student: "Sir, I love you more than words can wield the matter."

Second Student: "Dad, I can't possibly tell you how much I love you."

Third Student: "You demented old man! Am I telling you what you want to hear? What do I have to say to get a bigger share of the kingdom?"

Similarly, I spend a considerable amount of time blocking scenes, during which the class and I will try to figure out where each of the characters might be standing on stage, which entrances and exits would be used, and what kinds of stage movement could occur at specific moments in a production of the play.

I've gotten good results, too, from making a deliberately inflammatory statement, such as "Wives should always obey their husbands," and then asking the students to walk to one side of the room or the other depending upon whether they agree with the statement or not. The ensuing discussions, which often get quite vocal, have served as excellent introductions to various plays we have studied—in this particular case, *The Taming of the Shrew.*

Like many professors, I make extensive use of discussion groups, though I will often assign each group a different question or aspect of a play to consider, so that the ensuing full-class discussion is richer and more profound because all students have had an opportunity to voice their opinions in the group sessions. I've also had success with assigning students to become specific characters for a day (we then save time at the conclusion of the class period to guess who was impersonating which character), with staging mock trial scenes where we debate the relative guilt or innocence of certain characters (this works particularly well on *Romeo and Juliet*), with dividing up into acting groups and staging specific scenes, and with two other interesting staging techniques called "parallel scenes" (Flachmann, 1984) and "changing the w's" (Flachmann, 1993).

As is true with most good experimental educational techniques, the teacher must be willing—like Bottom in *A Midsummer Night's Dream*—to make an ass of himself by trying them in the classroom. Even our occasional failures, however, can bring forth spectacular results, and most teachers will soon find that the potential for insight and enthusiasm provided by these methods will far outweigh the risk of embarrassment.

HOW STUDENTS LEARN MOST EFFECTIVELY

These same theatrical teaching techniques, so useful and appropriate in introducing our students to dramatic literature, are also effective in a wide range of other courses at the high school and college level for a second, even more intriguing reason: The unique blend of physical and intellectual responses awakened by these pedagogical methods creates precisely the right balance of learning modes favored by many recent scholars who advocate the theory of multiple intelligences in their educational research. First proposed by Harvard psychologist Howard Gardner in his 1993 book *Frames of Mind*, the theory divides intelligence into the following seven comprehensive categories: linguistic (ability in verbal communication); logical-mathematical (the use of numbers); spatial (accurate perception of the visual-spatial world); bodily-kinesthetic (using one's body to express ideas or feelings); musical (skill with musical rhythm, pitch, and melody); interpersonal (sensitivity to people's moods, intentions, and motivations); and intrapersonal (self-knowledge). According to Gardner (1993), these seven intelligences work together in most people to solve problems, fashion products, create insights, or store knowledge. Since some of these intelligences (like linguistic and logical-mathematical skills) are located in the left hemisphere of the brain and others (like spatial and musical) involve the right hemisphere, teaching techniques that appeal to intelligences in each of these cerebral hemispheres are likely to engage a greater percentage of our student-learners and also to elicit a stronger response from individual students than single-intelligence stimuli are able to do (see also Armstrong, 1994).

If we write a few lines of Shakespearean verse on the chalkboard, for example, we will engage our students' linguistic intelligence, though none of the other six modes will be stimulated by such a one-dimensional classroom approach. On the other hand, if we ask two students to read the same lines aloud to each other, using appropriate movement and facial expressions as they do so, we are vastly expanding the range of intelligences to include all of the following: linguistic (reading, pronouncing, and understanding the words written on the page); spatial (the ability to imagine oneself as a partner participating in an ongoing conversation); bodily-kinesthetic (using one's body to move about the room and express feelings through gestures, facial expressions, and tactile relationships); musical (the capacity to hear and express the rhythms of spoken language); interpersonal (meaningful response to a partner's feelings); and intrapersonal (self-knowledge gained through the experience of acting out and analyzing the dramatic character's words and thoughts). Even the logical-mathematical intelligence might be engaged to some extent in this scenario if the students are aware of counting out beats in the fairly regular ten-syllable lines so characteristic of Shakespeare's mature verse.

WIDER APPLICATIONS

This educational theory of triggering multiple intelligences, which has worked so effectively in my Shakespeare classes, has served me nicely in other courses as well. In medieval drama, for example, I take my students outside, lay down bed sheets for stages, and block scenes from *Everyman* or *The Castle of Perseverance*, and in my composition classes I teach punctuation by taping oversized commas, periods, and quotation marks to my students' chests and having them leap from their seats to punctuate a row of students impersonating dependent and independent clauses. Similar techniques have even been useful in my judo and self-defense courses, where I deliberately mix intellectual instruction on the history and theory of martial arts with physical demonstrations of the throws, chokes, mat work, and falling exercises that are staple ingredients of the sport. As a teacher of judo for over thirty years, I have subconsciously incorporated many of its principles into my work in the English classroom, including traditional Oriental respect for the process of education, courteous interaction between instructor and pupils, genuine concern for the success of all students (regardless of their intelligence or skill level), and, most important, combined physical and mental stimulation that makes the subject matter of each course especially meaningful, exciting, and memorable.

On my campus, many other professors are using similar innovative teaching methods that involve their students' bodies as well as their minds. One of our physicists, for example, has his students learn about molecular weight and motion by having them run around the classroom, bump into each other, and veer off in oblique directions. A historian asks her students to present reports in which they dramatize important events from American history. One mathematician uses spatial visualization to introduce the concept of number theory by setting up a race track of chairs and having several students run around the track at different speeds. In our criminal justice program, a professor employs role-playing exercises in which students alternate pretending that they are crime victims and convicted felons; likewise, education professors simulate parent-teacher conferences by asking students to play each of these roles in the classroom. One of our biologists boasts that her students' physical hands-on laboratory work is much more important than her lectures because "in science, students learn best through experiments." Role playing is also used in several of our management courses, in which the professors have students act out both sides of a negotiation process between corporate managers and union representatives, and in sociology courses in conflict mediation, where students use play acting to learn how to resolve personality disputes. All of these professors at my university, plus thousands of other innovative faculty members throughout the nation, are using the same kinds of techniques to encourage their students to learn course material through an effective combination of mental and physical stimulation.

Whether the course is judo, Shakespeare, or something in between, I am a great believer in bringing together mental and physical stimuli—brains and brawn—in the educational process whenever possible. Only through this unique and effective combination of reason and emotion can our students truly take ownership of the knowledge we are paid to communicate to them. As actors have known for many years, the body has memory. As a result, long speeches are much easier to memorize when the blocking in the scene has been established through rehearsals with the director. Only at this point does the physical skill of navigating the stage in spatial patterns join with and reinforce the intellectual skill of understanding and learning one's lines. I have found this phenomenon to be valid in my own personal life as well. In fact, when I recall the most enduring, meaningful personal truths I have learned over the past fifty-three years, these moments of intellectual insight and clarity are always associated with some strong physical or emotional experience.

I remember vividly, for example, the delicious, almost tangible sensation of joy I felt when I saw my first live professional Shakespeare production, and I also recall the incredible emotional high of teaching my first college class. These memories are stored forever within my psyche through the powerful combination of intellectual and emotional stimuli. The trick of good teaching, I believe, is to remember the passion we first felt for our cherished academic fields and then to communicate to our students the elation, insight, and pure love of our disciplines. I try to do this by joining intellectual and physical experiences in my courses as often as possible, not only in the instruction my students receive but also in the behavior I model for them. If, as Shakespeare suggests, we always "suit the action to the word" in our classrooms, we will be able to reach not only into our students' minds but into their hearts as well.

REFERENCES

Armstrong, T. (1994). *Multiple intelligences in the classroom.* Alexandria, VA: Association for Supervision and Curriculum Development.

Flachmann, M. (1993). Changing the w's in Shakespeare's plays. In J. E. Davis & R. E. Salomone (Eds.), *Teaching Shakespeare today.* Urbana, IL: National Council of Teachers of English.

Flachmann, M. (1984). Teaching Shakespeare through parallel scenes. *Shakespeare Quarterly, 25* (5), 644–646.

Flachmann, M. (forthcoming). Think but this and all is mended: Reading Shakespeare (and other unnatural acts). In J. E. Davis & R. E. Salomone (Eds.), *Teaching Shakespeare into the twenty-first century.*

Gardner, H. (1993). *Multiple intelligences: The theory in practice.* New York, NY: HarperCollins.

12

Improving Teaching Through Teaching Portfolio Revisions: A Context and Case for Reflective Practice

JOHN ZUBIZARRETA

 *Professor of English and director of honors at Columbia College of South Carolina, John Zubizarreta was named the 1994 South Carolina Professor of the Year by the Council for Advancement and Support of Education (CASE) and the Carnegie Foundation for the Advancement of Teaching. He has also earned recognition for teaching and scholarly excellence from the American Association for Higher Education, the South Atlantic Association of Departments of English, the National Methodist Board of Higher Education, the South Carolina Commission on Higher Education, and Columbia College. In addition to his publications about literature, pedagogy, and portfolios, Zubizarreta has mentored faculty nationwide in developing portfolios to enhance and document teaching performance. An avid skier, he is also a former six-time national champion in whitewater canoe competition.*

In the context of higher education practices today, there are pressures from within and outside the academy for professors to document teaching competence, to record productivity, to tie research and scholarship to achievement in the classroom, and to demonstrate assessable accomplishment in student learning. These pressures have shifted the burden of faculty evaluation and improvement from anecdote to hard evidence, from the basically private and privileged professional life of past decades to a career under severe public scrutiny.

Faculty decisions about hiring, tenure, advancement, salary, grants, and merit awards are made increasingly not on the basis of accrued time in service, accepted reputation, or quality of research but on recorded evidence of continued growth in the many complex dimensions of the professoriate, particularly teaching. In the teaching profession, these changes have prompted a wave of interest in the benefits of reflective practice. Such a pressing national agenda suggests that professors committed to the kind of excellence celebrated by the CASE and Carnegie Professor of the Year awards are concerned seminally with finding faculty development strategies that blend the imperatives of clear, rigorous documentation and assessment with an intrinsic desire to improve teaching and learning.

As I experience it daily in my own teaching, reflective practice is grounded in the value of seeing teaching as an activity that is constantly in flux, an endeavor that challenges us 1) to examine *what, how,* and, even more importantly, *why* we teach, and 2) to question the assumptions, methods, materials, and goals of our teaching in order to test continually the extent of their influence on student learning. Model professors remain successful teachers probably because in large part they recognize the process nature of their craft. Seeking regularly to strengthen their impact on learning by engaging in meticulous, intentional research about their labor in the classroom, such professors demonstrate what Ernest Boyer (1990) calls the scholarship of teaching, which takes seriously the call to improve practice through careful reflection and action. Teaching, in other words, becomes not just vocation but vital avocation, not just work but essential intellectual pursuit.

A CASE FOR THE TEACHING PORTFOLIO
In the context of a professoriate with a growing, serious commitment to reflective practice, the teaching portfolio is a proven tool that offers not only an instrument for sound evaluation but also a process document that promotes continual revision and improvement of the teaching enterprise. The portfolio provides a vehicle for recorded evidence of performance and, more importantly, for the reflection, analysis, and action that are indispensable steps in a revisionary process of teaching enhancement.

Peter Seldin, the leading voice in portfolio development, served as my mentor in writing the first draft of my own portfolio, and his guiding collaboration has continued to shape much of my professional interest in how portfolios improve teaching. From his earliest book on portfolios (1991) to more recent publications on which the two of us have collaborated (1995), Seldin advocates strongly that the portfolio is "a living document that changes over time."

Seldin and I agree on the premier importance of regular portfolio revisions. Going beyond routine replacement of evidential materials in a file folder, these revisions stress in addition (or instead) a concise, written review of the relationship of present teaching performance to ongoing student learning. In the act of writing critically about current, actual teaching efforts and in constructing a rhetorical framework that compels the teacher to gather supporting materials, analyze information, draw substantial conclusions, and posit action plans for better practice, the teacher develops a habit of intentional improvement based on regular and timely portfolio revisions.

A TEACHING PORTFOLIO PRIMER

Ample information about the contents and format of a teaching portfolio may be found readily in Shore, et al. (1986), Edgerton, Hutchings, and Quinlan (1991), and Seldin (1991, 1993), which are the leading book-length sources for getting started on portfolios. Seldin's is the most cogent and practical model; it focuses on a compact narrative with supplementary materials that support and document the compressed information in the written body of the portfolio. An important note is that all the literature on portfolios advocates the collaboration of a mentor who helps guide the development of the process and who keeps the writer focused on the purpose of improvement throughout rigorous analysis of hard evidence.

A succinct reflective document of 8–10 pages, a sound portfolio gathers selected data from three major areas: 1) information from oneself, 2) information from others, and 3) products of student learning. Although they by no means exhaust the possibilities, here are some representative items that may be crucial in a particular professor's portfolio:

1. *Information from oneself:*
   Responsibilities, philosophy, methods, goals
   Teaching materials
   Teaching development activities

2. *Information from others:*
   Student and peer assessments and ratings
   Year-end evaluations by chair and dean
   Honors and awards
   Unsolicited letters

3. *Products of student learning:*
   Pre/post tests of learning
   Classroom assessment activities
   Student exams, projects, presentations, publications,
       essays in draft with instructor's formative feedback
   Alumni assessments

The information collected from the three broad areas is organized into main headings reflecting the various, selected facets of a teacher's work. For example, a recent draft of my own portfolio—written exclusively for my improvement—includes the following areas:

1. Statement of Teaching Responsibilities

2. Teaching Philosophy

3. Analysis of Strategies, Methods

4. Teaching Materials: Syllabi, Handouts, Exams, Essay Topics, Reading Lists, Web Pages and Sites

5. Collaborative Scholarship with Students

6. Assessment of Student Learning

7. Examination of Student Ratings

8. Survey of Peer, Chair, Dean Evaluations

9. Study of Impact of Improvement Activities: Conferences, Workshops, Committees

10. Teaching Goals

The narrative or reflective portion of the portfolio is meticulously documented by hard data, which is needed for clear, honest assessment and reasoned goals. Every significant claim about or analysis of teaching performance in the portfolio's narrative body is backed up by concrete evidence in keyed appendices. Thus, as the professor develops a section on methodology, for example, or on student evaluations or classroom assessment outcomes, the reflective statements are documented in an appropriately labeled appendix. To illustrate, if the instructor notes that a particular assignment proved significantly and uniquely to strengthen student learning of special disciplinary content, then the evidence in an appendix for materials might include the assignment sheet, auxiliary handouts, case studies, or models. Additionally, samples of selected student work in developmental stages might be included in an appendix for products of student learning. Such strong attention to both critical reflection and evidential information sets the stage for substantial improvement grounded upon research-based analysis of selected dimensions of teaching.

The potential bias of selectivity is diminished by three factors:

1. If the immediate purpose of the portfolio is merely evaluation, then selection of basically positive information may be appropriate and expected, but if the deeper motivation is improvement (as it certainly is in the case

of teachers dedicated to strengthening teaching performance and student learning), then selectivity is based not on such favorably culled materials but on fair and honest representation of particular areas targeted for enhancement.

2. The strong emphasis on documentation in the appendix demands scrupulous attention to detailed evidence. No amount of whipped up rhetoric, past reputation, or anecdotal testimony can substitute for concrete evidence, especially in the form of hard assessment of student learning, a key feature of a valid portfolio.

3. The crucial role of the mentor helps keep the faculty member intent on improvement through keen observation of recorded data and through collaboration on the steps needed for real development.

Faculty often fear that a portfolio is an exhausting, complete history of teaching that includes every minute detail of a professor's career. But remember that the portfolio is, instead, a selective profile of current teaching accomplishments and efforts. Depending upon the teacher's purpose for writing a portfolio, topics are developed and evidence gathered because they highlight an instructor's range of responsibilities, pedagogical values, strategic successes and disappointments, representative materials, evaluations, opportunities for improvement, and goals.

The mentoring process is a fundamental component of portfolio drafting. Indeed, the key to the conciseness and efficacy of such a process is the involvement of a trained and supportive mentor. With such a mentor, a faculty member can produce a valid and useful document in four or five days of concentrated work. I have been lucky to collaborate with Seldin on several occasions in workshop settings across the country. We have virtually a perfect record in helping numerous faculty to write—in a few days—portfolios dedicated to improved teaching activity that strengthens the quality of learning. As the professor revisits performance with improvement in mind, the succinct portfolio fashioned after Seldin's model offers a compelling profile that does not require wading though scores of teaching artifacts with accompanying narrative assessments. When collaboration involves a colleague from another discipline, and if possible, from outside the instructor's institution, the focus of portfolio development is more readily kept on teaching enhancement through meticulous, objective inspection of evidence.

Institutional support is also a crucial dimension of the portfolio process, and faculty are less resistant when they know that such teaching development activities are valued and rewarded. I believe that faculty need the encouragement and support of a formal workshop setting that signals an institution's commitment to instructional development and its administrators' recognition of the scholarship of teaching. Considerable experience with trying to mentor colleagues at my institution in an unstructured time frame has taught me that writing a portfolio piecemeal as time permits does not work. Four or five days devoted to concentrated writing and collaboration with a mentor provide the optimum occasion for development of an initial portfolio draft. Institutions should provide the resources needed to allow faculty to engage in the process successfully.

Another level of institutional resolve is when department chairs are recruited into the process of portfolio writing and into the complex task of understanding and judging portfolios. With such administrative involvement, the potential for stronger, more complete and effective evaluation is boosted, and the teaching in the department becomes more valued. Deans and other administrators, too, must be informed about the purpose, scope, strengths, and limitations of portfolios. Faculty investing in the importance of teaching in the mission of an institution need to take ownership of how and why portfolios enhance teaching and performance as a first step in introducing the concept on a campus. Later, as an instructor revises the portfolio to reveal growth, colleagues, chairs, and deans witness firsthand the authentic benefits of reflective practice.

HOW PORTFOLIO REVISIONS IMPROVE TEACHING: MY OWN CASE

The initial act of writing a portfolio has its own intrinsic merits in encouraging a teacher to discover potential areas for enhancement that often escape notice in the daily rigors of academic life. In my own case, writing flushes out the unseen and crystallizes the seen. It makes known in clear terms where I have been most successful and where effort needs redoubling. Writing also provides an indelible record of current performance, a baseline for renewal, challenging me to stay alert to the need for periodic revisions of my text and of my actual teaching and its impact on student learning.

As I develop new pedagogies, explore different methodologies, experiment with materials, and experience the successes and failures inherent in engaged teaching, my portfolio becomes the vehicle for analyzing the effects of my craft on student learning. "Out of sight, out of mind," the saying goes, but in teaching, if areas needing improvement are not openly examined in writing, I, for one, find it too easy to forget them in spite of the best intentions to pick up the task later, for too often later never comes.

Now let me offer two examples of how written portfolio revisions improve teaching. Significantly, both illustrations demonstrate the importance of collaboration in shaping revisions.

When I first worked with Seldin in producing a draft of my portfolio, I was pleased that my mentor extolled the virtues of my hard work and congratulated my meticulous emphasis on diverse sources of information about my teaching, which went beyond the usual student ratings and year-end self reports of most evaluation-of-teaching systems. Yet my draft conflated responsibilities, philosophy, strategies, and methods, a decision I made deliberately because, as I argued, I believe that *what* and *how* I teach are inseparably tied to *why* I teach as I do and to my *values* in teaching at all. My mentor pressed that I should extract my teaching values from the lengthy section and examine them more carefully in a distinct statement of philosophy. An expert collaborator, Seldin knew what he was doing, but I prevailed. By the time I got to the final draft of my portfolio, however, I realized why he was right.

As I made careful revisions, which took into account my mentor's suggestions on several key items, I began to notice that despite my disciplinary emphasis as an English professor— assigning essays, conferencing with students on successive drafts, and spending countless hours providing feedback on student writing—I had no real evidence in the form of student products that my efforts actually improved student learning. I graded essays; I returned them. I had never systematically and intentionally paid attention to assessing the outcomes of my teaching. My initial portfolio draft said much about my teaching ventures, but I had not addressed student learning.

At a later meeting, the mentor capitalized on my discovery and returned to the theme of writing a distinct philosophy. As I revisited my portfolio, I saw that my values were all in teaching as performance, inspiration, talent, labor, and dedication. My portfolio draft contained no word about learning or assessment and no deliberate inclusion of student products. The revelation was stunning but invigorating.

As a consequence of using the efficacious power of writing as a recorded process of discovery and criticism in updating my portfolio, I devised an action plan to study selected student works as a means of researching the effects of my methods, materials, and grading on strengthening course outcomes. My portfolio soon looked substantially different, separating philosophy as a distinct core that should connect theoretically and practically to all the other components of the portfolio. If, as in my case, such coherence is missing between, for instance, articulated values and products of student learning, then the revising process becomes the impetus for change: reflective practice in action.

My portfolio has since taken many turns. In adapting general teaching portfolio strategies to composing individual course portfolios, I have focused on the particular philosophy, methods, materials, evaluations, outcomes, and goals of one course to help me refine the teaching and learning in a single subject. Using the portfolio, again, as a vehicle for recorded evidence of teaching performance and extent of student learning, I recently discovered that over time my objective examinations in an upper-level literary critical theory course were not fairly gauging the students' knowledge.

In informal journal entries, most students were thoughtful, engaged, and reasonably secure in understanding the difficult course content, but the same students would perform poorly on examinations. I sent copies of two successive drafts of my reflective analysis of the dilemma, along with intentionally collected student products (remember I learned this lesson earlier!), to a colleague who taught a similar course at another institution. Enlisting the insights of a collaborator, I learned to combine take-home exams with in-class exams to provide students with an informal but still graded venue for studying for objective tests. The take-home exams helped bridge the students' enthusiasm for reflective writing in a journal with the imperatives of factual content knowledge. According to a recent revision of my course portfolio and the selected products in the appendix, the students' performance has improved markedly.

Portfolio revisions involve faculty in a method of earnest research about their individual teaching goals, objectives, and outcomes. Such a mechanism for improvement demonstrates a broad, genuine scholarship of teaching which recognizes that exemplary teaching perhaps only begins with inspiration and talent; the rest is hard work and systematic reevaluation. The process also reveals that conscientious and self-aware teaching is not separate from the intellectual, scholarly development of professors. The portfolio reconciles the perceived polarities of teaching and research, but only if it is engaged as a motivating contract for ongoing reflective practice rather than as a one-time hurdle for evaluation. Revision, to be sure, is the key to improvement, the basis for making a case for how the teaching portfolio fosters continual excellence in teaching.

TIPS ON MAINTAINING PORTFOLIO REVISIONS

Keeping up the momentum of improvement begun by the initial act of writing a teaching portfolio is not as easy as it seems, especially once the consuming duties of the semester take over. I confess that I often let slide many opportunities to write down my reflections at the height of a "teachable moment," the instant when I most immediately gain insight into a particular strength or weakness in my practice, which is the best time to articulate success or failure and to propose a goal for renewal. Yet, conscientious teachers can and do make time for crucial development activities as part of their commitment to exemplary teaching and their responsibility to student learning. Usually, such time is far less than the time devoted to the demands of research; yet the payoff is equally rewarding in the professional growth of scholar-teachers.

Here are some suggestions that may make the important step of regular and timely revisions of a portfolio more manageable and productive.

Use the appendices

Use the appendices as a convenient, self-defined filing system for hard-copy information and documentation. For example, the portfolio probably already has an appendix for materials such as examinations or handouts. As new materials are developed for the purpose of trying to improve student learning, pitch them into the appropriate appendix for future assessment. As evaluations come in at midterm or at the end of the course, store them in the corresponding appendix, where they can later be analyzed for patterns of improvement or areas of concern.

Don't reinvent the wheel

If year-end self reports are part of one's evaluation-of-teaching system, then combine the narrative revision of the portfolio and its assessment of quantitative information in the appendix with the required report. Find ways of making required assessment and evaluation activities integral dimensions of portfolio revisions, which, unlike most forms and data-driven reports, prompt genuine growth and intellectual engagement because of the power of reflective writing combined with the benefits of rigorous documentation.

Focus on selected areas for enhancement

Narrow the scope of improvement efforts and the amount of information analyzed in a revision. Identify, for instance, one particular assignment in one course and the role of the teacher's periodic, written feedback, tracking its potential for stimulating student learning over time among, say, three students of varying abilities.

Keep revisions detailed and specific

Conceiving of revision as a complete reshaping of all the fundamental components of a portfolio is intimidating and unnecessary. Rarely do we undergo such dramatic revelations about philosophy and practice that the entire portfolio must be recast. Remember that the portfolio is a process of continual analysis and improvement. Revise deliberately, a step at a time, for clearer evidence of steady, systematic renewal.

Use faculty development staff

Take advantage of faculty development staff to help identify areas for improvement and to suggest specific revisions of portions of the portfolio. Trained in implementing videotapes of teaching, peer review systems, teaching and learning styles inventories, and other strategies for improvement, faculty developers can introduce new modes of research into teaching that may prompt ideas for further revisions.

Use a mentor

Entrust a mentor to help guide the development of a portfolio through its various revisions. While collaboration with a trained colleague outside one's institution is often the best in the initial stage of writing a first draft of a portfolio, teaming with a colleague within or outside the department or with a department chair can help to create a useful perspective on the portfolio and to stimulate worthwhile revision. The corollary benefit of such collaboration is that teaching begins to grow in value across disciplines because of the cross-fertilization of serious commitment to ongoing improvement.

SUMMING UP

Other methods of strengthening the connection between teaching and learning exist and should, of course, be implemented just as carefully and widely as portfolio strategies. But if we professors take seriously the current call in higher education for more emphasis on accountability, assessment, and productivity, the model of reflective practice demonstrated by the teaching portfolio emerges as one compelling solution to the need for professors to improve the standards of teaching and learning in the academy.

As I posited earlier, reflective practice challenges us to reexamine consistently what, how, and, even more importantly, why we teach, with the aim of improving the impact of our practice on student learning. The labor of keeping up portfolio revisions is a small investment in creating a climate in higher education where teaching is valued and rewarded because professors can document on a regular and timely basis their commitment to enhancing the quality of education in our institutions. In other words, professors engaged in the demanding process of portfolio writing as a confirmed instrument of improvement of teaching and learning through methodical analysis of performance and through continual, meaningful revisions of their intensive work are the kinds of teachers most often recognized as professors thoroughly committed to the scholarship of teaching.

REFERENCES

Boyer, E. L. (1990). *Scholarship reconsidered,* Princeton, NJ: Carnegie Foundation for the Advancement of Teaching.

Edgerton, R., Hutchings, P., & Quinlan, K. (1991). *The teaching portfolio: Capturing the scholarship of teaching.* Washington, DC: American Association for Higher Education.

O'Neil, M. C., & Wright, W. A. (1991). *Recording teaching accomplishments: A Dalhousie guide to the teaching dossier.* Halifax, NS: Office of Instructional Development and Technology, Dalhousie University. Available on disk.

Seldin, P. (1991). *The teaching portfolio: A practical guide to improved performance and promotion/tenure decisions.* Bolton, MA: Anker.

Seldin, P., & Associates. (1993). *Successful use of teaching portfolios.* Bolton, MA: Anker.

Seldin, P., Annis, L. F., & Zubizarreta, J. (1995). Using the teaching portfolio to improve instruction. In W. A. Wright and Associates, *Teaching improvement practices: Successful strategies for higher education.* Bolton, MA: Anker.

Shore, B. M., et al. (1986). *The teaching dossier* (rev. ed.). Montreal, PQ: Canadian Association of University Teachers.

Zubizarreta, J. (1994). Teaching portfolios and the beginning teacher. *Phi Delta Kappan, 76* (4), 323–326.

Zubizarreta, J. (1995). Using teaching portfolio strategies to improve course instruction. In P. Seldin & Associates, *Improving college teaching.* Bolton, MA: Anker.

13

Creating Global Classrooms

MARK C. TAYLOR

 The Preston S. Parish Third Century Professor of Humanities at Williams College, Mark Taylor was educated at Wesleyan University, Harvard University, and the University of Copenhagen. The holder of fellowships from the Guggenheim Foundation, the Fulbright Foundation, and the American Council of Learned Societies, he is the author of many books and articles in philosophy and religious studies, including Altarity and Nots, which both received the American Academy of Religion's Award for Excellence. Taylor was named the 1995 U.S. Outstanding Baccalaureate Colleges Professor of the Year by the Council for Advancement and Support of Education (CASE) and the Carnegie Foundation for the Advancement of Teaching.

The arrival of the much-hyped information superhighway is transforming the landscape of higher education in obvious and not-so-obvious ways. While enthusiastic supporters welcome these developments as creating new opportunities for research and teaching, suspicious critics greet these changes as threats that call into question the very foundation of knowledge and the rationale for long-established institutions of learning. There are elements of truth in both points of view. The emergence of electronic and telecommunications technologies is not only changing what we teach but is transforming how we think, write, and communicate. It is as shortsighted to deny the significance of these innovations as it is to turn away from the possibilities they create.

Humanists frequently seem to be allergic to technology. Preferring splendid isolation to critical engagement, they are inclined to ignore the technological infrastructures upon which their own activities depend. The very division of the curriculum encourages this tendency. By separating the humanities from the social and natural sciences, institutions create walls where there ought to be windows of opportunity. The refusal to take technology seriously is both limiting and disempowering. Whether we like it or not, the information revolution is here to stay and if humanists do not develop alternative ways to deploy new communications technologies, others will do so for them.

Framing Cyberspace

Far from extrinsic or superfluous, technologies of production and reproduction constitute the matrices through which experience is mediated and knowledge is organized. Though most humanists freely admit the historical relativity of cultural systems, they tend to overlook the formative influence of technology on symbolic structures. Devoted to the mechanistic regime of print, they regard the advent of the electrosphere as a viral invasion threatening the very body of knowledge and life of the university. What is at stake, of course, is not knowledge as such but a particular way of organizing experience and processing information.

This point can be clarified if approached from a philosophical perspective. Immanuel Kant, among others, has taught us that experience is never raw but is always cooked. We have no direct access to the world because sensation, perception, and cognition are always mediated by forms of intuition and categories of understanding. Since Kant believed these forms and categories are not dependent on experience, he insisted that the structures of the mind are universal and unchanging. In a more contemporary idiom, one might say that the mind is hardwired. The stability of this perceptual and conceptual grid creates the possibility of organizing the flux of experience in coherent patterns that are meaningful. Though not immediately apparent, Kant's argument effectively translates Plato's theory of being into a theory of knowledge. As Plato's eternal forms bring order to chaotic matter, so Kant's unchanging categories organize unruly sensations. Whether conceived ontologically (i.e., in terms of being) or epistemologically (i.e., in terms of knowledge), the result of such form-giving activity is nothing less than the creation of the only world we can experience and know.

While many nineteenth- and twentieth-century philosophers accept Kant's criticism of the notion of the mind as a blank slate upon which the data of experience are directly imprinted, they remain suspicious of his claims for the universality of our mental apparatus. From Hegel and Nietzsche to Heidegger and Sartre, philosophers insist that systems of knowledge are psychologically, socially, historically, and culturally relative. While the mind might be preprogrammed, it is not necessarily hardwired. Since philosophers traffic primarily in ideas, they tend to view the reconfiguration of cognitive structures in terms of the implicit or explicit reformulation of organized concepts. This line of analysis represents an important advance on Kant's critical philosophy but does not go far enough. It is necessary to move beyond the confines of ideas to a consideration of the complex relays between the ways in which we shape experience and process information and knowledge on the one hand and, on the other, the technologies of production and reproduction characteristic of different societies and historical periods. Selves and groups are products of their technologies as much as technology is the product of individuals and societies. Thus, as technologies change, subjects and communities are transformed and, of course, vice versa.

THE PARADOX OF TECHNOLOGY

The transition from modernity to postmodernity involves a shift from mechanical to electronic means of production and reproduction. With this change, the forms of experience and structures of mental life are reprogrammed. New technologies simultaneously promote and subvert the Enlightenment longing for universality that inspired Kant's philosophy. A puzzling paradox lies at the heart of electronic telecommunications technologies. Stated as concisely as possible: The webs and networks that are drawing us together are also driving us apart. With the wiring of the world, lines of communication extend from the local to the global, and thereby bring distant persons and places even closer together.

There are both negative and positive sides to the increasing interconnection that information technologies entail. Two examples of problems created by compu-telecommunications underscore difficulties that must be addressed.

First, as we are drawn together in electronic webs and networks, we become vulnerable in previously inconceivable ways. While this vulnerability takes many forms, our growing exposure to electronic surveillance and the increasing susceptibility of vital communications networks to breakdown and disruption are particularly disturbing. The very strength of networks is also a weakness. The same technology that allows messages and currencies to circulate the earth at the speed of light provides a fertile environment for viruses that can infect the entire globe. In addition to this, the strength of contemporary communication links creates unprecedented possibilities for indirect management and covert control. From advertisers and politicians to intelligence agents and voyeurs, someone is always watching, listening, and whispering. Accidental disruption or purposeful intervention can lead to extraordinary problems.

Second, the spread of information technologies carries the potential for social inequalities resulting from the access or lack of access to information technologies. As in earlier generations social class and economic position were secured by possession or control of natural resources, in future generations they will be determined by access to information. The socio-economic implications of the distribution of information will influence relations among social classes within countries and the power structures that govern the interactions among nations. As new technologies expand, problems like these will grow more complex, and unanticipated difficulties inevitably will emerge.

While many critics cannot see beyond such problems, others maintain that information technologies harbor a bright future. As Marshall McLuhan insisted somewhat naively three decades ago, new media create the conditions for the formation of a global village in which citizens from various cultures come together to forge new forms of community. From the reformers of the Russian Revolution to the leaders of the Bauhaus, avant-garde artists and architects have long declared that technology brings with it the possibility of realizing utopian dreams. Many of the most important modernist experiments testify to an abiding faith in technology. But all too often, the enthusiasm for the latest technology is as problematic as the suspicion that leads people to turn away from innovation and seek a nostalgic return to traditional ways. What many enthusiasts who promote electronic telecommunications tend to overlook is that the very technologies that draw people together also expose their differences. While personal and cultural differences can, of course, be enriching, they can also generate conflict. As we are learning, the global village is not always peaceful. Contrary to expectation, proximity also creates distance and, thus, as we become more unified, we simultaneously become more divided. One of the most pressing challenges we face is to create structures and institutions that will enable us to establish connections without repressing differences and to sustain differences without destroying unity. Though the shape of the future always remains obscure, the challenge we are facing is coming into sharp focus.

Re-Forming Classrooms

As my awareness of the stakes of the information revolution has grown, I have been persuaded that the development of telecommunications technologies is too important to be left to commercial interests and market forces. Humanists, I have concluded, must overcome their technophobia and begin to devise ways to use new technologies in research and teaching. Toward this end, in the summer of 1991, Esa Saarinen, my colleague at the University of Helsinki, and I began to explore the possibility of creating a global classroom by using the latest telecommunications technology to team-teach a semester-long seminar. Though businesses had been experimenting with teleconferencing for several years, this was the first effort to use this technology for such an international seminar. Our goal was to integrate theory and practice by practicing what we were theorizing and developing theories about our practices.

As our plans unfolded, we encountered major practical problems. While administrators at Williams College and the University of Helsinki were intrigued by the idea, they were unwilling to commit the financial resources necessary for the seminar. Thus, Saarinen and I were forced to turn to private companies for support. Recognizing the educational value and commercial potential of this use of technology, Finish Telecommunications and Compression Laboratory Incorporated in San Diego provided the necessary equipment and advice free of charge. With this backing, we were able to mount a seminar entitled "Imagologies" in the fall of 1992. Throughout the semester, ten students from Williams and ten from the University of Helsinki met weekly for two hours to discuss a common syllabus, which included philosophers like Kant, Hegel, Nietzsche, Heidegger, Derrida, Jameson, Virilio, and Baudrillard, as well as topics ranging from postmodernism, televisual media, and video, to the electronic economy, telewriting, cyberwar, and virtual reality. Every session was initiated by one student from Williams and one from Helsinki who jointly planned the discussion in online exchanges throughout the week prior to the meeting. As the semester progressed, the entire class became engaged in intense e-mail conversations that were both public and private as well as academic and personal.

The seminar proved to be a great success: Indeed, I have never taught a course that generated so much enthusiasm. Part of the reason for the response, of course, was the novelty of the undertaking. Students realized that they were participating in a new venture and quickly grasped the educational potential and social value of our global classroom. Initially the technology was somewhat disruptive; the classroom felt more like a stage set than an educational environment. The theatrical aspect of the seminar was reinforced by frequent visitors who observed the class. Given a stage and an audience, some students inevitably felt obliged to perform. But after a few sessions, the technology because surprisingly transparent and the students less self-conscious. Our discussions then focused on careful analyses of difficult texts and elaborated imaginative interpretations of the media we were employing. When visitors overcame the dazzle of the scene, they were most impressed by the depth and seriousness of our dialogue.

By the middle of the semester, students were devising new ways to use the technology in class presentations. One Williams student, for example, began the discussion of Baudrillard's account of simulacra by pretaping her remarks and sending them to Helsinki as if they were being delivered "live." The feed was so seamless that the Finnish students did not realize what had happened until the situation was explained to them. This strategy enabled the student to make Baudrillard's points more effectively and more memorably than they are made either in Baudrillard's own texts or in scholarly commentaries on his work. On another occasion, students, having decided that cyberwar could be understood more impressively with audio-visual media than through prolonged discussions, created a video by collaging film clips from *Blade Runner* and *Terminator* with cuts from CNN's coverage of the Gulf War. By setting these images to heavy-metal music, they created an overwhelming sensory experience. During the session in which the video was transmitted, cameras were arranged in the Helsinki studio in such a way that, while watching the tape in Williamstown, we could also watch the Finns who were watching the video as well as watching us watch them watch what we had sent. In this case, pictures were worth more than thousands of words. No matter how many times one reads Guy Debord's *Society of the Spectacle*, the complexity and significance of specularity are unlikely to become more transparent than they did during that class.

The high level of class discussion was sustained in e-mail conversations. Throughout the semester, students wrote voluminously on topics we were considering in class. What was most impressive about these exchanges was the way in which students engaged each other in debate. Some of the most reticent students in the class were liberated in the electronic environment. In addition to responding to student questions and comments, Saarinen and I carried on a lengthy e-mail conversation about our experiment and the issues we were analyzing. We eventually reworked this material and published it as a book entitled *Imagologies: Media Philosophy* (1994).

My experience in this course not only reinforced my conviction about the educational potential of electronic telecommunication technology but also persuaded me that one of the most common criticisms of these new media is misguided. Critics often insist that electronic technology disrupts human relations and undercuts the sense of community by replacing "real" person-to-person contact with simulated or virtual presence. When applied to educational situations, this criticism implies that electronic technology significantly alters the teacher-student relationship by interrupting lines of personal contact and communication. In some cases, this criticism is justified. One of the most common uses of teleconferencing by universities is for distance learning in which communication tends to be one-way and non-interactive. It is obvious that in this kind of extended classroom or lecture hall, contact between teacher and student is difficult if not impossible. In most situations where this arrangement is used, however, the choice is not between presence or no presence but between instruction or no instruction. Reservations about this format do not, however, apply to all electronic teaching environments. In our teleseminar, electronic and teleconferencing technologies did not eliminate contact and interrupt communication; rather new media actually increased the contact between teachers and students as well as among students. While students are often reluctant to visit the office or to call on the telephone, they usually feel free to "talk" with their professors online. Having begun an electronic exchange, students frequently are eager to continue the conversation outside of class and in offices. In this way, virtual exchanges actually seem to create a desire for real contact. This tendency was powerfully demonstrated by the unexpected conclusion of the teleseminar. Reluctant to let go of the community we had formed, Saarinen and his students decided to visit Williams for a week in January. As I watched American and Finnish students meet on a cold winter night in the remote mountains of Massachusetts, I knew the global classroom had become a reality.

In addition to increasing contact among seminar participants, the electronic environment influenced the teacher-student relation in another important way. Students were much more willing to take the lead in discussions than in any other class I have taught. While the initial impulse to contribute might have been the result of the desire to see themselves on screen, students quickly overcame their exhibitionist impulses and became serious participants in a sustained dialogue. While I often use the strategy of beginning seminars with student position papers, it is usually necessary for me to assume a leadership role after the opening statement. In the teleseminar, the students were not only willing but were actually eager to contribute regularly.

Though becoming somewhat more common, the equipment for teleconferencing is still relatively rare and rather expensive. After researching various possibilities, we decided to use dedicated telephone lines instead of satellite hook-ups. Neither Williams nor the University of Helsinki had the necessary satellite equipment. Moreover, the cost-per-hour of satellite time is considerably greater than phone lines. In the few years since we offered the teleseminar, it has become clear that fiber optics is the way of the future. Recent advances in audio and video transmission over the Internet are promising but still involve significant problems. First, it is only possible to send images of talking heads. While several people can appear on the screen at the same time, each person is separated from the others. Consequently, the screen looks more like a collection of snapshots than a classroom. Second, images and sounds require considerable bandwidth not only at the points of transmission and reception but also at each stage along the way. If Internet traffic is heavy or messages encounter a bottleneck, the quality of the transmission suffers.

The ideal arrangement for the kind of global classroom we created is a teleconferencing studio. If the class is to be interactive, it is important to be able to project images of more than one person at a time. The effect of the simulated classroom is enhanced by cameras that can be manipulated by participants or technicians. In the most sophisticated equipment, cameras are mounted in the frame of the video monitors and can be directed from a seminar table in the classroom.

Funding for the development of electronic classrooms continues to be a problem. The novelty of our experiments enabled us to secure support from corporations. In most cases, it is now necessary for colleges and universities to raise the necessary funds. While many institutions are beginning to recognize the economic and educational potential of distance learning, it is important to develop multipurpose classrooms. The most efficient and profitable use of teleconferencing is for large classes in which an instructor's lectures are transmitted to distant sites. While not minimizing the significance of this kind of class, it is no less necessary to create interactive environments that are more conducive to smaller seminars.

In attempting to persuade administrators of the advisability of investing in teleconferencing classrooms, it is sometimes helpful to underscore the opportunities the technology creates for lectures and seminars offered by virtual visitors to the campus. With the spread of teleconferencing, it becomes possible to have people from anywhere in the world present their ideas and engage in discussion with faculty and students. For institutions with graduate programs, teleconferencing facilities enable outside critics to participate in reviews without having to travel. As people become more comfortable with the technology, new uses and applications will be developed.

FROM TELESEMINAR TO CYBERCOLLEGE

While persistent financial difficulties have made it impossible for me to offer another teleseminar, I have continued to explore alternative ways of creating global classrooms and deploying information technologies. In an effort to take advantage of the explosive spread of the Internet, one of the students who participated in the Helsinki project created a MUD (Multi-User Dimension), which we dubbed a "Cybercollege." In contrast to the teleseminar, which was an audio-visual interactive environment, the Cybercollege is a text-based virtual environment. In the Cybercollege, anyone with access to the Internet can participate in real-time exchanges whose format resembles synchronous e-mail messages. Though obviously different from televisual technology, the MUD has proven to be an extremely effective medium for teaching. The Cybercollege has made it possible for my classes to meet with students, faculty, and guests in other parts of the United States, Europe, and Australia. We have been able to have people visit our classes who never would have had the time to come to campus. As audio-visual transmission over the Internet becomes more efficient and sophisticated, such guest lectures and discussions obviously will become considerably more effective.

In spite of the success of the teleseminar, many of my colleagues at Williams remain puzzled by my interest in cyberspace and suspicious of electronic technology. Thus, when I was asked recently to present a faculty lecture, I decided to try to explain how I moved from Kant and Hegel to the electrosphere. Realizing that explanation alone would not be sufficient, I decided to demonstrate what I was discussing by presenting a multimedia lecture, in which I used slides as well as prerecorded and real-time video to illustrate points I was making. I also wired former students in California and participants in the Helsinki seminar to the lecture hall at Williams. I transmitted real-time video of the lecture over the Internet and relayed my voice with speaker phones. Students in Williamstown, in California, and in Helsinki logged on to the Cybercollege to discuss the lecture I was delivering. This electronic conversation was projected on the wall of the lecture hall. The impact of this presentation was immediate and lasting. By seeing this technology in action, people were able to appreciate its potential in a way that previously had not been possible. In the time since this lecture-demonstration, other members of the Williams community have begun to experiment with electronic technology in their teaching.

HYPERMEDIA

The most unsatisfactory part of the teleseminar was the formal written requirement for the course. At the end of the semester, we asked each participant to write an extended paper in which he or she used one or more of the philosophical texts we had read to analyze a noteworthy aspect of electronic technology or media culture. The students resisted the assignment and argued that the traditional seminar paper was inappropriate for the kind of inquiry we had conducted. Saarinen and I realized that they were right but at the time had neither the knowledge nor the means to support different projects. In recent years, I have been working with students to develop resources that will enable them to experiment with alternative textual formats. These efforts have resulted in a new course entitled "Cyberscapes," which continues to be a work-in-progress.

In Cyberscapes, I follow the procedure that proved so successful in the teleseminar by joining theory and practice. Class sessions are devoted to a consideration of readings that directly and indirectly bear on current cultural and technological developments. In addition to these formal discussions, students are required to participate in a weekly media lab in which they learn a variety of new skills and techniques. This media lab was developed and is taught by advanced undergraduate students. In the summer prior to the first offering of this course, I met regularly with two research assistants to plan the course. I organized the syllabus, and they were responsible for designing the labs. Borrowing a model from the natural sciences, I told my assistants that I wanted them to conceive a series of experiments and write a laboratory manual that explained how the experiments were to be conducted. By the end of the course, I expected students to know how to navigate the net, use the Cybercollege, and create hypertextual multimedia documents. I was most impressed by the imagination and creativity the students displayed in carrying out this assignment. Not only did they devise effective laboratory sessions and write clear procedures and instructions; they also repeated the gesture of uniting theory and practice or form and content by creating a hypertextual multimedia lab manual.

Having given my research assistants the opportunity to teach what they had designed, I elected not to attend any of the laboratory sessions. This decision rested on two assumptions: First, I have come to realize that students know more about this technology than I do; and second, I was beginning to suspect that these technologies create new possibilities for nonhierarchical relationships in which the line separating students and teachers becomes obscure. Indeed, one of the most interesting results of Cyberscapes has been the way in which the students have become my teachers. As faculty members venture into this unfamiliar territory, they must be willing to let students be their guides. There is no better way to become acquainted with new information technologies than by finding a good student and becoming his or her apprentice.

Teaching, of course, is always more difficult than it initially appears to be. The primary problem student instructors encountered was learning that they must begin at the level of the individuals they were teaching (especially when the student was their teacher) and then proceed slowly and deliberately to build from the ground up. The students in the class were remarkably patient and actually appreciated the opportunity to learn from fellow students. Indeed, as different students advanced at different paces, they began to help each other master the skills they were being taught. The result of this experiment was the creation of a cooperative atmosphere that proved to be unique in my teaching experience. This sense of community and cooperation extended beyond the lab meetings to classroom discussions and e-mail conversations.

Unlike the teleseminar, Cyberscapes does not end with a paper. The final assignment is to present a detailed analysis of texts and issues considered in the course in a hypertextual multimedia or hypermedia format. In other words, students are required to use skills acquired in the lab to probe questions raised in readings and discussions. Most of the research for their projects is conducted online. In addition to electronic texts, students draw on the growing body of audio and visual material available on the Internet. Some of the more enterprising students have supplemented online resources with images scanned from books and magazines and videos gathered from a variety of sources. The results of these efforts have been remarkable. The documents the students produce are imaginative, subtle, complex, and rigorous. One of the most impressive features of these projects is their effective integration of classical and popular texts and their startling juxtaposition of high and low cultural forms.

Hypertextual rigor is not, of course, the same as the rigor that characterizes traditional written documents. Having long insisted that the logic of electronic texts is not the same as the logic of the printed word, I have been startled nonetheless to discover how different these alternative media actually are. Students regularly develop remarkably effective nonlinear analyses, which are structured by principles of association that do not readily lend themselves to narrative recapitulation. Lacking a clear beginning, middle, and end, hypertexts are multilayered, open-ended, and interactive. Words, images, and sounds are collaged in ways that repeatedly release new insights. Today's young people think in images as much as in concepts; their imaginations, in other words, are as visual as they are verbal.

These points are important because they suggest that a noteworthy shift is taking place. Throughout the Western tradition, words and concepts have consistently been privileged over images and figures. While the former are correlated with thought and reason, the latter are associated with feeling and sensation. But this opposition is problematic because we not only think *about* images, but increasingly we think *with* images, too. There is, in other words, an inescapable cognitive dimension to the ceaseless play of images that surrounds us. In cyberspace, intelligence is no longer what it once was. Unless we learn to think, "read," and "write" differently, we will be condemned to illiteracy.

Postsigns/Signposts

You don't have to be a weatherman to know which way the wind is blowin' because the signs, they are a-changin'. Our era is undeniably a post-age: Something is passing away. But something new, something different, is also emerging. Though the metaphor is ill-conceived, the information superhighway is not a transient fad but is the shape the future is assuming in our midst. Instead of reacting to the new by trying to resurrect the old, humanists must realize that traditional ways of thinking and long-established institutions are inseparably bound to specific forms of textual production and reproduction that are rapidly fading. As technologies change, the world, as well as the subjects who inhabit it, are transformed.

One of the distinguishing features of contemporary experience is the increase in the rate of change. Speed has become a cultural value that is transforming the very shape of selves and societies. The world in which our students will live and work differs vastly from the world in which they are being educated. While transmitting the lessons of the past, effective teachers must remain open to the possibilities of the future. We must help students to cultivate ways of thinking, reading, and writing that will enable them to function effectively in the twenty-first century. Furthermore, we must labor to sensitize students to the urgent need to develop systems and structures that nourish productive interrelations while at the same time sustaining vital differences. I firmly believe that the creation of global classrooms in which teachers and students from around the world can come together to probe shared problems fosters mutual understanding and thereby contributes to the formation of a society in which our differences will enrich us rather than tear us apart.

14

The Community in the Classroom/The Classroom in the Community

PATRICK PARKS

Professor of English and director of the Writers Center at Elgin Community College, Patrick Parks was named the 1994 U.S. Outstanding Community Colleges Professor of the Year by the Council for Advancement and Support of Education (CASE) and the Carnegie Foundation for the Advancement of Teaching. He has also received the Illinois Community College Trustees' Association Outstanding Faculty Award and the Orrin G. Thompson Award for Excellence in Teaching from Elgin Community College. A writer as well as a teacher, Parks has received two grants from the Illinois Arts Council for his fiction and has published stories in several literary journals. He used his 1996 sabbatical to work on a novel.

> I grasp the hand of those next me, and take my place in the ring to suffer and to work, taught by an instinct, that so shall the dumb abyss be vocal with speech.
>
> Ralph Waldo Emerson
> *The American Scholar*

In the fall of 1992, Richard Jackson, a poet and professor at the University of Tennessee–Chattanooga, spoke to my creative writing students about the situation in what used to be Yugoslavia. Richard, who has spent considerable time there as a Fulbright scholar and visiting artist, told horrifying stories about atrocities and, in general, presented a dismal picture of the future for victims of the unrest. Outraged by what they had heard, the students wondered aloud about what they might do to help.

Seeing the students' genuine concern, I suggested that we compile an anthology of contemporary writing to raise funds for the victims. This undertaking, which was dubbed the "Sarajevo Project," began the following week with volunteers writing letters to authors across the United States asking them to contribute a story or a poem or an essay to the anthology and explaining that all the proceeds would go to a reliable relief agency.

Then we waited. At first, it appeared that the notion, noble as it was, would not meet with much support from the writing community. By mid-November, only a couple of pieces had been submitted, and it looked as if the project would fail. But later that month, when we returned from Thanksgiving break, we found that a half-dozen more manuscripts had arrived. From that point on, right up to and beyond our deadline—February 1—writers responded not only with stories, poems, and essays but with overwhelming enthusiasm and offers to provide any other kinds of assistance we might need. In all, forty-six authors from across the country contributed work.

Realizing that what they had piled in front of them—a manuscript six inches high—could and should become the anthology they had begun planning four months earlier, the students began the tedious process of typing every word into the computer and, at the same time, planned the next steps in getting the book into print. However, while the stack of untyped manuscripts grew smaller, the tasks involved in planning how to produce, market, and distribute the book grew larger. Money was needed to cover printing costs. Production of pages, cover art, and overall design needed to be considered. Contacts needed to be made with libraries and bookstores, churches and schools. Promotional materials needed to be written and designed. A reliable charity had to be identified. With each successive day, more questions were raised but few answers were given.

Gradually, as March gave way to April, and then April became May, the many questions were answered. A title was chosen (*Sarajevo: An Anthology for Bosnian Relief*), a book cover was designed, and text went from computer screen to completed page. As the months moved along, we also gained support from the Elgin Community College administration and faculty, and the community-at-large began to hear of the project. A publicity campaign was devised, and brochures announcing the book's impending publication were produced. Between four and five thousand pieces of literature regarding the anthology were mailed to college, university, and public libraries. We found a printer and, in early August, sent the manuscript off for production.

Again, we waited. But this time, there was plenty to do. Orders began to come in; one community college in Oregon wanted to use the anthology as a textbook and asked for thirty copies, maybe more. Contributing writers were contacted once more, this time to ask if they would be willing to participate in benefit readings to promote the publication. Space large enough to hold 2,500 copies of the book had to be found.

Finally, on September 13, 1993, cartons of books—84 of them—were unloaded. What had been an idea eleven months earlier was, at last, a reality. Since that time, we have sold about 1,500 copies and have sent $6,000 to Bosnia, with hopes of sending even more.

Although this project was unexpected—one that would not have come about had Richard Jackson not visited our campus—it still is a good example of how the world can be made part of the classroom and how the classroom can, in turn, be made part of the world. As a result of the Sarajevo Project, my students and I became very well-acquainted with the war in Bosnia and continue to be involved in efforts to raise money for Bosnian relief as well as to bring Bosnian refugees to the United States. As a result of the Sarajevo Project, people whose lives were shattered by the violence in Bosnia were able to buy food or fuel or to make their way to some safer place. Those who worked on the book and those who benefited from it will probably never meet, but all of the people whose lives have been changed, despite the miles separating them, share a bond as members of a single community.

COMMON EXPERIENCE AND COMMON EFFORT
ON A COMMON GROUND

In recent years—at least in the United States—the term *community*, usually used in place of its antecedent *team*, has become a buzzword among politicians and business people to encourage us all to pull together for a common cause. I suspect, perhaps cynically, that the change in terminology came about because too many of us felt that being a part of a team meant that our individuality was disregarded—even seen as detrimental—by the "coaches" in charge. *Community*, on the other hand, has a warmer, homier sound to it. We are—or want to be—part of a community because that is where we are welcomed and valued. But typically the two words are only interchangeable in this current lexicon in relation to improved efficiency; any positive emotions evoked by the friendlier community, in the minds of those who bandy it about in board rooms and press conferences and in advertising, do not extend beyond the confines of economic relevance. "Building communities," in this context, does not mean finding ways to live together better; it means finding ways to build a better machine, one composed of interchangeable human parts.

In his essay "Economy and Pleasure," Wendell Berry addresses this purely economic economy, and finds it lacking: "The great fault of this approach," he writes, "is that it is so drastically reductive; it does not permit us to live and work as human beings, as the best of our inheritance defines us" (1990, p. 135). Emphasizing competition rather than cooperation, he continues, means ignoring some basic guiding principles: "It is impossible not to notice how little the proponents of the ideal of competition have to say about honesty, which is the fundamental economic virtue, and how very little they have to say about community, compassion, and mutual help" (1990, p. 135).

For me, the notion that community has been appropriated to describe a desirable economic model is a disturbing one. I went into education, in part, because I did not want to measure my life in economic terms. That aim, I realize, was idealistic and perhaps even self-righteous (some might say hypocritical as well, given the ascendant influence of teachers' unions), but I wanted—and still want—to measure my success and happiness in some currency other than dollars and cents. For similar reasons, I chose to teach at a community college, believing that making higher education available and affordable to everyone is a worthwhile endeavor. I was also drawn to the idea that the institution would be an integral part of the lives of the people it served, that the relationship between community and college would be a symbiotic one. I might find the same thing were I to teach at a four-year college or university, but I've not yet been disappointed in my decision or my expectations.

When I started teaching, I don't think I consciously incorporated community into my classroom. The theme and concern were there, undeniably, but it wasn't until I came across the essays of Wendell Berry that I consciously realized its presence in what I do with my students. In "Writer and Region," Berry comments on the words of Emerson that are the epigraph for my essay, and Berry observes that Emerson "is not talking about a 'planned community' or a 'network,' but about the necessary interdependence of those who are 'next' each other. . . . We see how common work, common suffering, and a common willingness to join and belong are understood as the conditions that make speech possible in 'the dumb abyss' in which we are divided. This leads us, probably, to as good a definition of the beloved community as we can hope for: common experience and common effort on a common ground in which one willingly belongs" (1990, p. 85).

Getting to know the person attached to each name on my roster, learning about their interests and plans for the future, working to create an atmosphere where compassion and courtesy are as much a concern as the subject matter—for me all of those things are instinctive. In no small measure, they are also due to the fact that my first years of teaching were spent chiefly with high school freshmen and sophomores, a much more mercurial group of students than I would ever encounter at the college or university level. Not only did they tend to be more unkind to each other, but I also discovered that the students who whispered among themselves about sex were the same ones who were still losing baby teeth. Separating their lives outside of school from what we did in the classroom was impossible.

During the 1978–1979 academic year, I taught at a high school in Ely, Minnesota, a small town on the edge of the Boundary Waters canoe area and the border of Canada. In addition to its geographic isolation, Ely was also culturally isolated. Most of my students were only a generation or two separated from their families' European origins, and their values more closely resembled those of the old country than they did those of the United States. Having read an early edition of *Foxfire*, a student-produced collection of history, folklore, and heritage in Georgia, I proposed a similar project for my Ely class of college-bound seniors. Charged with recording the culture of their community, they interviewed grandparents and neighbors, parents and friends. They took pictures and drew illustrations. Some baked Slovenian bread and Finnish pastries, two built a log cabin, and one young man, whose grandfather was a Chippewa medicine man, learned traditional herbal cures. Every class period there was more to talk about, more to plan, more to write. When the students had all finished their parts of the project, we worked with the editor of the local newspaper, who donated her time and equipment and materials, to create our own little version of *Foxfire*, which we called *Northern Lights*. Though far less grand in scope than the book upon which it was modeled, *Northern Lights* was no less significant to the Ely students or to me.

As it turned out, our little book was significant to the community as well. The newspaper editor, without whose help and expertise the project would not have been completed, printed extra copies, which she sold out of her office, donating the money to the school. The students reported that their families were unanimously pleased and impressed, and dinner conversations revolved, more than ever, around their local traditions and histories. For me, taking out my copy to read reminds me of that place and that time and those students, and I am thankful that I was conscious of the lives my students led outside of my classroom and looked to find a way to bring those two worlds together.

THE STUDENTS' PLACE IN THE WORLD
The awareness of my students' being more than students carried over to my teaching at the community college. The people in my classes were older and their problems were different, but I was still unable—or unwilling—to detach myself from taking into consideration the full-time jobs they held while attending classes or the sick children at home who needed them more than they needed to hear about American Transcendentalism. At the same time, however, I needed to make sure they understood that the choices they made

were their own, that their education also needed attending to, and that I could accommodate their needs only so far as fairness to other students would allow.

From the outset, I tried to incorporate the students' lives into the curriculum as much as possible. Because I teach writing courses, I've been able to attach a variety of subjects and themes to their learning the craft of writing and could make the tasks more relevant to them by giving assignments that let them draw on their own experiences or issues of concern. As a result, in one class I received papers dealing with topics that covered everything from the politics of the rap group Public Enemy to an argument against a local landfill. With this kind of diversity, it became imperative for me to know something about the subjects my students were writing about. So I was obliged to listen to music, read local newspapers, and, most importantly, talk with the students to explore with them their roles in and responsibility to the community.

Shortly before the release of Nelson Mandela and the collapse of apartheid in South Africa, I taught an honors composition course focused on that country. The students wrote six papers during the semester, each dealing with elements of the South African political or social situation or, in some cases, with similar elements found in the United States. As a group, we read, discussed, and wrote about Mark Mathebane's *Kaffir Boy*, watched, discussed, and wrote about the film *A Dry, White Season*, and took a field trip into Chicago to view a traveling collection of African art and artifacts. Individually, the students engaged in research on apartheid, the homelands, the Afrikaans and the Afrikaner language; they also investigated American economic ties to the country and scrutinized U.S. support of the South African government. One student arranged for a public showing of Spike Lee's *Do the Right Thing*, led a discussion following the movie, and then wrote an insightful essay in which she described and evaluated the reactions of the racially mixed audience.

The day Nelson Mandela was released from prison—it was several months after the course had ended—I received a phone call from a student in the class who wanted to make sure I had heard the news. He had written letters to the South African government on Mandela's behalf, and I could hear in his voice not only joy but pride as well; he had done something that helped to save a man's life and a country's future. Interestingly, three of the students enrolled in this course have studied abroad in the past few years, and one student just completed two years of Peace Corps service in Guatemala.

The thematic approach to our honors composition courses has continued among other faculty who have taken their turn teaching the class, and all agree that the concentrated focus provides for much richer discussions, more thoroughly researched papers, and, in general, more awareness of the world. Gender roles, science and technology, art as a form of political expression, Chile, the former Yugoslavia, and the environment have all served as focal points in this course. As a department, we are also designing a similar composition course that would have a service learning component: The students enrolled would be engaged in community service, and all of their writing assignments, reading, and research would center around their service experiences.

Such approaches involve both delight and danger. Often, I find out that my students' views are not my views, and I'm hard-pressed not to proselytize, worried as I am that their beliefs are restrictive and not well-formed. At those times, however, I recall Wendell Berry's observations about his former teacher, Wallace Stegner, and the role Stegner played in the classroom:

> A teacher leading his students to the entrance to [the] community [of recorded human experience], as would-be contributors to it, must know that both he and they are coming into the possibility of error. The teacher may make mistakes about the students; the students may make much more serious ones about themselves. He is leading them, moreover, to a community, not to some singular stump or rostrum from which he will declare the Truth (1990, p. 50).

Leading them to the entrance, however, may not be enough. Sometimes, it is necessary to bring into question the values and beliefs of our students. Again, it was Berry who started me thinking about the long-term effects of my teaching on students. In "The Loss of the University" (1990), he criticizes institutions of higher learning for not attending to their mandated task of making "not just trained workers or knowledgeable citizens but responsible heirs and members of human culture" (1987, p. 77). Our obligation, he believes, is to develop human beings who are equally adept at "good work and good citizenship," and we professors can do that only by accepting responsibility for our influence on students:

> If, for the sake of its own health, a university must be interested in the question of the truth of what it teaches, then, for the sake of the world's health, it must be interested in the fate of that truth and the uses made of it in the world. It must want to know where its graduates live, where they work, and what they do. Do they return home with their knowledge to enhance and protect the life of their neighborhoods? Do they join the upwardly mobile professional forces now exploiting and destroying local communities, both human and natural, all over the country? Has the work of the university, over the last generation, increased or decreased literacy and knowledge of the classics? Has it increased or decreased the general understanding of the sciences? Has it increased or decreased

pollution and soil erosion? Has it increased or decreased the ability and the willingness of public servants to tell the truth? Such questions are not, of course, precisely answerable. Questions about influence never are. But they are askable, and the asking, should we choose to ask, would be a unifying and a shaping force (1987, p. 96).

CREATING COMMUNITIES

Developing our students into good citizens, I believe, is an essential part of higher education. As Berry suggests, we professors should assess our role in helping students to assume new and greater roles in their communities. That work can start with the fostering of a healthy, bountiful learning environment, one that encourages active participation in the learning process and is grounded firmly on the principles of "community, compassion, and mutual help." In that kind of environment, where interdependence and a common purpose are given equal status with subject matter, meaningful learning will occur, learning that will last long after the term has ended.

Integrating the same spirit of community into the curriculum will also enhance our students' understanding of their place in the world. One increasingly prevalent means of accomplishing this integration is service learning, but there are other options available that can provide opportunities for students to make valid and valuable connections between what goes on in the classroom and what goes on beyond the classroom walls. Course content can provide direction for the kinds of activities that might promote making these connections, but that does not mean that a larger context cannot be created which includes but is not limited to prescribed subject matter. In my case, one of the most exciting and interesting projects came out of a need to remedy a chronic dilemma.

After teaching fiction writing for several years, I had become frustrated in my attempts to find some way to address the basic tenets of story writing when the work I was receiving ran the gamut from science fiction to romance, family drama, or horror. The basic elements (for example, plot, character, and point of view) were present in each type of story, but the chief concern of the students was how to write their kind of story, and in workshop/discussion sessions, they often tended to critique, say, a coming-of-age story using criteria appropriate to a "whodunit." Rather than trying to translate from one genre to another each time out, I decided instead to find common ground upon which all the fiction submitted during the semester would be based. I knew about another teacher who had his students devise a fictional town inhabited by people whom the students had created. It sounded like a great idea, so I tried it with a class.

We began by laying out the place, deciding on its geographical location, its proximity to other towns, the nearest metropolitan center, the nearest body of water, and any other factors we could think of that would help us to understand why people might have settled there and why they stayed. Once that part was completed, the students created the town's history. They dreamed up local legends and began filling the businesses and houses with people. By the third week of the semester, students were calling each other outside of class to see if they might "borrow" a character for a scene or to make sure their version of an incident did not conflict with someone else's. Before class, the students met to trade gossip about the citizens of Babel (the name they came up with for their community) and to ponder the town's past, present, and future. Story built upon story, characters roamed from one student's work to another, and by the time the semester ended, each student had a thick three-ring binder filled with his or her work and that of classmates.

Not only did this semester-long experiment result in better stories, it also gave my students a chance to look elsewhere for inspiration. Rather than imitate plots and copy characters from their reading, they came to class with sketches drawn from their own neighborhoods and families, real people from real life turned into fictional characters. By the time the course ended, they also understood what it took to make a community, what kind of problems exist, how people cause and resolve those problems, and how important it is for people to rely on each other. They learned about relying on each other as students as well, creating among themselves a community more tightly knit than any I have ever had in a class. Two of the women in the class were so pleased with their work on Babel that they continued to write stories about the town, exchanging their manuscripts with each other and making sure that I got copies, too.

Because of the students' willingness to take part in this experiment and because of the success we all enjoyed (I contributed my share of community pieces, too), I'm certain that I'll have future classes create a town of their own design. The next time around, though, I'll know enough to talk about the idea of community at the outset and to encourage even more investigation by the students into their own communities so that we understand even better what it is that brings and holds people together.

As both a teacher and a student, I have held to the notion that education requires participation, that unless a teacher provides opportunities for a student to become actively engaged in the learning process and the student takes advantage of those opportunities, no real, important learning transpires. What we have instead is a rather lifeless exchange of information, which lasts only as long as the term in which it occurs. Connecting subject matter to the real world and showing how the subject matter is made manifest beyond the walls of the classroom are central to creating a bountiful learning environment. It is also vital to make connections within that environment, connections between teacher and students and among the students themselves. Key to each of these connections is the idea of community.

From the very first day of class, I make it clear that we're all in the learning process together and that the only way we can succeed is if everyone does his or her part in helping to create an atmosphere of acceptance and excellence. I let the students know that they've got my respect as human beings and will keep that respect if they assume responsibility for themselves. I tell them that, at this level in their education, they should learn to be divergent rather than convergent thinkers, that they should use the opportunities presented to them to explore and examine the world in as many ways as they can. I also explain that, while everything they learn may not seem practical at the time, their learning will still be worthwhile. I want the students to be excited about their learning and to savor the experience. And I want them to know that once they've finished their college education, their place in the world will be different than it was. Expectations of them will be higher. Their responsibilities will be greater. Their contributions will be more important.

Concentrating on community as both learning environment and course content reinforces for the students their present and future roles as citizens, as human beings who will look to others for help and will, in turn, provide help when asked. But can I be certain they will assume that role and the responsibilities that accompany it? Can I be certain that what I have asked them to do, and participated in with them, will make a difference in their lives? I may not know for many years. As Wendell Berry notes, "A teacher, finally, has nothing to go on but faith; a student has nothing to offer in return but testimony" (1990, p. 54). I hope that those testimonies, when they come, assure me that I have done my job well and that my students feel they are better for it. As a teacher, I can find no higher purpose in my work.

REFERENCES

Babbitt, J., Feucht, C., & Stabler, A. (Eds.). (1993). *Sarajevo: An anthology for Bosnian relief.* Elgin, IL: Elgin Community College.

Berry, W. (1987). *Home economics.* New York, NY: North Point Press, Farrar, Straus and Giroux.

Berry, W. (1990). *What are people for?* New York, NY: North Point Press, Farrar, Straus and Giroux.

Wigginton, E., & his students (Eds.). (1991). *Foxfire: 25 years.* New York, NY: Doubleday.

15

Teaching
as Subversion

TEOFILO F. RUIZ

Born in Cuba in 1943, Teofilo Ruiz was educated at the City College of New York, New York University, and Princeton University, where he took his Ph.D. in 1974. Presently he is a professor in the department of history at Brooklyn College and the Graduate Center of the City University of New York. He has held fellowships from the National Endowment for the Humanities and the American Council of Learned Societies. A frequent lecturer in Europe and South America, Ruiz is the author of more than thirty articles and five books, including Crisis and Community, *which in 1995 received the* Premio del Rey, *the American Historical Association's biennial award for the best book on Spanish history. Ruiz was named the 1994 U.S. Outstanding Master's Universities and Colleges Professor of the Year by the Council for Advancement and Support of Education (CASE) and the Carnegie Foundation for the Advancement of Teaching.*

There are many who seek knowledge for the sake of knowledge: that is curiosity. There are others who desire to know in order that they themselves be known: that is vanity. Others seek knowledge in order to sell it: that is dishonorable. But there are also some who seek knowledge in order to edify others: that is love.

I came upon this statement by Bernard of Clairvaux, a Cistercian reformer in twelfth-century France, as I prepared my remarks for a memorial at Princeton in 1987 that honored my own teacher, Joseph R. Strayer. I thought then, as I do now, that the quotation reflects what is and ought to be the essence of teaching, with one significant omission. This concept of teaching—the imparting of knowledge as love, as caring for one's students and discipline—is central to our pedagogical mission. Yet the continuous questioning of accepted beliefs, what Bacon called the "idols of the cave, of the market place, of the tribe," is a necessary counterpart to teaching as love. Regardless of how kind to and loving of our students we are, as teachers we fail them if we do not also foster their intellectual independence, if we do not help them to think critically about what they learn on their own.

Many attributes go to making a successful teacher: tolerance, good humor, and the ability to convey information, to engage students, to capture their interest, to encourage intellectual autonomy, to bring innovative pedagogy to the classroom. I also want my students to learn without fear and to be rewarded for their individual efforts. Very good students should be directed onward to widening intellectual horizons; those who are not as gifted or who do not wish to pursue a scholarly life ought to have, at least once, the knowledge of having succeeded, of having mastered some area of research, regardless of how small, and of having shared fully in the pleasure of intellectual discovery. I have found many students who never thought of themselves as gifted, but who became deeply engaged with the experience of learning when given an opportunity.

Teaching is caring, but it must also be the continuous challenging of one's own and one's students' values. In a very real sense, teaching must be subversive; that is, it must include a willingness to question and criticize, and at times even to undermine, established orthodoxies. Both teachers and students must be agents and targets of this subversion. Together, they must question the material they teach and learn, while reexamining their perceptions of the world and of themselves. In this essay, I offer a brief reflection on the present state of education in the United States, a more detailed explanation of what I mean by teaching as subversion, and some suggestions about how to encourage students to question the material, the teacher, and, most important, themselves.

On Teaching

Why and how I teach are questions I do not treat lightly, for they explain what has been an important part of my life for more than two decades. For all of us who have chosen teaching as our metier, this choice has been made, in most cases, out of a deep commitment to a life of inquiry, of transmitting culture, of sharing one's knowledge and doubts with our students and colleagues. At its best, teaching is a vocation, a calling to a specific kind of life, chosen in spite of its limited financial compensation or, in this country, its often low social status. Let us be honest: At present in the United States, education in general and teaching in particular are under severe attack.

In 1995, partly because of the CASE and Carnegie award for teaching, and partly because of my experience of teaching concurrently at Brooklyn College and Princeton University, I have come face to face with realities that have radicalized my thinking about teaching, equality, and the future of education in this country.

First, while in Washington, DC, to receive the CASE and Carnegie award as one of the four 1995 Professors of the Year, I was asked to teach three seventh-grade classes in a junior high school in the inner city. This school, only a few minutes away from the White House, Congress, and the National Gallery of Art, sits in the middle of a devastated neighborhood not unlike the ghettoes of New York, Newark, Detroit, or Los Angeles.

Surrounded by a high metal fence, with metal detectors and metal gates, the school was like a warehouse, its classrooms separated only by low, mobile blackboards. Two of the teachers in my three classes were absent. On the walls there was no art, nothing beautiful, only handwritten cardboards with slogans about violence, drugs, and AIDS. No real learning could take place in that environment.

I was so angry that I discarded the lecture I had prepared and attempted to talk to these children, all of them African-American plus a few Latinos, about power, equality, and justice. It was hopeless. The immense majority of the children had long been turned off from education, from any meaningful discourse. At fourteen years of age, most of these young lives were already cast into dead-end pathways. Is it, then, so difficult to explain why Washington, DC, has one of the highest incarceration rates in the world?

As I was being given the CASE and Carnegie award, my own institution, Brooklyn College, suffered and will continue to suffer draconian financial cuts. In New York, public education as a whole is not a high priority; prisons are. Providing minorities, immigrants, and the poor with an affordable college education—the traditional mission of the City University—is being abandoned. With funding drastically reduced and with new teaching positions scarce, the present climate is not favorable to learning. This hostile attitude toward education and teaching is not restricted to those in government, but pervades large and important segments of the nation, if not the country as a whole. The reality is that we are well on our way to creating two distinct educational paths: one for the elite, another for the masses. Although elite education has always been part of this country's pedagogical realities, the distance between elite institutions and those such as Brooklyn College has now widened beyond reason or fairness. Teaching at Brooklyn College and at

Princeton in the spring of 1995, I was appalled by the contrast between the opportunities students have in the latter institution and the obstacles they face in the former—and it was not a question of the disproportionate difference in the abilities of the students, but of the disproportionate difference in the conditions under which they live and learn. When I left Princeton more than twenty years ago, the distance between these two institutions was not extreme; today I cannot see the other shore.

The unwillingness to fund educational facilities, to expand our mission, is common throughout the nation, and thus it is reflected in popular culture. Mass entertainment seldom idealizes what we do as educators. All to the contrary, our tasks are often ridiculed. Popular films glorify stupidity, ignorance, and the triumph of chance. They do very well indeed at the box office.

TEACHING AS SUBVERSION

As I see it, the deplorable state of education in this country requires us, more than ever, to instill in our students a critical perspective. There is a renewed need to question not just what our students learn, but how and why they do so. What we need in the classroom is a thorough discussion not only of our respective disciplines but, above all, of our values. My experience in more than twenty years of teaching at Brooklyn College and elsewhere throughout the country is that a good number of our students come to us with a passive attitude towards the material they are studying and towards learning in general. Will it be on the exam? Should I write this down? These are questions we have all heard in our classrooms. This approach to learning reflects the values of a capitalist economy, of the market place: How well can I do by working and learning as little as possible? We should not, however, blame the students for behaving as they have been taught to do; rather, we should blame ourselves for acquiescing to this attitude.

This same uncritical and reluctant approach to knowledge is often found in the students' political and cultural values. Not too many of our students are well-informed about what goes on in the world or in the nation; not many care either. Their values and perceptions of the world and community have been handed down by their families, by primary and secondary schools— which, with some exceptions, insist on measuring students' intellectual promise by their ability to regurgitate information—and by friends and religion. Too many students lack a world-view arrived at by reflection, by that process of inquiry and self-examination that allows for an informed opinion and for free choice. Such as it is, their perspective is more like a comfortable garment, often worn out of fear of questioning the validity of their beliefs or the authorities who handed them down.

I am not suggesting here that we overthrow the values and beliefs of our students; I am not arguing that they must see things as I do or follow my lead. That would scare me. We should stay clear of philosopher kings. All to the contrary, what I am arguing for is a process of inquiry and criticism that all of us, teachers and students alike, should undertake while developing our points of view and before embracing specific values or discarding them. That process entails a continuous subversion of handed down ideas and established authorities. And even when we come close to reaching some conviction, we must continue to question. Paraphrasing Nietzsche, one can say that there is no honor in upholding one's convictions; rather, the honor lies in questioning them. To me, the essence of democracy, of civilized dialogue, resides precisely in the willingness to question oneself.

As scholars, we make our living by arguing with and undermining (or attempting to undermine) previous points of view. Original scholarship—that is, research that goes beyond the slavish rehashing of previous knowledge—is always subversive. If we set such standards for our scholarly life, why not then for teaching our students?

I realize that we also have a duty to impart information. This responsibility is certainly the case in the exact sciences and even in history, a very inexact science indeed. In the classroom, we must come to some agreement as to what is known, a necessary foundation for all subsequent knowledge. But there it should stop. If postmodern theories teach us anything, they teach us about the ambiguity of knowledge, the fragility of language itself. Our students, therefore, must be encouraged to question what they learn, to challenge their teacher's opinions, and the authority of texts. What I am asking for is very simple: that we develop a critical outlook in our students, the ability to read and think critically. Without these attributes, we will not have thoughtful citizens.

Below I list some of the techniques I have used. Teaching, however, is a very personal activity, and each teacher must devise an approach that will fit his or her personality. As a teacher, I tend to be theatrical, very dramatic in class; yet some of my most vivid memories as a student are of being awakened to intellectual life by magisterial lectures, which were delivered in a most traditional manner. As teachers, we must play to our strengths and seek to capture our students' attention, to engage them in this process of questioning. If some of the following ideas seem peculiar, remember that they work for me (or, at least, they work sometimes); they are among the best ways in which I reach my students.

SUBVERTING THE TEXT/SUBVERTING THE DISCIPLINE

In our different disciplines, we have what one might call normative texts. In high school and, lamentably, even in college, our students are often taught to enshrine these pillars of national, religious, and pedagogical orthodoxies. We have granted such written work and teachers' lectures a kind of authority that often goes unchallenged in the classroom and in public discourse. In my introductory core course, "The Shaping of the Modern World," I target some of these foundational texts—for example, the Declaration of Independence, the U.S. Constitution, and the *Communist Manifesto*—and examine them from diverse perspectives. Although one must not ignore the promise inherent in such texts and their value as inspiration for later political developments, it is also important to contextualize them. My students at Brooklyn College, to give just one example, are often shocked to realize that the words "all men are created equal" in the Declaration of Independence would not have included anyone in the class, which is composed mainly of women, immigrants, racial minorities, and the poor. The perspective on women, slaves, and the poor provides us with an altogether different understanding of one of our "sacred" texts. The points that I try to make throughout the semester include the following:

1) Several interpretations—sometimes conflicting ones—are available

2) Students must make up their minds about what the document means, but only after they have examined all the available evidence and points of view

3) All texts are contestable

On the first day of class, which is the most critical day in the entire semester because it sets the tone of the course, I seek to introduce the notion that undermining authority is desirable. In particular, I do so by demonstrating that I am not an unimpeachable source of knowledge and truth. For example, in my introductory courses, where the students usually do not know who I am, I may come to class and write the following on the blackboard: Professor Stephen Dedalus, Comparative Literature 57, The World of James Joyce. The students move restlessly in their seats, gripped by the terror of finding themselves in the wrong class. I begin to describe how we are going to discuss Joyce's *Ulysses*. Finally, one of the students dares to raise her or his hand and ask whether she or he is in the wrong class; others join in, showing me the class schedule indicating that "Core 4" (History) meets in that classroom at that hour. I look appalled, confused. I apologize to the class, pick up my notes and leave. After one or two minutes, I jump back into the classroom, erase the blackboard, and tell them: "You must not believe everything you hear or everything you read."

This opening does not always work. I have had classes in which half of the students got up and left the room "because the teacher must be right." I had to run down the hall after them and bring them back to class. Then, right away, I begin to discuss authority—how we, students and teachers alike, must not accept anything without questioning its validity. Not all students wish to question, or learn to do so. Many prefer to play it safe, to go along for the sake of the grade. They do not believe that I am in earnest. Teachers play it safe, too. But we accept ideas and authority without question at our peril.

I do not let up. Throughout the semester, I will say things that are totally invented or preposterous, the kind of things reason indicates to be impossible. The students will write them down, and then I will challenge them to understand that what they have just written down as truth is a fabrication. Sometimes students will object to my points of view, to my interpretation. The more they do, the more I praise and reward them.

I am not of one mind about this little play that I have just described. My partner argues with me constantly about my first-day theatrics. She argues that some students get up and leave because they are smart and quick. They have absolutely no reason to think that I will deliberately mislead them (that goes against the parameters of my job and the rules by which all of us, the students and I, are playing). The quicker they go, the smarter and more assertive they are. There is a point to these objections, which I am willing to concede. On the other hand, my theatrical opening usually leads to laughter, relaxes the students, and creates a classroom environment in which dissent is more acceptable.

SUBVERTING THE STUDENTS

By subversion I do not mean political subversion, although, occasionally, some of that would not hurt. What I mean by subversion is the questioning of received beliefs that students tend to accept as knowledge. Most young students and many adults in the United States have difficulties discerning between belief and knowledge. What I seek to do in the classroom is to question what the students think they know and how they have come to hold their values. Learning is essentially a process of unlearning, of shedding of what Plato calls images. Although it insists on a universal Truth that few today would accept, Plato's *Republic*, which is mostly about epistemology, remains essentially correct as to how we move from belief to knowledge.

After entering with them into heated debate, which is often provoked by my outrageous statements, I tell my students that I will always be where they are not. If they agree with me, then I will change sides. But discussion in the classroom—in which students and teachers alike are forced to defend their points of view and to think about their ideas critically—can only take place in an atmosphere where the students are assured that they will suffer no reprisals, but, to the contrary, will be rewarded for independent thinking.

The teacher must encourage the student to challenge him or her continually. The only requirements are that the discussion be carried out with an open mind, that the arguments be coherent and reasonable, and that the student participate not to score rhetorical points but to search for some common ground of understanding. I cannot even remember how many times students have convinced me to change my mind, nor how often I have admitted to being wrong in class. We cannot subvert our students if we do not begin by subverting our own authority.

SUBVERTING THE TEACHER'S AUTHORITY

Many of the examples I have given above are also aimed at lessening the distance between teacher and students. Let's face the truth. In the classroom there is a clear hierarchy that runs counter to our own efforts to allow a free exchange of ideas. We professors are the "experts." We give the grades. We have great power, and, at times, I fear, we abuse and exercise that power to the detriment of our students. As teachers, we all wish to have the respect and admiration of our students, but that respect must be earned anew every day, and that respect has to be reciprocal. Where and how we stand or sit in class, how we address our students, how we are addressed by them play an important role in that complex process of creating an atmosphere that fosters critical thinking and questioning. These factors may seem utterly ancillary to intellectual exchange, but I argue that they all play a most important role in determining how students respond to our challenges.

On the first day of my classes, I come all dressed up in coat and tie, which I slowly remove as I teach and point out that certain types of clothes are symbols of power, parts of a symbolic code in a discourse of difference. I never sit or stand behind a desk or lectern. Rather, I walk among the students to the very back of the class, so as to reach the last rows in the classroom. No one can hide in my class. I address the students by their first names, and I explain why I do this, and why they should address me in an equal manner.

If I earn the students' respect, that should happen because I work hard, because I know the material, because I care deeply for them, and not because I have a title, a desk to hide behind, and a coat and tie. Isn't this, after all, what our duty to our students is or should be?

16

A Story Waiting to Be Told: Narratives of Teaching, Scholarship, and Theory

DIANA COOPER-CLARK

Born in Kingston, Jamaica, Diana Cooper-Clark is now a Canadian citizen who lives in Toronto. Since 1970, she has taught English and humanities courses at York University, where she also tutors individual students at the university's Centre for Academic Writing. Cooper-Clark's publications include two books, Designs of Darkness: Interviews with Detective Novelists *and* Interviews with Contemporary Novelists. *Her third book,* Writers on Writing: Perspectives on the Contemporary Novel, *is underway. In addition to the teaching awards she received from York University in 1992 and 1994, Cooper-Clark was named the 1995 Canadian Professor of the Year by the Council for Advancement and Support of Education (CASE) and the Carnegie Foundation for the Advancement of Teaching.*

When I started to win teaching awards, I was unaware of the sniper's bullet lurking on the edges. People began asking me questions that they had never asked before: "What is your philosophy of teaching?" "Why are you the 'best' teacher?" My answers to these questions seemed akin to holding water between my fingers. Although those questions gave me pause at first, they set off a chain reaction of feelings and thoughts about my career. When teaching, I had always just "done it" and presumably done it well. Now I wanted to find a language to explore and explain more fully what I do when I teach.

My narrative about teaching is one of tensions, paradoxes, and repeated reconciliations. My pedagogy and its relationship to teaching and scholarship, practice and theory, are like the spreading rhizome, a mass of roots that shoots

166

out above and below and does not look like other roots. Pedagogical theory is not an isolated entity. It is, as Borges has said about books, an axis of innumerable relationships. But I did not know this when I started to teach. I realize now that this teaching narrative is one of my untold stories, a story that I was unable to tell before.

WORLDS WITHIN WORLDS

No one trains university professors. They do not go to teachers' college. Most professors of my acquaintance, and I include myself, do not read books or journals about pedagogy; they read for their disciplines. When a colleague invited me to teach at York University in 1970, I was paralytic with fear. In desperation, I went to the library to get some tips. As strange as it might seem, I borrowed the novels *Good-bye Mr. Chips* and *The Prime of Miss Jean Brodie*. Needless to say, they didn't give me any tips.

Initially, my training as a teacher relied on the models of my great teachers, my knowledge and scholarship, and an openness to the gifts of my students. The teachers who had touched my life were very different, but they had several things in common. Either consciously or unconsciously, they understood that to interest someone else they had to be interested. Their teaching came out of a superior devotion to learning. They were like china night-lights, those small lamps whose outsides have one painted scene and whose insides have another. When such lamps are lit, the inner and the outer merge. The two pictures come together to form worlds within worlds.

The knowledge of my best teachers and how they imparted it to us were all of a piece, seamless, eloquently resonant and resonating through my life. Although some of these teachers have retired and some have died, they live on in me. They live on in my students also. The expanding relationship between my emblematic teachers, myself, and my students is like a single plant of winter rye grass that can send forth 378 miles of roots with 14 billion root hairs (Dillard, 1974, pp. 163–164). One such expanding relationship is the one I have with a former student, Mary Beattie, who is a professor in the faculty of education at the University of Toronto. Mary's insightful book, *Constructing Professional Knowledge in Teaching* (1995), is the narrative of her inquiry that led both to enriched professional knowledge and skills and to reformed and restructured personal and practical knowledge. In this book, she kindly refers to me as one of her important teachers. In turn, she has been a valuable student and teacher to me.

I wonder if my teachers formulated a teaching philosophy. It has taken a lifetime in the classroom before I could struggle through and articulate my own theory of teaching. Part of the problem is that pedagogy is more experiential than prescriptive. Theoretical discourse joins forces with the personal. I did not go from theory to practice; my theory evolved from practice.

KINETIC KNOWLEDGE AND TEACHING AS ART

Paradoxically, teachers and students can link both central and peripheral vision. Central vision is conscious, linear, and objective; peripheral vision is unconscious, lateral, and subjective. The unification of these two ways of seeing does not have to lead to cognitive dissonance or to an erosion of academic respectability. The curriculum, pedagogy, and practice of institutions explicitly and implicitly cite scholarship and its method as analytical, empirical, and stable. The deconstruction of these assumptions is significant in a multicultural world that comprises differences of race, ethnicity, language, gender, class, sexual preference, and age, to name some of the infinitely expanding divergencies. But we need not recklessly demolish the center in order to construct a new vision. Regardless of how we de-canonize our contexts of teaching, method, and scholarship, even radical pedagogy relies on the centers it challenges for its determination and form.

At the heart of my teaching is an awareness that the real voyage of discovery consists not solely in seeking new landscapes, but in having new eyes, to re-word Marcel Proust. Teaching is fluid, overflowing those categories in which we attempt to confine it. Scholarship and teaching are a matrix that embrace the oppositions of Jean-Francois Lyotard's admonishment to stop the terror of the theory and Jacques Derrida's reminder to acknowledge theory as an adventure of vision. Bertrand Russell suggested that human beings created ideas so that they wouldn't have to think. But ideas are not bloodless. Because knowledge is kinetic, not static, teachers cannot find a motionless, winning formula for theory and practice. The world of the mind and the imagination is not reductive, not ultimately a final examination. My pedagogy constantly changes as I evolve, my students metamorphose, knowledge transforms, and perspectives alter, as light to a prism. Teaching cannot be proscribed because it is a winding path, a labyrinth, an art. As J. Schwab has perceptively said:

> Teachers will not and cannot be merely told what to do. . . . Teachers are not . . . assembly line operators, and will not so behave. Further, they have no need, except in rare instances, to fall back on defiance as a way of not heeding. There are thousands of ingenious ways in which commands on how and what to teach can, will, and must be modified or circumvented in the actual moments of teaching. Teachers practice an art. Moments of choice of what to do, how to do it, with whom, and at what pace, arise hundreds of times a

school day, and arise differently every day and with every group of students. No command or instruction can be so formulated as to control that kind of artistic judgment and behavior, with its demand for frequent, instant choices of ways to meet an ever varying situation (1983, p. 245).

Individual and collective contexts intertwine and unravel through the multiplicities of many cultures, many biographies, and many stories. If we shake a kaleidoscope, there, reflected and refracted in the mirrors, is another arrangement of the fragments. Within our classrooms, students and teachers engage in what Walter Pater called "that strange, perpetual weaving and unweaving of ourselves."

PASSION, PREPARATION, AND BLUES SINGERS

I do not believe in arbitrary and rigid boundary lines between academic and personal development, between the writing process and other academic skills, between artificially separated disciplines, or between scholarship and teaching. I believe, rather, that the relationship between student and teacher, focused as it is on intellectual life, is a mutually enriching one, with each partner in the educational process learning from and teaching the other. Students and teachers are like major and minor keys in music or like a sonata for two instruments. They are both important. I want to share the exciting experience of the intellectual life with my students and consequently empower them. I am not using the word "intellect" in what I consider to be its archaic definition, "the power of knowing as distinguished from the power to feel and to will." In our classrooms, or so I would like to think, knowing is an act of integration.

I approach my teaching by constantly keeping in mind the question, "What do I want to learn?" That question leads me to teach what I feel that I need to know, in order to be informed about and engaged with the world of knowledge, which is my immediate responsibility, and with the larger world that will be affected by my understanding and commitment. My teaching comes out of the passions of my life. Thus, preparation and passion meet. I adopt a holistic approach, encouraging students to think better in order to feel more intensely, and vice versa. I teach my students what they know already, but don't know that they know, so that knowledge becomes an integral part of self understanding. But at the same time (following the Latin root of the word *education*, "to lead out of") I seek to lead them out of themselves to an engagement with the entire world.

I am not the repository of the Milk of Truth, and my students are not empty vessels that I fill up. Remembering Schwab's metaphor of the teacher as artist, I think of myself as a blues singer. In a sense, blues singers don't need an audience because they are singing to themselves in order to find themselves and get in touch with what they know. If there is an audience, they don't simply listen to the blues. They must experience the music and become participants. I like to think that often happens in our classroom. When I'm singing, students get in touch with what they know, substantiated and supported by whatever knowledge and methodologies I can share.

THE TYRANNY OF THEORY AND THE
CONJUNCTION OF THE SCHOLARLY AND THE PERSONAL

I certainly disagree when Paul de Man asserts that "teaching is not primarily an inter-subjective relationship between people but a cognitive process in which self and other are only tangentially and contiguously involved. The only teaching worthy of the name is scholarly, not personal; analogies between teaching as various aspects of show business or guidance counseling are more often than not excuses for having abdicated the task" (1982, p. 3). I do not have a resistance to theory, but I do oppose the tyranny of theory. Should I warn the student who needs help to finish her first-term essays—because her father murdered her mother before Christmas and then her aunt attempted suicide—that "teaching is not primarily an inter-subjective relationship"? Should I tell the Italian-Canadian student who is working two jobs to stay in university, helping to take care of his grandfather with Alzheimer's, and struggling because English is a second language that our relationship is "a cognitive process in which self and other are only tangentially and contiguously involved"? When I was barely coping with the care of two dying parents and an only sister suffering with cancer, teaching a triple full-time professor's load as a single mother, trying to interpolate my feeling and thought worlds, would de Man accuse me of being personal and not scholarly?

Elliot W. Eisner has taken a very different approach. He writes about "the feeling of alienation, of being torn between the canons of the academic world and the exigencies of the practical" (1988, p. 18). Furthermore, Eisner has discussed the hegemony of propositional discourse in education theory and research. He asserts that "the language of propositions is typically a class language. That is, it focuses upon categories of events and objects and thus generalizes more than particularizes" (1988, p. 16). Here is the crux of the contention between the "scholarly" and the "personal." De Man's propositional language does not place theory in the life of teachers, students, and the classroom. It prefers to generalize rather than to particularize.

Consider the following case. Many of my students have a "fatal flair for false passives," like the main character in E. Annie Proulx's novel *The Shipping News*. I located a lesson in psychological history to help them. The current curricular focus in my departments—English and humanities—is largely on marginality. After I explained the grammatical problems of the passive voice, I connected it to the experience and concentration of their subject matter. In this case, the material was on women and African-Americans. Several students in this particular class were people of color, and half of the class was female. I argued that history had placed these people in a construct of passivity. It was time to make them active and the subject in the students' sentences. The next set of essays were approximately 65 percent free of the passive voice. De Man's disjunctions between cognition and self, the scholarly and the personal, were conjunctions in my teaching theory and practice.

What are de Man's criteria for "show business"? I had assigned oral presentations in my English course on American literature. One student, Sudha Nayani, discussed the problems of translating native material. She chose a Chippewa song, "The Approach of the Storm," which appears in *The Norton Anthology of American Literature*. The text provided both the Native American version and the English translation:

> Abitû'
> Gicîguñ'
> Ebigwĕn'
> Kabide' bwewiduñ'
>
> (From the half of the sky
> That which lives there
> Is coming, and makes a noise)

The song was flat and unanimated on the page. Sudha wanted to capture the original meaning, question the interpretation, and maintain what she called the mechanics, such as alliteration and rhyming, which were lost in the English translation. She felt that she had to hear the song, not merely read it. She spent hours in the music library listening to Frances Densmore's original 1910 recordings of Chippewa songs. Sudha rehearsed singing "The Approach of the Storm" in native dialect, although she, herself, comes from India. In class, she began her analysis of the text by singing. This approach was a revelation to the other students and to me. In this form of analysis, we could see and hear what we had not seen and heard before. Sudha's singing brought out the sound of the impending storm, unheard on the textbook page. She explained that reading the song concealed the onomatopoeia. The English word "noise," even if read aloud, gives no sense of the storm. She showed how natives mispronounced words to fit the music because the music was more important than the words. This observation stimulated me to other thoughts about native cultures. Language is a living dynamic in the aboriginal world. Sudha triggered knowledge in me. Because of her, I remembered that native languages have several words for "wood," unlike English, to signify the difference between living and dead wood (a tree as opposed to a table, for example).

De Man's dismissal of show business and guidance counseling suggests that he valorizes cognition at the expense of the body's other intelligences. Within his purview, cognitive power bureaucratizes and institutionalizes scholarship, as though thinking does not occur in other modes. Teaching is not a task, and I am not a taskmaster. Elitism and exclusion spill out from his observations, and they are antithetical to what I consider the true dynamics of the classroom. The fusion of mind and body, of central and peripheral vision, of the objective and the subjective, of the rational and the irrational does not have to lead to a mindless group grope or to thinking and writing that are thin. To the contrary, my students and I bait our hooks for Leviathan.

THE RICHNESS AND POVERTY OF PURE THEORY
The dispute in the academic world between objective knowledge and what Suzanne Langer has called non-discursive forms of knowledge is contested terrain. For instance, Einstein felt that scientific theory was too poor for experience; Niels Bohr felt that experience was too rich for scientific theories. Theory and experience coalesce in my teaching practice. My course on fantasy looks at devices, techniques, and forms of fantasy that construct alternative realities. The texts in the course are interdisciplinary; they comprise examples from literature, film, music, history, and the visual arts.

One of my students was a geography major. He was having difficulty with the major essay and the fantasy course in general. He was an intelligent student who was both comfortable and successful in his field. But his training in statistical research and quantitative analysis did not help him in the fantasy course. He, and the majors in science and mathematics, were apoplectic at the course's treatment of these disciplines as imaginary constructs. I wanted to help him find a subject and form that would connect his interests and expertise to the requirements of the course.

I asked him if he worked with maps in geography. He did. So I suggested that he do his paper on maps and fantasy, and I brainstormed ideas with him. Maps, like fantasy, are neither objective nor value-free. They are someone's vision of reality, a combination of the imagination and the intellect. I had read a fascinating book on maps by Peter Whitfield (1994). He argued that the act of representing reality in maps was not too different from the act of representing it in art or literature. It was the same impulse to crystalize, comprehend, and therefore to control aspects of reality.

A number of fantasy texts in the course had maps or theories of voyaging—for example, Jonathan Swift's *Gulliver's Travels*, Tolkien's *The Lord of the Rings*, the film *Casablanca*, and a discussion of Galileo. The geography student's essay included *Gulliver's Travels*. He argued that maps mirror the minds of the society or the individual from which they spring. The visual space of maps reflects a navigational, scientific, religious, political, national, or colonizing cosmology. He connected the rationality and irrationality of maps to central themes in the novel and the fantasy course. He analyzed the ways in which the implication of voyaging in maps related to the transformation of character, whether individual, scientific, or national, Gulliver, the Royal Society, or England.

I teach in both the day and the night programs in my university. In the night program, students must take four general education courses, one of which is in humanities. Many of the students are mature students with full-time jobs. When I taught a course called "Business: Its Tradition and Culture," I knew from experience that 90 percent of the students would be business administration or related majors. Most of them were in their second, third, or fourth years. They had put off the humanities requirement because they were afraid of a discipline that seemed too alien to their concentration and background. When they saw the word "business" in the course's title, they swarmed to it. After they saw the course's outline, however, many were in shock. The course's texts included film, literature, history, and psychology. Among others, the texts included: Thoreau's *Walden*, which advises corporate climbers that the cost of a thing is the amount of life you have to spend to get it; Marx's *Communist Manifesto*, which analys the alienation of labor; Stowe's *Uncle Tom's Cabin*, which reproves the marketzeplace of slavery; Balzac's *Eugenie Grandet*, which reveals the consequences of miserliness; Fitzgerald's *The Great Gatsby*, which exposes the promise and the betrayal of the American Dream; and Keneally's *Schindler's List*, which illuminates the atrocities of bartering with human life. In an effort to ground the course both in academic discourse and in the world to which it refers, I brought in executives from The Body Shop to discuss their community-based agenda, as well as the head of personnel from Ontario Hydro to explain employment equality and affirmative action.

In conjunction with *Schindler's List*, I took the students to a Holocaust museum and invited a survivor to speak to them. I discussed Nazism as capitalism gone mad. I used the language and the concepts of the course to rework business ideas such as "work" and its articulation in the concentration camps (*Arbeit macht frei*). I reinterpreted the designation "salesman" to incorporate Oskar Schindler's redefinition of what that idea means in a world where human life is a commodity.

In this course, I also brought the issues and texts of the course to the students' primary world in a special project. In addition to the course's two essays and a final examination, I divided the students into groups of five. Each group had three months to create their own business. Whatever business the group created had to respond in whatever way they wished to the ideas in the course and to a list of twenty issues. The groups could either incorporate or reject them, but their companies had to engage the focal points. These concerns addressed course topics located in business and its social context. Some of those issues involved the environment, organizational hierarchy and whether or not it should exist, day care, architecture as it relates to working conditions, gender, physical capabilities, age, and more.

Over a period of five weeks, the students presented their companies to us. I marveled at their ingenuity. All of the groups clarified their objectives and the structure of their companies. Each handed in a ten-page prospectus, written not in business language but in response to the course's texts. The class then debated the merits, theories, practicalities, and disadvantages of their businesses. For example, one presentation described a T-shirt company that amalgamated the needs of the business with the environment. This group wore the products their business had made. The colors were so outstanding that we immediately challenged them on their dyeing process. They patiently explained that the colors were vegetable dyes. Another group created a bakery whose mission statement was to produce delicious and nutritious goods while proactively integrating with the environment. Their report included organizational charts, a company history, and pre-recession growth projections as well as discussions of corporate structure and participation, environmental responses, management philosophy, employee benefits, an architectural plan of the company layout, safety issues, profit sharing, and many more specifics and rationales. This group presented their company dressed as chefs. They had all baked examples of their goods for the benefit of illustration.

Overall, the class felt that this project helped them in team building and in assimilating the texts and ideas of the course. Many of the students said that they used the ideas generated in class in their own workplaces. Five students out of twenty-five changed their majors to English or humanities.

In the classrooms of my life, both my students and I have learned to share and love knowledge rather than crudely and ruthlessly to compete for it. We have learned that the love of ideas should not become love of power and dominance. Eisner has written about the miracles of stunning teaching. Those miracles happen when student and teacher journey together. I will continue as an explorer of consciousness and, in the end, I say to my students what Seamus Heaney's literary ancestor said to him in *Station Island* (1984): "You listened long enough. Now strike your note."

REFERENCES

Beattie, M. (1995). *Constructing professional knowledge in teaching: A narrative of change and development.* New York, NY: Teacher's College Press.

de Man, P. (1982). The resistance to theory. *Yale French studies, 63.*

Dillard, A. (1974). *Pilgrim at Tinker creek.* New York, NY: Harper.

Eisner, E. W. (1988). The primacy of experience and the politics of method. *Educational researcher, 17* (5), 15–20.

Schwab, J. (1983). The practical 4: Something for curriculum professors to do. *Curriculum inquiry, 13* (3), 239–265.

Whitfield, P. (1994). *The image of the world: 20 centuries of world maps.* San Francisco, CA: Pomegranate Artbooks.

17

Feminist Pedagogy: A Voice of One's Own

ROSEMARIE TONG

 *The Thatcher Professor in Philosophy and Medical Humanities at Davidson College, Rosemarie Tong teaches courses in many fields: feminist thought; philosophy of law; genetic and reproductive technology; and ethics, with special emphasis on bioethics and medicine. She is the author of many books, including* Feminist Thought: A Comprehensive Introduction, Feminine and Feminist Ethics, *and* Controlling Our Reproductive Destiny: A Technological and Philosophical Perspective *(coauthored with Larry Kaplan). Tong has been a consultant for the American Council of Learned Societies, the National Endowment for the Humanities, the Fulbright Foundation, the North Carolina Medical Society, and various curricular programs involving women's studies and bioethics. She was named the 1986 U.S. Professor of the Year by the Council for Advancement and Support of Education (CASE) and the Carnegie Foundation for the Advancement of Teaching.*

In reflecting upon how, what, and why I teach, I have noticed several things about myself, but none so revealing as the following two: First, I am firmly convinced that good teaching is as much about examining one's self and relating it to others as it is about disseminating the content of one's discipline. Second, I am decidedly committed to those techniques of teaching that cluster under the rubric of "feminist pedagogy." In this essay, I hope to articulate what I understand by feminist pedagogy and to persuade more of my colleagues to use its techniques.

Differences Between Women's Pedagogy and Feminist Pedagogy

Feminist pedagogy is not to be conflated with women's pedagogy—that is, *women's* supposed way of teaching, whether this way of teaching is biologically determined or, more probably, socially constructed. Heavily influenced by the work of Carol Gilligan (1982), Nel Noddings (1984), and Mary Ann Belenky et al. (1986), advocates of women's pedagogy claim that, on the average, men and women establish truth claims and answer moral questions in decidedly different ways. In their estimation, men favor 1) a kind of knowing that separates the subject from the object, and 2) a type of moral reasoning that emphasizes individual rights and the importance of treating everyone the same—that is, justly. In contrast, women favor 1) a kind of knowing that links together the subject and the object, and 2) a type of moral reasoning that stresses responsibilities to others, the value of relationships, and the need to treat each individual differently—that is, with care. Advocates of women's pedagogy make the further claim that these supposed gender differences predispose men and women to teach differently. As they see it, men's mode of teaching is paternal, authoritarian, aloof, demanding, and adversarial. It is geared toward generating a competitive struggle for excellence in which there are clear winners and losers. In contrast, women's mode of teaching is maternal, nurturant, caring, sensitive, compassionate, and attentive. It is structured to develop a cooperative community of teachers and students who share their knowledge with each other.

Objections to the claim that women teach differently than men are several. Over and beyond the obvious objection that some men have a "female" style of teaching and that some women have a "male" style of teaching, critics first observe that there is no *one* way that all women teach—that what has passed as *women's* way of teaching is typically a white, heterosexual, middle-class women's way of teaching, unmediated by important differences of race, sexual orientation, class, and so on. Second, critics note that, historically, women's "maternal" way of teaching has actually been more militant than nurturant. For example, in an article on late nineteenth- and early twentieth-century elementary and high school teachers, Madeline R. Grumet writes that when women entered the teaching field *en masse* in the nineteenth century, they imported into the classroom not the "intimacy, spirituality, and innocence" of the mother-child bond but cagey strategies for controlling their sometimes unruly charges. The world was nasty and brutish. Competitive husbands, fathers, and sons had to be restrained somehow, and the task of restraint fell to wives, mothers, and daughters. Gradually, the school system became patriarchy's primary means of control, and "virtuous" women—

that is, women willing to order, center, rank, and line up their charges, to teach them how to be obedient workers and docile citizens—became patriarchy's best teachers (Grumet, 1981, pp. 165–184). Third, and finally, critics caution that in the same ways that it is risky for women to subscribe to an ethic of care or an epistemology of connectedness, it is also risky for women to subscribe to a pedagogy of uncritical nurturance. To tell women that they should be carers, that they should forge close connections with those to whom they are related, is often to urge them to give to others more than they should (Hoagland, 1989).

FEMINIST PEDAGOGY

For all the reasons above, I think that feminist pedagogy is quite different from women's way of teaching, especially if the latter is sentimentalized. Like several related nonfeminist pedagogies, feminist pedagogy tends to be interdisciplinary, experiential, and process-oriented. Feminist teachers are interested in connecting rather than in separating the disciplines; in showing students how learning in the so-called Ivory Tower relates to doing in the so-called real world; and in focusing on how they teach as well as on what they teach. What distinguishes feminist pedagogy from other interdisciplinary, experiential, and process-oriented ways of teaching, however, is its focus on the politics of gender. Whenever it makes pedagogical sense, feminists seek 1) to ask the so-called woman question (Does principle x, policy x, practice x harm or benefit women?); 2) to raise all people's, but especially women's, consciousness about gender oppression in their private and public lives; and 3) to motivate all people, but especially women, to change the principles, practices, and policies that prevent or impede true equality between men and women.

Feminist pedagogy as interdisciplinary

To say that feminist pedagogy is interdisciplinary is not to claim that all feminist teachers do or should teach in an interdisciplinary program. Rather, it is to stress the fact that, when the opportunity presents itself, feminist teachers are ready, willing, and able to break the boundaries that separate one academic discipline from another. The disciplines are exactly what they proclaim themselves to be: rules, regimes, prescriptions for asking certain kinds of questions in certain ways to get certain sorts of answers. When people from different disciplines try to approach a common problem in an interdisciplinary manner, they sometimes get new and better answers to old and hard questions. What they *always* get, however, is first the opportunity to challenge the assumptions, methodologies, and conclusions of their own and each other's disciplines, and second the opportunity to collaborate, corroborate, and cooperate in ways that will help each of them to see what is colloquially referred to as the whole picture.

My own experiences with feminist interdisciplinary teaching have enabled me to overcome some of my moral and intellectual myopia. At Williams College, for example, I had the opportunity to teach "Feminist Thought" with gifted professors in the departments of English, economics, psychology, and political science. Although all of us were feminist teachers, each of us raised the "woman question" differently depending on her or his academic home base. For instance, when it came to a topic such as pornography, I wanted to analyze the truth value of claims such as "pornography is to sexism as segregation is to racism." My colleague in economics, however, wanted to focus on who buys and sells pornography, while my colleague in English wanted to know what distinguishes an artistic representation of sex from a pornographic one. They asked questions such as: "Do men really buy more pornography than women do?" and "Does it make a difference whether a male heterosexual or a lesbian produces a nearly identical film on sado-masochism among lesbians?" In contrast to the rest of us, my colleague in psychology wanted to know what kind of men prefer violent pornography and why. Is it only extremely aggressive, women-hating men who enjoy "slice-and-dice" films, or do many mild-mannered husbands and lovers also find these films sexually arousing? Finally, my colleague in political science wanted to discuss the First Amendment status of pornography. She asked whether pornography is true speech or simply a series of moanings and groanings emitted by human beings in the heat of passion.

After listening to my colleagues separate lines of inquiry in this one course, I have never been able to raise all and only philosophical questions about pornography and its role in maintaining gender oppression. The abstract questions of philosophy need the concrete frames of reference that the sciences and other disciplines in the humanities provide, just as much as the details of varied humanities fields and the facts of the sciences require the generalizations and classifications of philosophy. Moreover, my first experience with interdisciplinary teaching left me unable to enjoy teaching alone quite as much as teaching with others. Moving between the role of teacher and student, as one typically does in interdisciplinary teaching/learning, makes one ever sensitive to how hard (and wonderful) it is to be a student as well as how hard (and wonderful) it is to be a teacher.

Feminist pedagogy as experiential
To say that feminist pedagogy is experiential is to say that it denies both the theory-practice dichotomy and the contemplation-action dichotomy. *Discussing* the tensions between physician paternalism and patient autonomy is

one matter; *observing* these tensions played out between a particular physician and a particular patient is quite another. When students actually hear patients refuse to follow their physicians' treatment recommendations, they begin to understand just how *human* the struggle between paternalism and autonomy is, a struggle many of them are experiencing in another form as they break away from parental authority.

Both nonfeminist and feminist teachers committed to experiential education probably teach courses such as the ones we teach in Davidson College's medical humanities program. Carefully prepared students, many of them pre-med, are given the opportunity to intern with physicians who treat AIDS patients, for example. Since these students go on rounds with their mentors, they are often privy to discussions that end with a patient's demanding an experimental drug that a physician refuses to prescribe, or with a patient's insisting that he or she be allowed to die what a physician regards as an unnecessarily premature death. Suddenly, the students who championed the value of physician paternalism *über alles* are no longer sure that the doctor knows best. Similarly, the students who set the value of patient autonomy over all other values become less confident that patients' preferences should always have the final say. In short, as a result of their clinical experiences, what was initially crystal clear to students in class becomes foggy and even muddy.

Unlike nonfeminist experiential teachers, however, feminist experiential teachers do more than provide their students with internship experiences. Feminist teachers also encourage their students to reflect upon their real-world experiences, inviting them to comment first on the gendered and then on the raced and classed dimensions of these experiences. For example, as my students recount what they have observed about the conflict between physician paternalism and patient autonomy in the clinic, I ask them questions such as: "Are women or men more inclined to refuse treatment?" "Are physicians more likely to respect a man's or a woman's decision to refuse treatment?" "Are female physicians any less paternalistic than male physicians?" "Do women worry more about being a 'drain' on their families than men do?" "Are physicians more likely to view men's or women's decisions as rational?" More often than not, these questions—phrased in terms of gender—catch students off guard. As they become accustomed to raising the "woman question" (or the "race" or "class" question), however, students begin to see facts they had previously overlooked—facts that make a difference in assessing how free a patient is or how "knowing" a physician is.

Feminist pedagogy as process-oriented

Process-oriented teaching is as much of a challenge to the academy as are interdisciplinary and experiential teaching. Process-oriented nonfeminist as well as feminist teachers are convinced that there is a regrettable tendency for teachers to become so concerned about covering the material that they leave no time for the kind of discussions or question-and-answer exchanges that challenge students to reflect deeply on the context of their classes. Process-oriented teachers realize that their message will fall on barren ground absent good faculty-student communication. In other words, unless teachers know who their students are, they will not be able to understand why some students sit stony-faced while other students do all the talking, or why some students roll their eyes or snicker when other students venture an opinion. Similarly, unless students know who their peers and teachers are, they will have trouble voicing their deepest questions for fear of revealing themselves to unsympathetic strangers.

Like all process-oriented teachers, feminist process-oriented teachers are sensitive to classroom dynamics, but they are particularly focused on how their own as well as their students' gender, race, and class affect learning and teaching. Feminist teachers claim that unless both teachers and students realize how their gender identity affects their ability to teach well or learn well, they will never understand what went wrong (or right) in a certain class. Students will fail to realize, for example, why they loved or hated the discussion in a course on Southern women writers, or why they regarded a teacher as the best or worst one they ever had. Similarly, teachers will not be able to identify why they failed to get a discussion going in one of their classes, or why the topics of greatest interest to them were dismissed by some students as "boring" or "a waste of time."

PITFALLS OF FEMINIST PEDAGOGY

In the preceding discussion, I have sought not only to make some distinctions between otherwise similar feminist and nonfeminist teachers, but also to present a favorable view of feminist teachers. Unfortunately, feminist pedagogy has a dark side as well as a bright side. Feminist teachers, like all teachers, can easily abuse their power as teachers: They can manipulate or coerce their students into seeing the world as they see it. For this reason, I agree with feminist philosopher Kelly Oliver that to be truly feminist teachers, teachers must 1) "challenge their students and their beliefs without disempowering them"; 2) "undermine their own position of authority within the institution without undermining their effectiveness as teachers"; and 3) "examine their own political, or consciousness-raising, agenda, as a possible mode of domination itself" (Oliver, 1989, pp. 82–87).

Always challenge; never disempower your students

To point out to a student, for example, that he (or she) has some incredibly nonfeminist, indeed antifeminist, points of view without making him (or her) feel foolish or worse is to accomplish no simple task. When one of my "Feminist Thought" students recently announced to the class, "Date rape isn't real rape—it's just a sexual misunderstanding," I wanted to tell him to sit down and keep quiet. But I didn't. Although I believe it is my responsibility as a feminist teacher to challenge such a student, I do not believe that I have a right, not even as a feminist teacher, to express contempt for him. Instead of censoring a student with a wrong-headed view, I ask him how he came to the conclusion that date rape is not real rape, and why he thinks I probably disagree with him. Although I refuse to let him off the hook, and although I permit other members of the class to take him to task, I try to reassure him that his position is not absolutely groundless. I concede, for example, that some women do permit men to take sexual liberties with them before they suddenly draw the line, and that it would probably be better if these women behaved differently. Nonetheless, I point out in no uncertain terms that just because a woman says "yes" to some things does not mean that she cannot say "no" to others. Usually such concessions and observations lead students with unreflective views to soften their positions, and to admit, for example, that just because a woman is partially responsible for creating a volatile situation does not mean that she forfeits her right to extricate herself from it. I count such admissions as progress towards the kind of world I wish to create.

Always be an effective teacher; never be an authoritarian teacher

The second challenge to feminist teaching that Oliver mentions—undermining one's position of authority within the institution without undermining one's effectiveness as a teacher—is equal to the first. Whenever I indicate to my students that I can learn from them as much as they can learn from me, or that I am less than omniscient, I risk my credibility as a teacher. I risk even more of my credibility, however, when I reveal my feminist (and other) commitments to my students, identifying the ways in which they shape my value system (I happen to teach a variety of ethics courses). Nevertheless, taking this risk can be rewarding indeed. More often than not, I manage to earn my students' respect. They come to realize that I am not interested in dazzling them with what I know but in motivating them to learn as much as they can. They also discover that I am not a female chauvinist but simply someone who is especially concerned about the ways in which gender (or race or class) alternately empower and disempower people. When students start learning because *they* want to learn and not because they fear me or want to please me,

I feel worthy of the title Teacher. Similarly, when students report that the tools of gender analysis (or race analysis or class analysis) have helped them to understand reality in better as well as in deeper ways, I feel that I have served them especially well. Truly effective teachers enjoy being surpassed by their students; they have no need to proclaim their vision *the* best possible vision. That need is the scourge of the authoritarian teacher.

Always empower your students; never dominate them

The third challenge that Oliver mentions—namely, the willingness to examine one's own political or consciousness-raising agenda as a possible mode of domination—is extremely difficult to meet. Recently, several of my friends and I were discussing politics. We got on the subject of the role of the Roman Catholic Church in Latin America. One of my friends, an advocate of liberation theology, said that many priests and nuns were effective advocates for the disadvantaged. In response to this observation, one of my other women friends exploded. She exclaimed that as far as she was concerned the world, but especially women, would be much better off without the Church. The Roman Catholic Church, she insisted, was one of patriarchy's primary tools of oppression, and anyone who failed to realize this was suffering from self-deception. No matter what anyone said in response to this comment, my friend dismissed it as an instance of false consciousness. She would hear nothing about the complexity of the Church's role: that there were liberating as well as oppressive, repressive, and suppressive tendencies within it. As far as she was concerned, the issue was utterly simple. "The Roman Catholic Church is patriarchal—end of story," she concluded, chastising several of us for observations such as, "Sure, the Church's official policy on sexual issues is antifeminist, but in practice, especially in developing nations, many nuns and priests are the first to dispense contraceptives." As she saw it, to make such observations was to defend the Church and strengthen patriarchy. Part of me, the part that fears being complicit, admired my friend, so strong in her convictions, so unwilling to compromise. Another part of me, the teacher part, did not admire my friend. I speculated that were she a teacher, she might have a tendency to proclaim her views as truth with a capital "T"; and this, even on behalf of a good cause, is a mode of domination.

FEMINIST PEDAGOGY AS FOCUSED ON POWER

As must be clear to readers by now, feminist teachers are particularly concerned about power axes in the academy, particularly about power axes among students (Briskin & Coulter, 1992, p. 258). Since students are gendered, raced, and classed subjects, they bring differential sorts of power and privilege to the classroom and reproduce gendered (and raced and classed) power dynamics in their interactions with others. These dynamics shape their class participation and sense of entitlement in the classroom. Although student interactions can be affirming and supportive, just as frequently they can involve destructive competition or dismissal of each other's perspectives. Regrettably, feminist teachers are not always able to channel student power dynamics in positive rather than negative directions. The power of students—especially white, middle-class, heterosexual, male students—to shape classroom dynamics is not always amenable to intervention by even the most skilled feminist teachers. Feminist teachers have to recognize their limits as they struggle to interrupt their students' thoughts—to make them aware of how they are using, abusing, misusing their power. Indeed, feminist teachers have to learn what to do when their creative power is threatened by the destructive power of one or more of their students. For example, I recall feeling badly after one particular class. I had noticed two of my male students laughing hysterically in the back of the room as I sought to defend a woman's gestational relationship to her child as possibly a more important criterion for parenthood than a man's genetic relationship to his child. As I let myself focus on these two young men's faces, I began to lose my train of thought. It took every ounce of my psychic powers to finish my lecture as forcefully as I had begun it.

FEMINIST PEDAGOGY AS FOCUSED ON GENDER

As much as feminist pedagogy is about power, however, it is not about just any kind of power. If it were, it would be extremely difficult to distinguish feminist pedagogy from the liberatory pedagogy of Paulo Freire, author of *Pedagogy for the Oppressed* (1987), and Ivan Illich, author of *Deschooling Society* (1988). These thinkers are very concerned about how civil authorities in particular use the schools to tame, to domesticate, to dispirit children. What these authors do not urge teachers to do, however, is to use gender as the primary category of analysis. For them, class is the primary category of analysis. And that is to be expected. One must begin from where one's primary commitments are in order to communicate effectively. If one is a Marxist, one must begin with the assumption that class is the root of all evil; but if one is a feminist, one must begin with the conviction that, as Christine di Stephano (1990, p. 66) has argued, gender is a more basic difference than even class or race. As feminists see it, there is no escape from either the fact that we are gendered or the consequences that maleness and femaleness have on our lives. Certainly, there is no way for a feminist to teach without emphasizing the role that gender plays in shaping men's and women's respective perspectives on reality.

That gender and its accompanying dynamics of power are still largely ignored in the academy became clear to me again when one of my colleagues and I discussed Kurosawa's film *Rashomon*. In this Japanese tale, a husband and wife traveling through the forest are attacked by a bandit. The husband is killed, the wife raped. Through a series of flashbacks, the director shows us four people's different perspectives on the event. The bandit recounts the classic male fantasy of rape: She fought at first, but once he started, she loved it. He fights her husband in hope of winning her as the prize. Yet when she runs away, he forgets her, because he feels no attraction to a cowardly woman. He declares to the police that she was not worth chasing. The wife's story of her violation is quite different. She claims that after the bandit raped her, he left her crying on the forest floor. When she looked to her husband for compassion, she found only hatred and contempt in his eyes. She begged him to kill her, to do anything but look at her with those eyes. He, however, remained stonily silent; and she, realizing his condemnation of her, ran away in undeserved disgrace. The dead husband, speaking through a medium, testifies that his wife agreed to run away with the bandit after he raped her. In fact, she asked the bandit to kill him, as she could not go with the bandit as long as he lived. The bandit, disgusted by such female treachery, offered to kill or spare her, as the injured husband saw fit. Noble to the end, the husband let her flee from the scene of *her* crime. The final version of the story comes from a witness, a firewood gatherer who stumbled on the scene while walking through the woods. On his account, the bandit first tried to gain the woman's love and promise of marriage, but ultimately rejected her after her husband called her a shameless whore and refused to fight for her. After all, if rape is seen as a power struggle between men, and the husband refuses to risk death for the woman, he takes all of the adventure out of it!

I saw *Rashomon* as a movie about the horror of rape, the powerlessness of women, and even a confirmation of the kind of view Catherine A. MacKinnon (1987, pp. 198–205) has articulated: namely, that in a patriarchal society all sexual intercourse should be viewed as rape unless proved otherwise. The four stories recounted above are ultimately one and the same story about women supposedly "wanting it," "getting it," and then claiming that they didn't want it, after all. While talking with a male colleague, however, he mentioned to me that, for him, *Rashomon* was simply a story about truth: a philosophy of law classic. Just as in a court of law different witnesses tell different stories, the director masterfully shows us how different truths are seen with different eyes. The facts of the case forever elude us. Objectivity is continually melting into subjectivity. Enamored with the mystery of the myriad nature of abstract truth, my colleague was eager to downplay the horror of the concrete, even of the young woman's rape. Indeed, he told me that it did not matter what the film was about. It could be about anything provided that it let his class discuss the differences between reality and interpretation. Indeed, it would be better if the film did not involve rape, since every once in a while the women in the class got sidetracked by the rape issue.

When all is said and done, then, I gladly admit that the feminist teacher is always attuned to the ways in which issues of gender and also race and class have shaped and are shaping the human experience. There is no way to avoid gender in genuine teaching. It affects the way our students dress, speak, reason, think, and, yes, learn. Until gender (and also race and class), understood as embedded systems of power relations, are truly exploded, we feminist teachers will have a *political* commitment that distinguishes us from other excellent teachers who share our *intellectual* agenda about interdisciplinary, experiential, and process-oriented education.

We feminist teachers cannot miraculously think the fact of bi-polar, dichotomous gender relations out of existence. We know this. We can hope, however, to act invidious gender relationships out of existence. Actions, and not simply thoughts, will ultimately liberate us from the narrownesses of mind and the constrictions of heart that disempower us by setting male against female. It is this conviction that guides much of my feminist teaching, and that convinces me that all teachers should embrace at least the spirit, if not the letter, of feminist pedagogy.

REFERENCES

Belenky, M. F., Clinchy, B. M., Goldberger, N. R., & Tarvie, J. M. (1986). *Women's ways of knowing: The development of self, voice, and mind.* New York, NY: Basic Books.

Briskin, L., & Coulter, R. P. (1992). Feminist pedagogy: Challenging the normative. *Canadian Journal of Education, 17* (3).

di Stephano, C. (1990). Dilemmas of difference. In L. Nicholson (Ed.), *Feminism/postmodernism.* New York, NY: Routledge.

Freire, P. (1987). *Pedagogy of the oppressed.* New York, NY: Continuum.

Gilligan, C. (1982). *In a different voice.* Cambridge, MA: Harvard University Press.

Grumet, M. R. (1981). Pedagogy for patriarchy: The feminization of teaching. *Interchange on Educational Policy, 12* (2–3), 165–184.

Hoagland, S. L. (1989). *Lesbian ethics.* Palo Alto, CA: Institute of Lesbian Studies.

Illich, I. (1988). *Deschooling Society.* New York, NY: Harper & Row.

MacKinnon, C. A. (1987). *Feminism unmodified.* Cambridge, MA: Harvard University Press.

Noddings, N. (1984). *Caring: A feminine approach to ethics and moral education.* Berkeley, CA: University of California Press.

Oliver, K. (1989). Toward thoughtful dialogue in the classroom: Feminist pedagogy. *APA Newsletters, 89* (1), 82–87.

18

The Liberal Arts and Civic Education: Grounds for Inspired Teaching

RALPH KETCHAM

The Maxwell Professor of Citizenship and Public Affairs at Syracuse University, Ralph Ketcham specializes in American political history. Among his many books are Individualism and Public Life: A Modern Dilemma *and* Framed for Posterity: The Enduring Philosophy of the Constitution. *He has written and edited numerous works on Benjamin Franklin and James Madison, including a biography of Madison that was nominated for a National Book Award in 1972. Ketcham has lectured and taught in England, India, Japan, China, and Mexico. In the 1990s, he has spent summers in Hungary and Russia, where he helps teachers to improve materials and methods for civic education. Ketcham was named the 1987 U.S. Professor of the Year by the Council for Advancement and Support of Education (CASE) and the Carnegie Foundation for the Advancement of Teaching.*

Inspired teaching can happen at the most meaningful level only when the lesson to be learned is of deep importance and interest to both the teacher and the student. Without that essential, no amount of brilliant classroom presence, sophisticated technology, or skillful methodology will produce inspiration or lasting, significant impact. Such impact can take place when the subject may seem rather narrow and specialized, and indeed it is often even heightened by a focused intensity; the teacher and student thus share a sense of discovering and pursuing something new and creative. But even in these specialized situations, there must be at least some connection to the questions of most profound concern to the student: Who am I? What is the world like? Why am I here?

These questions are most directly addressed in that part of education usually termed general or liberal. This area is where the school and the teacher open up and articulate for students the inherent curiosities they possess as human beings. By the time students reach college, they have usually faced such questions, or perhaps merely found themselves with puzzling, unarticulated versions of the questions, and, at least implicitly, they have pursued some answers to them. In any case, as human beings they are ready for and in need of a further consideration of both the questions and the answers, and they need to be guided by good teachers.

Even the most specialized or vocationally oriented course must in some fashion relate itself to the larger questions if it is to strike the most resonating, responsive chord with a student's curiosity and thirst. Most directly, though, courses that are part of what has traditionally been termed a liberal arts education address these questions and offer special opportunities for inspired teaching, which is possible only if the teacher understands and shares an interest in the questions.

To make the inspiring moments happen, teachers must first have a subject matter of consuming interest and importance to them, and then have a motivation, intensity, and skillfulness in conveying the subject and its significance (that is, its capacity to enlarge student understanding of big questions). The formal, curricular arrangements encouraging such moments can be and are varied indeed. In fact, considering those arrangements and especially insisting upon the basic qualities that most create opportunities for inspired teaching may well be the most important and creative task of any college or university faculty.

THREE CHARACTERISTICS OF LIBERAL EDUCATION

Perhaps the best way to grasp the essence of liberal education is not to think of it so much as a certain substance or content, but to concentrate on three characteristics that its courses—whatever their content—always need to possess: They must be *profound, integrating,* and *radical.* When these qualities are emphasized, liberal education will be in tension with at least the more pretentious claims of specialized, vocational, and critical studies, because such claims tend to obscure the wider meaning of the word *education* itself (to educe; draw forth). A look at how three characteristics of liberal education—profound, integrating, and radical—can be evoked generally, and particularly in pursuit of civic education, reveals most fundamentally the grounds of inspired teaching.

In a sudden burst of insight, a graduating university senior recently responded—profoundly—to a question that is often inane: What advice would you give to high school seniors who are preparing to go to college? "Spread yourself thin," the university student advised, "know a little about a lot. Specialization is far too transient. Hail the Renaissance children! Avoid vocation, and indulge education. 'Let early education be amusements. You will then be able to find out the natural bent.' Plato said that," the graduate continued, "and if I had stayed a photography major, I never would have known it."

It must be profound

What does it mean to be profound? Educationally it means to read and be exposed to the good, deep stuff that challenges and then enriches and enlarges the most important concerns one has about oneself and one's world. Its essence is found in the best works of art, literature, history, and philosophy the world around. If one asks, "Why read the works of Shakespeare or Thucydides or Melville or Confucius or Kawabata or Virginia Woolf or Rousseau or Burke or Dostoyevsky or Vaclav Havel or Joyce Carol Oates or Toni Morrison?" the answer in each case is the same: They are profound. They probe the human psyche, revealing its depths, torments, and potential in ways that compel understandings to be stretched and deepened. Big questions have been opened and explored. The mind thus touched can never again be quite as content with triviality.

The canon of such works is not fixed, since it is continually being added to by rediscovery and creation, but the standard remains the same: Humanity has been enriched. Hamlet and Prince Genji and Captain Ahab and Alyosha Karamazov and Morrison's Sethe belong to us all because they stand for something in the deepening of our own lives and souls. They enlarge our freedom not only by opening doors but also by revealing exciting, poignant, or terrifying ways we might go through them. Are we not then liberated in the most profound sense?

To teach such works is itself an inspiration; it offers opportunity and stimulus not so readily available in less profoundly humane materials. Though all subjects do not obviously welcome the use of such works, the teacher, seeking to give greater possible significance and impact, can with sensitivity and ingenuity give deeper meaning to nearly any inquiry—the best teaching scientists and engineers, for example, do this.

It must be integrating

The requirement that liberal education be integrating is of heightened concern in our age of specialization and of reductionist or deconstructionist studies, because the inherent tendency to examine the trees closely, which is all right up to a point, nevertheless ends up incomplete and unsatisfying. One prominent executive made the point in remarking that, in this world of specialized scholars, sophisticated think tanks, and elaborate bureaucracies, there were far too few "experts in the situation as a whole." This deficiency is apparent enough in the realms of scholarly inquiry and public policy, but in a way it is even more poignantly harmful to young minds seeking meaning in the world they inhabit.

As teachers, we must recognize that no matter how important and challenging and brilliantly presented any specialized courses might be, random assemblages of them will seldom amount to more than that. Study after study of college-student reactions to undergraduate distribution requirements reach the same conclusion: The effect is simply incoherent and chaotic. Students find such requirements a waste of time, and they learn implicitly that things don't add up. One student's program at a prestigious university without a core curriculum included courses in "Arctic Archeology," "Anger," "Counseling," and "The Unsolved Problems of Biology"—all splendid courses by themselves, the student thought, but taken together they remained merely sparkling parts.

There are, to be sure, beguiling justifications. The faculty gets to teach whatever idiosyncratic courses suit its fancy (and are relieved of the burden of planning and teaching survey and foundational courses), while students have the freedom to choose courses as they please. Things are open-ended, diverse, and creative, with everyone free to pursue individual interests. But a serious flaw is at least as apparent: There is neither pattern nor effective guidance to help students "get it together"; there are no systematic, required courses to give students foundations, big pictures into which they might then fit the specialized pieces. Large, integrative works are likely to be neglected as attention focuses on the results of the latest research. Connections among things are likely to receive less emphasis than the examination of the parts. Even less likely is the explanation of pattern and purpose and cosmology, not with the idea of imposing orthodoxy, of course, but simply to give students the repeated experience of confronting and considering such integrations—surely an important part of the desire by humans to know about the world they live in. It may be that the whole is greater than the sum of the parts, and students need to have instruction acknowledging that. The enlightening, stretching experience one has in confronting integrative minds such as Max Weber's or Arnold Toynbee's or Joseph Campbell's or Cornel West's or Marguerite Youcenar's needs to be an incessant part of higher education. That sort of material is likely to educe inspired teaching. Indeed, it requires such teaching, and together the material and the teaching are likely to produce inspiration in students. At any rate, it is clear that this sort of broad understanding of the world that

Thomas Jefferson, for example, got from reading Cicero and Locke and Gibbon must still, in ways suited to the twenty-first century, be part of the intention of liberal education. Institutions of higher learning and their faculties have that inescapable responsibility—and opportunity.

It must be radical

Liberal education must also be radical. It should open up to students something of the range of potential and alternative that humankind has envisioned, explored, and attempted for itself through time and across space. Only thus can one be free of the confines of one's own (narrow) world and begin to imagine and pursue a brighter, more beckoning one, however practically difficult its realization might be. Such radicalness as much searches the present as the past, as much the distant as the close at hand, and as much humankind's inward as outward journeys in pursuit of aspirations that might liberate and ennoble life. In advising Peter Carr, his young nephew, about religious and philosophical studies, Jefferson urged him first to "divest yourself of all bias in favor of novelty and singularity of opinion.... Fix reason firmly in her seat, and call to her tribunal every fact, every opinion.... Neither believe nor reject anything, because other persons, or description of persons, have rejected or believed it. Your own reason is the only oracle given you by heaven, and you are answerable, not for the rightness, but uprightness of the decision" (Peterson, 1975, pp. 425–427). Unless students experience the exhilaration that goes with such honest inquiry, with such openness to "novelty and singularity of opinion," they risk forever being confined within their biases, limitations, and shortsightedness. The experience of such exhilaration and openness is the highest purpose of multicultural studies.

In his *Letters to the Young*, Peter Kropotkin wrote that young people should ask: What kind of world do you want? What do you need to know? What are you good at? What do you want to work at to build that world? He urged the young to demand that their teachers help them learn those things. That is, if the young are to be truly liberated, they must have visions set before them and paths pointed toward the realization of fuller and better ways to live. Writing in 1793, near the end of his life, Immanuel Kant made this important point: "No idea does more to lift the human spirit and to fan its enthusiasm than the very idea of a pure moral character.... If constant use of this view were made a principle of private and public education, the state of human morality would improve in short order" (1974, p. 54). To read the likes of Plato, Thoreau, Marx, Margaret Fuller, Martin Luther King, Jr., Gandhi, and Emma Goldman, great envisioners of ideals that challenge orthodoxies and open minds to alternatives, is also an essential part of true liberal education.

We see the scope of this need when we recall that the words *theory* and *theater* both derive from the Greek *thea*, which means *the act of seeing*. In the company of Aristotle and Shakespeare, of Hannah Arendt and James Baldwin, students can be led to the act of seeing dimensions and depths previously unknown to them.

Liberal education means, then, to bring students to a liberating sense of the nature of the world they live in and of their own potential as human beings. It would thus seem self-evident that such education would have to be profound, integrating, and radical. For to be shallow, fragmented, and conventional is to miss the nature of the world and of our human potential. Education of that kind leads to trivial answers to big questions such as "Who am I? What is the world like; what might it be like? Why am I here?"

Liberal education means not merely the absence of restraint on a student's inquiries but more profoundly that the student's mind is furnished with deep and integrating and radical questions and aspirations. That point was made with poignant force in 1996 by the reformer/revolutionist Daw Aung San Suu Kyi, who was quoted in the *New York Times Magazine* shortly after her partial release from six years of house arrest in Burma-Myanmar. Asked whether she was finally truly free, she replied:

> Well, I am acting as though I'm free. I do what I think I should, but to be free? What does that mean?... I think to be free is to be able to do what you think is right [Confucius, Jesus, and Hegel, among others, have made the same point], and in that sense I felt very free—even under house arrest. Because it was my choice. I knew I could leave any time. I just had to say, "I'm not going to do politics any more." But it was my choice to be involved in the democracy movement. So, I was perfectly free" (Dreifus, 1996, p. 34).

A truly liberal/liberating education gives one a sense of high ideals drawn from a wide exposure to them, and then a sense of efficacy about how to be involved in the real world. Could a teacher possibly have a higher aspiration, or inspiration, than to nourish such senses?

CIVIC EDUCATION

The idea of liberal education has a special meaning in the public life of a democratic society. Liberal education is required by all people in a democracy—whatever their particular skills or group identities or walks of life—so that they can perform properly in their public office as citizens. Jefferson put it simply in his 1779 proposal for a system of primary education: All citizens thus "would be qualified to understand their rights, to maintain them, and to exercise with intelligence their parts in self-government" (1944, p. 52). Such education, he explained to John Adams after each had served as president of the United States, "would raise the mass of the people to the high ground of moral respectability necessary to their own safety, and to orderly government" (1959, p. 387). To skeptics who thought this idealism too high, Jefferson replied, "If we think [the people] not enlightened enough to exercise their control [over government] with a wholesome discretion, the remedy is not to take it from them, but to inform their discretion through education" (1955, p. 93).

In the 1840s, Horace Mann (1969, pp. 195–202) picked up Jefferson's argument when he pointed out "a republican form of government, without intelligence in the people, must be, on a vast scale, what a mad-house, without superintendent, or keepers, would be, on a small one." Thus, he affirmed, "one of the highest and most valuable objects, to which the influence of a school can be made conducive, consists in training our children in self-government." Mann argued that the development of rational intelligence, the training of young people so that they might rise from poverty and ignorance, the instruction in the processes of government, and the inculcation of a morality suited to public enlightenment were all vital parts of a system of universal public education.

Thus, Mann's theory of public education was an idea guided fundamentally by education's public purpose. He advocated in Massachusetts a system of education funded by the state (thus public in one sense), and he intended those schools to be open to every child (thus public in yet another sense), but even more he was intent on the stake the public had in preparing young people to be good citizens. Public education, then, whether conducted in state-supported or in privately operated schools, was essential for every young person because each would become a member of the public and thus require education for that role. The public and not the private benefits of universal education loom largest. Colleges and universities have the responsibility to be the capstone of this education in civic matters, a responsibility that both stimulates and requires inspired teaching.

Considering the concern of Jefferson and Mann to train young people in self-government, what should be said about education for citizenship as the twenty-first century approaches? Following the distinguished philosopher Joseph Tussman (1960), I would suggest that we begin by regarding the citizen in a democracy as an office holder in government. That is, in discussing, voting, and acting in a self-governing society, the citizen is part, actually one of the ultimate parts, of the government itself. Thus, the citizen's role differs only in degree from that of any elected or appointed official, or even from that of a monarch in a society ruled by one person. This role's essential obligation, as we expect (though don't always receive) from all office holders, is to develop perspective and habit that put the public interest, the good of the country as a whole, above private, selfish, dynastic, class, race, gender, or any other partial interests. In educating young people for "the office of citizen," we must start and end with nourishing the essential, public-spirited stance expected of any public official. The skills of data collection, policy analysis, and communication taught by social scientists are important and useful, and the nourishment of cultural and group identities can be vital and constructive. Standing by themselves, however, they leave the political decision-maker, the citizen, without guidance at crucial points. That guidance can only properly come from an enlarged and disciplined way of looking at public affairs.

Such an idea of citizenship has an ancient and honored lineage and thus offers teachers of history and philosophy inspiring opportunities. This idea was central to Aristotle's argument that good government depended on the public virtue of those who ruled (all the citizens in a constitutional polity) and to the Renaissance's "civic republican" model, which required an independent, reasonable, and responsible citizenry. It was also central to Jefferson, Mann, and other North American proponents of democratic citizenship. All attended primarily to the "quality of the parts," the nourishment of the vital "public spirit," as well as to the practical skills of those who would take part in self-government. The need for public spirit and proper perspective remains as strong as ever.

The teaching of such a perspective needs to be, and can be, woven into every level of education, but it should also be the explicit focus of "participation in government" courses. For example, for seniors in high school (an ideal time because "the office of citizen" begins then for most Americans), a Supreme Court case such as *New Jersey v. T.L.O.*—it focused on the right of school authorities to search student purses—can teach the vital lessons. Students readily understand the issue and are keenly alert to both the rights of students and the responsibilities of authorities to maintain a good learning atmosphere in the school. The facts can be grasped easily and the implications discerned quickly. Even the arguments supporting the Court's opinions are, with careful explanation, within the understanding of most students. The students' attention can be drawn not so much to the legal technicalities of the case or to the issue of the "correct" opinion, but to the broad view and careful reasoning of the justices on both sides of a split (5–3) decision. That is, students can learn how to approach public questions: First, how to understand the facts and issues, then to see the lines of thought reasoned consideration can take, and finally to discern responsible judgments. They can learn primarily not what decision is "right," or how the technical processes of adjudication work, or even what the principles of constitutional law may be, but what the proper perspective of the participant in government involves. With this perspective in mind, students are ready to practice it in examining other public issues (crime, for instance, protection of the environment, or world trade policy), in doing their own community research projects, and in considering and trying out various active participations in public life.

Colleges and universities can provide the same opportunity and fulfill the same responsibility by offering (perhaps even requiring) more sophisticated courses keyed explicitly to the sorts of public understandings and issues students will face as citizens. One eastern university with a strong tradition for training in citizenship has developed, for example, two team-taught courses, one domestically oriented toward "Critical Issues" such as justice in education and political gridlock, and an internationally oriented one on the "Global Community," which looks at cultures around the world. By requiring faculty from various departments to develop and teach these courses together, and by asking a wide range of the student body to listen, talk, and write together about key issues and communities, the opportunity for inspired teaching—profound, integrating, and radical in ways highly relevant to students—is heightened. In fact, the public perspective foundational to both of these courses is itself a kind of inspiration that can really come only from that kind of teaching—and thus such courses may be at the same time a spur to inspired teaching.

Another important part of education for "the office of citizen" includes attention to the development of responsible freedom and self-government through the study of Western civilization. Study of what Walter Lippmann called "the tradition of civility," the attitudes and practices essential to the process of democracy over the centuries, the growth of free government in Anglo-America, and the ideas undergirding constitutional democracy would help students understand the rich connotations of democratic citizenship. In any case, it is clear that constructive participation in free and democratic government must be grounded in some understanding of the evolution, principles, and practices of such government. These elements define, we might say, the liberal core of the public-spiritedness basic to all civic education. This understanding need not imply overall "superiority" of Western culture (in fact ongoing global studies would be raising profound challenges to any such notion). It would simply be a foundation for understanding the particular political culture—a democratic, constitutional polity—that North American students will be part of and hence need to understand and know about, even if their inclination is to raise fundamental challenges about that culture. A liberal education will furnish grounds for doing that, too.

Lest this approach seem unduly utopian about the capacity of human beings to achieve a public-spirited posture, let us remember the possibly even greater utopianism of 1) supposing that all is OK in democratic societies when *no one* is expected or even encouraged to achieve such a perspective, or 2) thinking that it can be sufficient simply to open up the political process to all people, groups, and interests and then to deconstruct and analyze various policies. Such a dynamic might work well, or at least be the best we can do in a free and pluralistic society, but in our interdependent world, it is less and less likely to suffice. In our day, problems of global ecology and world peace require the forethought, reasoned approach, and concern for the good of the whole central to "the office of citizen." Instead of being naively optimistic about human nature, the encouragement of the human potential for a vision beyond the merely subjective and the narrowly selfish may be the only practical thing left for us as the twenty-first century approaches.

Once again the task and responsibility of teachers to tie together the liberal arts, public education, and good government stands out. Political leaders have much to do to enhance and promote "the good society." They need a thorough and sophisticated education in arts, letters, science, philosophy, and public right to fulfill the demanding tasks before them. To choose and support such leaders properly, and to be able to judge and replace them when necessary, the people also need to be well educated for their public responsibilities. The more the principles of the liberal arts permeate all levels of education, and the more people have access to the higher forms of liberal studies, the more cultivation of public virtue there can be. Good government that can fulfill the human potential for an ennobled life and the public interest depends on the widespread existence of such public virtue among all society's officers—from presidents and senators to every citizen.

Genuine human fulfillment requires a liberal/liberating education that opens up the profound insights, the integrating perspectives, and the radical alternatives that allow human life to transcend the limitations of ignorance, self-concern, and struggles for survival. In a self-governing society, the public spirit necessary to fulfill "the office of citizen" means largely to possess a sense of a wider, universal context and to project it into every public deliberation—from neighborhood conversations and primary and high school classrooms to college and university courses and national election campaigns. Whenever possible, therefore, and especially in every young person apprenticed to and eventually filling the office of citizen, inspiring teaching needs to nourish understanding of what the general good can be.

REFERENCES

Dreifus, C. (1996). The passion of Suu Kyi. In *New York Times Magazine*, January 7.

Jefferson, T. (1944). Autobiography, 1821. In A. Koch & W. Peden (Eds.), *The life and selected writings of Thomas Jefferson*. New York, NY: Modern Library.

Jefferson, T. (1955). Jefferson to W. C. Jarvis, September 28, 1820. In E. Dumbauld (Ed.), *The political writings of Thomas Jefferson*. Indianapolis, IN: Bobbs-Merrill.

Jefferson, T. (1959). Jefferson to John Adams, October 28, 1813. In L. Cappon (Ed.), *The Adams-Jefferson letters*, 2 vols. Chapel Hill, NC: University of North Carolina Press.

Kant, I. (1974). *On the old saw: That it may be right in theory, but it won't work in practice*. Trans. E. B. Ashton. Philadelphia, PA: University of Pennsylvania Press.

Mann, H. (1969). Annual reports (1845 and 1848). In S. A. Rippa (Ed.), *Educational ideas in America: A documentary history*. New York, NY: McKay.

Peterson, M. (Ed.). (1975). *The portable Thomas Jefferson*. New York, NY: Viking.

Tussman, J. (1960). *Obligation and the body politic*. New York, NY: Oxford University Press.

19

What Teaching Teaches Me: How the Holocaust Informs My Philosophy of Education

JOHN K. ROTH

Fresh from graduate study at Yale University, John Roth joined the Claremont McKenna College faculty in 1966. CMC has been his academic home ever since, but he has also taught in Switzerland, Austria, Japan, Israel, and Norway. Roth's honors at CMC include the Huntoon Senior Teaching Award, the Crocker Award for Excellence, which he has received three times, and the President's Award. Dedicated to writing, Roth has published more than twenty books and hundreds of essays, many of them focused on the Holocaust. His writings include the text for the permanent exhibition at Holocaust Museum Houston, which opened in that Texas city in March 1996. From 1992 to 1994, Roth chaired the California Council for the Humanities. Presently he serves on the United States Holocaust Memorial Council, which governs the United States Holocaust Memorial Museum in Washington, DC. The Council for Advancement and Support of Education (CASE) and the Carnegie Foundation for the Advancement of Teaching named Roth the 1988 U.S. Professor of the Year.

A Fulbright fellowship took me to Norway during my 1995–1996 sabbatical. My Norwegian work included reflection on the Holocaust, a subject that has been at the center of my academic and personal life for a long time.

The Holocaust was the systematic, state-sponsored persecution and murder of nearly six million Jews by Nazi Germany and its collaborators. They slaughtered two-thirds of Europe's Jews and one-third of the world's Jewish population. More than half of the dead came from Poland, where the Nazi annihilation was 90 percent complete. The Holocaust hit Jewish children especially hard. Up to 1.5 million of its victims were under fifteen. Of the European Jewish children alive in 1939, only 11 percent survived.

Although Jews were its primary victims, Nazi Germany's genocidal policy also destroyed millions of other defenseless people. Roma and Sinti (Gypsies), Poles, and the handicapped were targeted for racial, ethnic, or national reasons. Millions more, including homosexuals, Jehovah's Witnesses, Soviet prisoners of war, and political and religious dissidents were also oppressed and put to death under Nazi tyranny.

HOW THE HOLOCAUST AFFECTS ME

Norway's chapter in the Holocaust seems small, even insignificant. For me, however, neither of those descriptions is accurate. Even if Norway's Jewish population was minuscule compared to Poland's, the destruction of Jewish life in Norway was more thorough than in many other Nazi-occupied countries. My Norwegian encounters with the Holocaust can start to show what teaching teaches me.

Constructed in the late 1930s, my Oslo apartment in 1995–1996 was down the street from Kirkeveien 23. Since a relatively new building now stands at that address, Kirkeveien 23 meant little to me until I learned that hundreds of Norwegian Jews were sent to that location when roundups took place around the country in the early morning of Monday, October 26, 1942. Later some of those same Jews were imprisoned at the Grini concentration camp, which was situated only a few minutes by train from my flat.

While pursuing Holocaust studies in Norway, I also visited the country's secondary schools to consult with teachers who have responsibility for teaching American history and literature to Norwegian students. Often those schools contain memorials to Norwegians who were killed by the Nazis. Among their names are those of Jewish students—Feinberg and Jaffe, for example—who were taken from their schoolrooms by Norwegian police while their classmates and teachers stood by.

Some of those children were in the largest transport of Norwegian Jewish prisoners that left Pier 1 in Oslo on November 26, 1942. Those Jews sailed aboard the *Donau*, a German troopship that became available for the deportation. Their Norwegian citizenship was revoked the moment the ship departed. It was intended that none of these 532 people would see Norway again. Few did; there were less than twenty survivors. Most of the deported Norwegian Jews were gassed at Auschwitz instead.

Some Americans visit the Resistance Museum in Oslo, but probably few Americans who spend time in Norway know very much about the places I have mentioned or the history they contain. It is almost by chance that I have come to care about them myself. Yet not a day of my life—in Norway or anywhere else—now passes without feelings, thoughts, and visions that create post-Holocaust encounters with the Holocaust for me. As I think about how easily my experience might have been different, I wonder how it has turned out the way it did. As I wonder, I also know that I must try to find out more about the Holocaust, its history and implications, because that event has more to teach me and perhaps my students than any other part of human history.

What I mean

To draw out what I mean, recall how William Styron begins *Sophie's Choice*, his controversial novel about the Holocaust: "Call me Stingo," wrote Styron, "which was the nickname I was known by in those days, if I was called anything at all" (Styron, 1979, p. 4). A fictional but not unreal American character, Stingo hails from the Presbyterian South, but "in a place as strange as Brooklyn" (1979, p. 25), he becomes aware of what Ida Fink, an actual survivor of the Holocaust, called "a certain time not measured in months and years" (Fink, 1987, p. 3). Her measures of time, Fink explains, have been words like "roundup" or "action," words that spelled Nazi Germany's Final Solution of the so-called Jewish question.

A gifted woman, Ida Fink was born in Poland in 1921. She survived the Holocaust in hiding, eventually emigrated to Israel, and went on to become a distinguished writer. In stories collected in a moving book called *A Scrap of Time*, she excavates what she describes as "the ruins of memory" (Fink, 1987, p. 3). Stingo gradually does the same as Styron's novel weaves together the scraps of time that created *Sophie's Choice*.

Stingo's experience climaxes in Washington, DC. "We walked through the evening in total silence," he recalls. "It was plain that Sophie and I could appreciate neither the symmetry of the city nor its air of wholesome and benevolent peace. Washington suddenly appeared paradigmatically American, sterile, geometrical, unreal." The reason, Stingo adds, was that Auschwitz "stalked my soul" (Styron, 1979, p. 493).

Stingo's experience in Washington, DC, would have taken place nearly fifty years ago. Although the city is still paradigmatically American and its symmetry remains, much about the nation's capital has changed. On one hand, there may now be less an "air of wholesome and benevolent peace" than there was then. On the other, perhaps there are today more people walking through the evening in total silence. For now Americans not so different from Stingo visit the United States Holocaust Memorial Museum and thus, like Stingo, they may find—at least for a while—that Auschwitz stalks their souls, too.

Although a generation younger than Stingo, I identify with him. Like so many of my American peers, I grew up Christian in the United States—too young to be much aware of World War II, barely hearing of Auschwitz afterward, and knowing practically nothing about the Holocaust for a long time. Yet I increasingly think of myself as a post-Holocaust American.

A stalked soul

Auschwitz stalks my soul. How that happened involves encounters that have included matters of chance, but also face to face meetings, and conflicts that rivet my attention. Key elements in those encounters are found in my previous Fulbright experience as a lecturer in American studies at the University of Innsbruck, Austria, in 1973–1974. Personally as well as professionally, that year proved to be of immense importance to me. Not only was I trying to interpret American life to Austrians by exploring the American Dream, another topic that has occupied much of my teaching life. During that Innsbruck year, I also worked on the writings of Elie Wiesel, an Auschwitz survivor who became a brilliant writer and went on to receive the 1986 Nobel Peace Prize in Oslo.

Coincidentally, I had begun to study Wiesel's writing in the summer of 1972, when my second child, Sarah, was born on the Fourth of July. The collision I experienced then between my good fortune—fatherhood, a promising academic career in the United States, soon a Fulbright appointment—and the destruction of family and hope explored in Wiesel's European Holocaust reflections left lasting marks upon me. In ways that I scarcely could have imagined at the beginning of my teaching career, my philosophy of education became increasingly informed by the Holocaust.

As I look back on my life as a professor, which is now entering its fourth decade, I see that it has been spent mostly in study of injustice and suffering, pain and death, the dark side of history and the questions it raises. I also understand that my calling as a teacher has often emphasized bearing witness and protest for those whose voices have been silenced and whose lives have been laid waste by human blindness, hate, and violence.

Although I am a philosopher, I do not pursue this work in abstractly philosophical ways but by immersing myself in the particularity of history and the details of its stories. Specifically, for about twenty-five years, I have taught an annual course on the Holocaust. Focused on the perpetrators who engineered that disaster and on the bystanders who aided and abetted them, as well as on the victims and the relatively few rescuers who worked heroically to get people out of harm's way, this course is the most difficult and important one that I offer at Claremont McKenna College.

Disturbing and rewarding, my Holocaust teaching keeps teaching me. That claim is true for multiple reasons: The particularity of the Holocaust emphasizes insights that humankind overlooks or ignores at its peril. Study of the Holocaust makes a decisive impression on my students. It also profoundly affects my teaching practices. In fact, the Holocaust's impact influences not only how I teach the Holocaust but how I teach in any time or place.

FIVE THEMES

What Holocaust teaching teaches me can be illustrated by five themes that govern my work. Each one can inspire teaching. After reflecting on them briefly, I will describe some teaching practices that the five themes encourage me to use. Those practices can also play important parts in inspiring teaching.

Questions are more important than answers

Answers aim to settle things, but their ironic, even tragic, outcome is that they often produce disagreement, division, and death. People are less likely to savage and annihilate each other when their minds are not made up but opened up through questioning. The Holocaust shows as much: Hitler and his Nazi followers "knew" they were "right." Their knowing made them killers.

Answers to questions have their place; it can be essential, too. Nevertheless questions deserve lasting priority because they invite continuing inquiry, further dialogue, shared wonder, and sensitive openness. Questions can relate people to one another, especially students and teachers; they may focus concern about the common good in ways that answers alone rarely can.

Inspiring teaching depends on silence

Commonly we teachers talk too much. True, good teaching depends on the spoken word, but inspiring teaching also depends on silence, on sensing when not to speak, on recognizing that in some times and places keeping silence is the best one can do.

Keeping silence involves a rhythm, because silence also must be broken. I often miss key beats, but Holocaust teaching keeps me aware of the importance of finding the right blend of speech and silence. If my students and I study a text such as *Night*, Elie Wiesel's classic memoir about his boyhood in Auschwitz, my challenge is to set the context so that his text—including the awesome silence it contains—can speak to the students for itself. In setting that context, questions are more important than explanations or answers, because they break silence but not too much.

Less can be more

Author of an impressive study of the Holocaust called *The Destruction of the*

European Jews, Raul Hilberg is arguably the world's preeminent scholar of the Final Solution. In style and substance, his scholarship intensifies feeling, deepens emotion, and increases sensitivity. To be significant, any encounter with the Holocaust must have those results. Indeed those elements are both causes and effects of inspiring teaching in any time or place.

Hilberg's example teaches me, however, that such intensification and deepening do not depend on overtly emotional appeals, which study of the Holocaust can provoke so glibly. Hilberg shows that there is no substitute for a quiet, restrained, even understated matter-of-fact description of the Holocaust's detail. Less can be more when the point is to generate more light than heat, especially when that goal places a premium—as Holocaust studies should—on producing insight about the differences between right and wrong, good and evil, justice and injustice.

Take nothing good for granted

The Holocaust warns us. It teaches that nothing good should be taken for granted. The Holocaust's "truths" denied basic human equality and human rights. Nazi Germany's antisemitism and racism identified "life unworthy of life" and then targeted it for annihilation. Those policies were the antithesis of life, liberty, and the pursuit of happiness.

Holocaust teaching teaches me that human life has paid an incredibly high and deadly price for racial classifications and the almost unavoidable racist thinking that follows from them. In particular, the Nazis' genocidal mentality understood the "logic" of racism. That "logic" entails that if you take seriously the idea that one race endangers the well-being of another, the only way to remove the menace completely is to do away, once and for all, with everyone and everything that embodies it.

The thoroughness with which the Nazis and their collaborators tried to destroy even the small Jewish population of Norway shows how seriously that "logic" was taken. Such awareness teaches me to emphasize Elie Wiesel's insight: "If we stop remembering," he warns, "we stop being" (Wiesel, 1985, 1:368).

Inspiring teaching happens in spite of despair

Holocaust teaching teaches me that despair is a teacher's constant companion. How could it not be?

Most teachers are idealists. However jaded we may become, most of us became professors because we wanted to mend the world. That hope, however, encounters discouragement aplenty. History, especially Holocaust history, provides it. So does teaching, which is a less than reassuring activity when humankind's future is at stake.

We are all beginners every day. No matter how hard we teachers try, indifference persists, prejudice remains, ignorance endures, and no place on earth guarantees safety from the destruction that such forces can unleash. Education's gains take place against stiff odds; learning is not a matter of evolutionary progress. Every year, every class, means starting over because wisdom does not accumulate. "Never again!" the Holocaust makes some people say. Yet it is questionable whether the world has learned that lesson. Racism and genocide are only two of the scourges that still scar the earth.

Holocaust teaching makes me more melancholy than I used to be. It makes me realize how much despair lurks around every classroom door. Even more, however, Holocaust teaching teaches me that those recognitions are not the conclusion, but instead they must be the beginning of inspiring teaching.

My friend Jim Quay, executive director of the California Council for the Humanities, helped me to understand this point when he honored me with a poem upon my retirement from the Council in 1995. The words he wrote for me, I believe, apply to caring professors in every time and place:

> The scholar bends on his hands and knees over the
>   deep hole of history.
> His light spills into the darkness, as he looks for
>   reflections
> Far beneath the surface.
> It's work he does at night, better to see the faint
>   glint,
> And without gloves, better to grasp the stories waiting to be
> Plucked from oblivion.
> This work can only be done by a hopeful man willing to
>   be sad.
>
> Sometimes he cuts his fingers on a fragment, sometimes
>   his vision blurs,
> Or he loses his balance, falls, and sits all night,
> Rocking in the darkness, until voices of the living
>   lead him home.
>
> When, during the day, he discusses dreams with his
>   students,
> The ashes on his pants and the scars on his hands
>   make them listen,
> Make them believe.
> Their faith in dreams is the gift of a hopeful man
>   willing to be sad.

My students make me listen, make me believe, as their voices lead and teach me. My students do so, in particular, by telling me what happens as they study the Holocaust. One student, for example, could have been speaking for many of her peers when she ended her final essay with a poem that reflected on the visit to Dachau that had led her to take the course on the Holocaust after she returned from a semester abroad:

> The dead do not rest easy here.
> Neither do little children
> who cry when carried through the gates.
> We must come and pay homage
> see what our hands wrought
> if not directly,
> by sins of omission.
> Before, I did not understand.
> I still do not, and yet now I have seen.
> That in itself brings pain.
> But birth is painful and Dachau
> was my birth.
> Now both man and God exist
> in a region that explodes reason
> and I do not accept either
> without questioning.
> I find I was blind to much, now I struggle to see.
> I am a toddler, learning to crawl,
> watching for sharp stones
> in a world that is new to me.

As the poem suggests, Holocaust teaching contains a rhythm that my students describe repeatedly. Even though they may not brim with optimism when they enter the Holocaust class, my students still experience shock as they begin to confront the shadows of the Holocaust—even if they already bring some knowledge of that history with them. As the semester moves along, shock gradually edges toward despair as we trace the twisted road to Auschwitz that winds all through Western civilization and exposes one dark chapter of human history after another. Nevertheless, the students do not end their journey in that darkness. Nor do they allow me to do so.

Holocaust teaching teaches us all that despair does not deserve the final word. To let despair have its way would be to give Hitler a posthumous victory that he must not have. Thus, despair can move beyond itself. Returning in spite and even because of disillusionment, determination rebuilds to keep trying again to mend the world.

TEACHING PRACTICES

I believe that renewing determination in spite of despair is a key ingredient of inspiring teaching in any time and every place. In addition, I find that some teaching practices can be especially helpful in encouraging that movement. They do not rely on the latest technology but on two teaching practices that are as traditional as they are important: essays and tutorials. Both underscore the importance of questions and silence. As they provide occasions for showing that less can be more, they can also teach that nothing good should be taken for granted.

Inspiring teaching depends on writing

My teaching emphasizes writing. In my Holocaust teaching, but not only there, I urge my students to write, rewrite, and write some more. For in the silent grappling with questions that writing requires, insight emerges as it can in no other way.

Students need to write in different ways, but my teaching introduces students to the discipline of writing short, reflective essays. In a less-is-more style, these essays encourage students to gain mastery and perspective on the substantial reading we always do, to explore their own angles of vision, and to see that every answer leads to other questions, which is a discovery that can teach us, among other things, to take nothing good for granted.

In each of my courses, but especially in the one on the Holocaust, I plan a sequence of question-based topics that form the parameters for the students' reflection. My aim is not to direct what the students will say or how they will say it. Instead I hope that the topics will lead to lines of thought that deepen incrementally both the students' understanding and their senses of wonder. As I read and evaluate what the students write, I find that such results take place not only for them but also for me.

Each topic begins with a quotation from the reading we have done. Then it poses a series of questions that the students can ponder as they think best. The essays are brief. No more than four or five double spaced pages, I tell the students, nudging them to make every word count. There is much to learn in discovering what can be done with only a few hundred words. That discipline creates its own instructive tensions between speech and silence, between what can and cannot be said. A sequence of the six essay topics from one of my recent Holocaust classes illustrates an adaptable form that can be used in a wide variety of courses.

1. "I want to talk about a certain time not measured in months and years" (Fink, 1987, p. 3). Write an essay that addresses these questions: In light of the work we have done thus far, what do I want to say about the Holocaust? Can this event be measured in months and years? Is your answer basically yes or basically no? Say why. Then indicate what you take to be the most important question that your answer entails and suggest how you would start to respond to it.

2. "The purity of German blood is essential for the further existence of the German people" (from "The Law for the Protection of German Blood and German Honor of 15 September 1935"). Do the words quoted above make sense? If your answer is basically no, then why did such ideas become so powerful in Nazi Germany? If your answer is basically yes, then what more does your study in the course thus far lead you to say in response?

3. "Few examples could illustrate more effectively the notion of choiceless choice" (Langer, 1989, p. 230). In your study thus far, what is the most telling example of "choiceless choice" that you have encountered? Why does this example loom so large for you? How does it affect you? What does it teach you about the Holocaust and about the post-Holocaust world in which you live?

4. "What, then, is one to conclude?" (Browning, 1992, p. 188). What do you conclude from your study in this portion of our course? Why do you respond as you do? What do you take to be the most important implication(s) of your inquiry about these matters?

5. "The tree is still there" (Keneally, 1983, p. 394). As you pause at this point in your study of the Holocaust, what is "still there" for you? Why do you respond as you do? What do you take to be the most important implication(s) of your inquiry about these matters?

6. "I have told you this story not to weaken you but to strengthen you. Now it is up to you" (words from a veteran prisoner of the Sachsenhausen concentration camp, quoted in Berenbaum, 1993, p. 3). Looking back at all that we have done this semester, write an essay that addresses these questions: Having encountered "this story," do you feel strengthened? If your answer is basically yes, indicate how you feel strengthened and why you feel that way. If your answer is basically no, indicate why and then say how you would describe your feeling differently.

Tutorials strengthen inspiring teaching

I evaluate the essays in terms of the quality of the students' writing, the richness of their illustrations from and allusions to the assigned reading, and the specificity and depth of their reflection. Whenever possible, I amplify and extend the evaluation process through tutorials, which intensify inquiry by driving it deeper.

Neither a class nor a seminar, a tutorial can be organized in various ways. I have found, however, that the following plan yields sound results. Students are paired to meet with me for an hour or more in my office or some other comfortable room. Prior to our meeting, the two students exchange their papers, and both give a copy to me. The students and I read the essays and prepare written comments about them before the tutorial takes place. That way valuable time is saved because the essays do not have to be read aloud.

The tutorial begins with one student making a five-minute oral response to the other's essay. The aim of this response—indeed the aim of the entire tutorial process—is less to criticize and more to encourage the writer to explain, expand, and defend the main points that he or she wants to make. As the writer responds and conversation between the two students ensues, I listen mostly but intervene to clarify and coach. Midway through the tutorial, the students reverse their roles, and we explore some more.

At the tutorial's conclusion, the written comments prepared earlier are shared. I give no grade at this time, but the students revise their essays in light of the tutorial discussion and the written comments. I comment further on those revisions, and then award a mark. As circumstances permit, the next time the students have a tutorial with me, their partners will be different. That procedure gives the students more varied perspectives on their work.

For student and teacher alike, this tutorial style is as demanding as it is rewarding. It raises questions and responds to them in penetrating ways. It uses and breaks silence effectively. The intensity it builds reveals how less can be more. Its practice illustrates the point that neither a sound essay nor a worthwhile tutorial can be taken for granted. Both require diligence and discipline on everyone's part. Writing has to be done on time, and discussion has to be carried out conscientiously or the whole process collapses. In addition, the tutorial method builds strength as students discover that they can cope with their uncertainties by opening themselves to others and by experiencing the support that such sharing can produce—support that is particularly welcome when the students' sharing leads them to find that their work contains more strong points than weaknesses. Such outcomes are especially important in Holocaust teaching, where despair is always close at hand, but they deserve to be the goal that inspires all the teaching that we professors do.

A POSTSCRIPT

Has the world learned from the Holocaust? Sadly, one response must be: Not enough. Reasons for that response include "ethnic cleansing" in the former Yugoslavia, mass murder in Rwanda, upsurges of antisemitism around the world, the tenacity of racism in the United States, and even the persistence of so-called scholars and propagandists who deny the realities of the Holocaust. These results make it more important than ever to teach and learn the Holocaust's lessons better. The alternative is to give up in despair, which only plays into the hands of powers that waste human life.

Nothing that Holocaust teaching teaches me is more important than the realization that the Holocaust was not inevitable and that no events related to it ever are or will be. The Holocaust emerged from decisions and institutions made by ordinary human beings who were responsible for their actions and who could have acted differently and better than they did. Points akin to those can be made in much of the teaching that we do, but the Holocaust in particular teaches those lessons to me. If we learn what the Holocaust has to teach us, we will keep teaching—no matter what the odds—to heal wounded human relations and to mend the world's broken heart.

REFERENCES

Berenbaum, M. (1993). *The world must know: The history of the Holocaust as told in the United States Holocaust Memorial Museum.* Boston, MA: Little, Brown and Company.

Browning, C. (1992). *Ordinary men: Reserve police battalion 101 and the final solution in Poland.* New York, NY: HarperCollins.

Fink, I. (1987). *A scrap of time and other stories.* New York, NY: Schocken Books.

Hilberg, R. (1985). *The destruction of the European Jews.* 3 vols., revised and definitive edition. New York, NY: Holmes & Meier.

Keneally, T. (1983). *Schindler's list.* New York, NY: Penguin Books.

Langer, L. (1989). The dilemma of choice in the deathcamps. In J. K. Roth & M. Berenbaum (Eds.), *Holocaust: Religious and philosophical implications.* New York, NY: Paragon House.

Styron, W. (1979). *Sophie's choice.* New York, NY: Random House.

Wiesel, E. (1985). Let him remember. In I. Abrahamson (Ed.), *Against silence: The voice and vision of Elie Wiesel.* 3 vols. New York, NY: Holocaust Library.

20

The Carnegie Professors of the Year: Models for Teaching Success

Trained in journalism, organizational communication, and higher education administration, John R. Lough is the undergraduate coordinator for the department of management at the University of Georgia in Athens, where he advises hundreds of students and teaches courses about the principles of management. Lough also teaches in supervisory-level to executive-level training programs and maintains an active consulting practice with manufacturing and service organizations. His numerous books and articles reflect research interests in leadership selection and development, curriculum development for colleges and schools of business, and identification of behaviors associated with superior teaching. The latter topic led to research on the Carnegie Professors of the Year. His essay reports findings from that study.

I became a student of teaching while enrolled in Ronald D. Simpson's University of Georgia class on instructional processes. I was already a student and teacher of management and the improvement of managerial practice. It was in Simpson's doctoral seminar, however, that I came to consider ways in which we might combine what we know about teaching college students with what we know about measuring and improving the performance of the business enterprise.

In the field of strategic management and business policy, there is a planning technique known as "benchmarking." This technique, also known as "best-practices benchmarking," is a process that allows a company or business unit to measure its operations profile against those of other companies that are considered the "best-in-class." Benchmarking centers on a company's recognition that it can continue to improve by learning from other companies. This method of competitive analysis certainly provides no grand revelation. It would seem only commonsensical to identify that which is best in one's market or industry, find out why it is best, and then copy it or learn from it. This is the basic rationale underlying the focus of this essay and its purpose to expand or, at least, to clarify further what we know about the characteristics of good teachers and good teaching.

LOOKING FOR THE "BEST-IN-CLASS"

In the course of the seminar to which I referred earlier, I happened across an article entitled "Part Mentor, Part Friend, All Inspiration," which appeared in the November 24, 1993, issue of *The Chronicle of Higher Education*. This feature described the person, teaching practices, and philosophy of Dr. Vincente D. Villa, professor of microbiology and holder of the Dishman Chair in Science at Southwestern University in Georgetown, Texas. Professor Villa had just been named the 1993 U.S. National Professor of the Year by the Council for Advancement and Support of Education (CASE) and the Carnegie Foundation for the Advancement of Teaching.

Over the next few days, I revisited the article, fascinated by this incredible story of dedication, boundless energy, and simple love of the art and science of sharing knowledge and intellectual development with undergraduate students. It occurred to me that useful insights might be derived through an examination of the background and teaching practices of Dr. Villa as well as those of his predecessors as Carnegie U.S. Professor of the Year award winners. What I expected to find would be a set of common background traits and a set of common teaching practices that might form a kind of "best-in-class" profile by which we might measure our own teaching performances. This profile might also serve as a blueprint and standard for the training of those who aspire to be good teachers and scholars.

My first step was to contact the Council for Advancement and Support of Education (CASE) in Washington, DC. Kim Hughes, Senior Communications Program Coordinator–External Affairs, turned out to be my main source of extraordinarily useful information regarding previous winners and the criteria used for their ultimate selection. Some of the winners, as one might expect, were much easier to reach than others. Complicating factors revolved around retirements, job changes, and sabbaticals. One of the previous winners had died in 1992. In research that covered the Carnegie Professor of the Year competition from its inception through 1993, I was ultimately able to contact, either by phone or letter, all of the living U.S. National Professors of the Year—there were twelve of them—whom CASE and the Carnegie Foundation for the Advancement of Teaching had honored.

It would be a gross oversight if I failed to point out how responsive and facilitating each of these contacts were. On reflection, however, I should not have been surprised, given the nature of the kind "beasts" whose nature I was examining. Each winner was simply asked to supply me with a curriculum vita and any course syllabi they had readily available. As I suggested above, the response was staggering. I then drafted for each of these individuals a brief questionnaire, to which I received a 100 percent response. The questionnaire focused on background issues and specific teaching or professorial practices. From these data sources I expected to construct my profile of the superior teacher.

There is nothing new about the profiling of outstanding teachers. Each American campus seems to have its own teacher of the year recognition in some form or fashion. There are also state and regional awards meted out to those who have distinguished themselves in the classroom. Likely, each of these award winners is interviewed and described in the campus and local presses. Pithy quotes from the teachers, the students they teach, and the administrators who hired them are given precious column inches.

Other works of a more scholarly bent seek, among other things, to describe what it is that makes an outstanding teacher outstanding. Twenty years ago, in an article entitled "The Superior College Teacher from the Students' View," Kenneth Feldman listed nineteen characteristics of outstanding teachers (1976, pp. 243–288). These characteristics included such qualities as stimulation of interest, the instructor's enthusiasm for subject area or for teaching, an instructor's preparation and organization of the course, clarity and comprehensibility, and the instructor's fairness. In their powerful volume on undergraduate education, *Inside College*, Ron Simpson and Susan Frost cite "Seven Principles for Good Practice in Undergraduate Education" (1993). These principles encourage such general practices as student-faculty contact, active learning, the giving of prompt feedback, the communication of high expectations, and respect for diverse talents and ways of learning.

Ten years ago, Peter Beidler of Lehigh University, himself a Carnegie U.S. Professor of the Year award winner, edited a volume for Jossey-Bass (1986) which provided other award winners and award finalists the opportunity to offer their views on teaching and the profession of teaching. He sought to reveal something about these concepts of teaching and learning, from the people who ought to know best, through the responses of these honorees to a set of wide-ranging questions:

- What professor most influenced you?

- How does your teaching relate to the real world?

- How do you view the multiple obligations of teaching, research, and service?

- What single quality, skill, or attitude do you want a student to have after one of your classes?

- What are the most important ways students learn?

- How do you keep from getting bored as a teacher?

- What best advice can you pass on to a beginning teacher about how to teach?

- Why is teaching the right profession for you?

Beidler was right when he noted that "the world rarely asks good teachers" about the issues involved in student learning and what constitutes good teaching. This work proved an excellent showcase of the wisdom and guidance of these particular honorees.

We also have learned (not surprisingly) that good teachers can make a big difference in student learning. As Ernie Pascarella and Pat Terenzini revealed in their encyclopedic work, *How College Affects Students* (known affectionately as "Moby Book"), increased interaction between student and faculty can positively influence the acquisition of subject matter knowledge, attitude and value change, changes in religious commitment, development of general cognitive skills, institutional persistence, and changes in humanitarian and civic attitudes, among other things (1991).

All of these efforts have advanced greatly our knowledge and appreciation of superior teaching. In each work the reader is treated to revealing and penetrating expositions of the attitudes, beliefs, and philosophies of what a good teacher is and what he or she influences as seen through the eyes of both student and teacher. This information is useful and necessary to the process of setting standards and defining developmental goals and objectives. However, my expressed goal was to capture best practices—that is, the specific behaviors, actions, and techniques employed by outstanding teachers in the complex process of encouraging student learning. I also wanted to deal with certain myths that seem to prevail when we consider those who are generally regarded as outstanding classroom teachers. For example, there is the myth that the best teachers are found only at those places where good teachers can survive and prosper—the small, private, liberal arts college. There is also the myth that a teacher can be outstanding only in a small-class environment or in a situation of low student-teacher ratios. Finally, there is the myth that one who is an outstanding teacher conducts no meaningful published research and has no significant academic life beyond the classroom. Thus, my purpose here is to define, in terms as specific and instructive as possible, those backgrounds and best practices of the superior teachers while simultaneously describing the richness of the breadth of academic contributions made by this very elite group of professors.

BACKGROUND INFORMATION

One of my initial hypotheses was that an examination of the biographical data of the Professor of the Year award winners would reveal something both common and telling about how each of these exemplary individuals got to be where they are or were at the time the award was earned. Each award winner was asked questions regarding such areas as parental occupation and education, family size, size of community in which the individual went through primary and secondary schools, number and order of siblings, and character of one's educational experience. It was not surprising to find that there was a rich diversity in the social and educational backgrounds of these individuals who would ultimately achieve the highest honor their chosen profession could bestow.

The honorees come from families that represent all sectors of economic life and all sociological classes. They are the sons and daughters of architects, physicians, bakers, carpenters, restaurant owners, farmers, factory workers, and teachers. Exactly half of the parents attended college. Interestingly, more than half of the Carnegie winners grew up in communities of fewer than 5,000 inhabitants. They ranged from only children to one of six children. If there was any common characteristic here, all but two were either the only child or the oldest child, blessed (or cursed) with all the baggage that birth position carries. All but one received their primary and secondary education through a public school system. Based on responses to the questionnaire used in this study, there appear to be no strongly governing background characteristics among the winners.

The career path to becoming a professor for these individuals is represented by as much diversity as is found in their respective social backgrounds. One fact is for certain, however: None of them set out to be a professor. Early on, only one wanted to be a teacher at any level. For many, the decision to teach was made in graduate school. For one, the decision was not made until age 40, after a divorce left this person with no money and no job. For others, the decision was reached by way of some special experience as an undergraduate, while in the military service, or while teaching high school.

One might have expected that this group of teachers might have shared the experience of a highly personalized undergraduate education of the sort found at the typical small liberal arts college. While about a third of this group did attend such a school as undergraduates, the others were spread out over junior colleges, small state universities, large urban institutions, and large state universities.

Out of the wide ranging information sought and received through the survey instrument used, one compelling fact was that all but one of the award winners' academic backgrounds were in the arts and sciences, about evenly distributed among the humanities, social sciences, and sciences. With the lone exception of a civil engineer, there was no professional school representation—in terms of educational background or current teaching discipline—among the award winners represented in my study. I will leave to future research the potential question of why the traditional liberal arts methods might tend to provide the better academic foundations for superior teachers.

AGE, TEACHING EXPERIENCE, AND ACADEMIC RANK

One common characteristic of the group centers on their many years of experience in the teaching profession prior to the winning of the national award. All of the winners were over 40 years old, with the average age at the time of the Carnegie award being 50 years. All but one had reached the rank of full professor or were holders of an endowed chair. At the time of their respective award winning, each teacher had averaged almost twenty years of teaching since earning the doctoral degree.

What is striking about these data is that this pinnacle of success in the teaching profession was achieved at a time in one's life when, typically, enthusiasm for teaching and research begins a steady decline. A 1992 study by Daniel Kinney and Daniel Smith, which focused on the faculty at a private "Research I" institution (institutions that offer a full range of baccalaureate programs, are committed to graduate education through the doctorate, give high priority to research, award fifty or more doctoral degrees each year, and receive annually $40 million or more in federal support), found that teaching effectiveness, based on student evaluations of teaching, generally goes through a period of decline beginning around age 43 in all fields, even though for the humanities it starts a slight upward trend around age 52.

This relationship between age and teaching effectiveness is reinforced by an earlier examination of faculty career development by Roger Baldwin and Robert Blackburn (1991), which defined five distinct career stages in a college or university teacher's life:

1. Assistant professors in the first three years of full-time college teaching

2. Assistant professor with more than three years of college teaching experience

3. Associate professors

4. Full professors with more than five years until retirement

5. Full professors within five years of formal retirement

Characteristics and experiences of these five stages of the academic career showed that, at stage four (the stage at which all but one of the Carnegie award winners were at the time of their selection), there was a reduced enthusiasm for teaching and research and a questioning of the value of the academic career. While this characterization is based on generalized inferences from the self-reported data resulting from the study, it probably accurately represents the condition of most college faculty at this career juncture. It is significant, therefore, that this group of outstanding teachers is not only teaching well, but teaching enthusiastically and well enough to win a national award of tremendous importance.

John Kremer (1991) has suggested that at those institutions where research is an essential determinant in salary and promotion decisions, assistant professors are forced to devote their energies singularly to research activities, often at the expense of teaching. As these same faculty move on through associate professorships, however, they may enlarge their efforts to include teaching and service, partially in an effort to avoid burnout and stagnation. This career development stage might partially explain the relatively advanced ages of the Carnegie winners.

CONTRIBUTIONS TO THE DISCIPLINE

The prevailing myth in the academy is that teaching and research are mutually exclusive activities. Stated more precisely, if one is to be an outstanding teacher, then meaningful research will be absent. The twelve Carnegie award winners included in my data base presented credentials that strongly counter this assertion. Of course, it is important to note that the criteria for Carnegie award selection include a superior research record. It was no surprise that a review of the curriculum vitae of all the U.S. national award winners in my study revealed that each had made, and was continuing to make, significant contributions to the literature in his or her chosen field.

Nearly all of these professors had published books on subjects of interest, averaging six published books for each winner. In terms of book chapters and refereed journal articles, the achievements were even more weighty. The awardees averaged more than 58 such publications with one winner authoring more than 200 articles. These outstanding teachers also averaged more than 35 paper presentations at professional meetings and more than 15 research grants or fellowships each. Unquestioningly, these figures represent records that likely would win research awards for their respective owners at most institutions.

Staying abreast of the latest research in his or her respective discipline also seems important to each of these professors. All subscribe to the academic journals of their fields, averaging more than seven such journals each.

SIZE OF INSTITUTION AND CLASSES TAUGHT

Another currently held myth concerning the character of superior teachers is that they teach only small classes in which it is easy to get to know and become more personal with the students. Again, the data show that, with this group of professors, this is not at all the reality. While these professors do, at some time during their typical teaching year, teach classes of 8 or 10 students, nearly all teach classes that may range between 100 and 300 students. For example, one of the award winners with whom I spoke directly talked about the special problem of engaging and involving students in a large (160 students) class. He said:

> I initiate contact. I get in their faces. I offer tons of eye contact. I vary speed and volume of voice. I walk around a lot. I stop for questions, and I call on students at random.

This group of outstanding performers has apparently found some suitable method of working with large numbers of students in a caring and personal way.

A related reservation many have of teacher award winners is that they all teach in institutional environments highly conducive to good teaching—low student-teacher ratios and overall small enrollments. It is true that a majority of the Carnegie winners were teaching at schools of fewer that 10,000 students. However, at least one-third were teaching at schools that average over 22,000 students. The range of teacher-student ratio was 1:7.4 to 1:16.7, with an average ratio of 1:11.4. It is significant to note that, at the time of the award, all but two of the winners were on the staff at independent colleges and universities, although most of these are doctoral degree granting institutions of some size.

The important point of this discussion is that all of the Carnegie winners teach in institutional environments that are fairly typical of those in which all teachers function, and that they are not neglectful of any of the consuming obligations related to their research and to their respective disciplines.

SPECIFIC TEACHING PRACTICES

The final section of this essay focuses on the critical area of interest on which my study was based: those actual teaching-related behaviors by which others may be benchmarked. The behaviors considered center on syllabus makeup and design, attendance requirements, office hours, general availability, policies on socializing with students, and other miscellaneous techniques associated with teaching activities.

Syllabi

The course syllabi used by the Carnegie winners vary widely; however, several common themes prevail. The syllabi are written with rather detailed precision. Clearly stated course objectives and requirements are a hallmark. Typically, there is a rather precisely laid out day-by-day schedule showing specific reading assignments as well as other significant requirements and due dates. There is also great specificity regarding such issues as makeup exams, attendance, and the like. For instance, the following examples from one course syllabus refer to makeup exams and due dates for assignments:

> There are NO makeup quizzes. The only excuse for missing a
> quiz will be confinement in a hospital or student health.
> PLEASE STUDY. Do not ask for an extension; to grant it
> would be cruel of me, and I hate to be cruel.

Even with the injection of subtle humor, the precision of the requirements for the students in this course is unquestionable. Such "rigidity" of standards is characteristic of the Carnegie honorees. Usually the requirements for special projects or assignments are thoroughly described to minimize ambiguity. One syllabus that referred to a special project as part of the course requirements included a six-page, single-spaced supplement devoted to very precise directions about parameters, methods, and deadlines.

Each of the syllabi includes varying messages regarding the accessibility of the professor for the enrolled students. Typically, there are specific references to phone numbers at office and home, e-mail addresses, and office hours.

Another common characteristic of the course syllabi is their specificity in describing grading standards. One example looked as follows:

> Your grade will be determined on the basis of your perfor-
> mance in the following areas:

Quizzes	100 points
Exams	200 points
Laboratory	100 points
Final Examination	200 points

Grading Scale:

A = 540 points or more
B = 480 to 539 points
C = 420 to 479 points
D = 360 to 419 points
F = 359 points or less

Class participation grades are often a nemesis for both student and teacher. For students, they represent a troubling ambiguity. For teachers, they are often the proverbial battleground for grade disputes with borderline students. Notice the attempt at precision provided on one syllabus:

> The papers will count roughly one third of your final grade, the written exercises roughly one third, and the class work roughly one third. By class work I mean a subjective mix of your boldness, eagerness, cooperativeness, sense of humor, cheerfulness, grace, and kindness to others.

Very often these syllabi included specific notes and suggestions regarding student success in the course. Clearly these teachers want every student to be a star in the class or at least to achieve to one's highest level of ability. One syllabus highlighted a series of twenty features of the course coupled with the rationale for the inclusion of that feature in the course. An example follows:

Special Feature	*Reason for Feature*
Weekly quizzes taken directly from homework with "instant" grading and the opportunity in class to learn the material missed on the quiz with help from the instructor.	To encourage each student to study chemistry on a regular basis and to provide a mechanism that allows the student to assess what he or she knows and the time to remediate, with help from the instructor, before the student is so far behind that he or she cannot catch up.

Other syllabus notes are designed to improve each student's chances for success; they include suggestions on how to study, prepare for class, and how to take notes:

> Spend at least six hours outside of class each week on reading, pondering, writing down points that are puzzling or confusing, and thinking up two examination questions that you are required to bring to the Friday discussion each week.

> As you read each week's assignment, make an outline of its major points. On average, this should be between one and two pages long.

> On taking notes: don't overdo it. Better you should listen. Write down only the basics; then refer to the text (or the instructor) for clarification. Furious copying of vocal gems will do little good.

Connectedness

Announced office hours were a fixture on every syllabus. Students were encouraged to connect with the teacher in every way possible. During the terms in which they were teaching, the Carnegie winners made themselves available to students for extraordinary periods of time. All but two of the teachers were in their on-campus offices more than 20 hours per week. More than one-third of them exceeded 40 hours of availability. Two were on-campus and willing to meet with students over 50 hours per week! For most of these teachers, virtually all of their in-office time is open for student visitation. One professor who listed only 10 hours in the office noted that he lived on campus and allowed that he, therefore, was actually available much more than his posted hours might suggest. On a related issue, all of the Carnegie professors allow students to call them at home, although two teachers who post rather full hours discourage such calls except in cases of a student emergency. Typically, these teachers allow calls until ten or eleven o'clock at night. The overriding point is that students' contacting of the professor at home, at night, is frowned upon only in very rare cases.

An extension of the notion of connectedness between student and teacher involves the various ways of socializing outside of class. When asked whether they regularly invite students into their homes, all but one of the Carnegie winners responded affirmatively and, in the instance of the one "no," that teacher consciously sought other opportunities for encounters with students outside of class. Besides in-home gatherings, these teachers experienced frequent associations with the students (and former students) through field trips to other countries, breakfasts and lunches, attending student functions, presentations, and athletic events, going to parties, making joint trips to national meetings, and staffing the office with as many students as possible. This distinguished group of teachers apparently got to be that way by what they do outside the classroom with their students as much as by what they do inside the classroom.

Attendance

It may seem contradictory that these teachers, who strive with so much energy to facilitate the growth of equally energetic and independent learners, would place so much premium on attendance and punctuality. Another way of putting it is that the notion of freewheeling, intellectual exchange often runs counter to the seeming rigidity of mandatory attendance. All but two of the teachers require attendance at all classes. Perhaps this next syllabus note best captures the norm:

> You must come to all classes. No "free" cuts are permitted.
> Please treat this class as if it were a job. If an emergency pre-

vents your coming to class on a certain day, let me know ahead of time and plan to turn in any required work before class time. When in doubt, communicate. Never simply fail to show up for class and then wait until the following week to see me.

Even when absences are allowed, the standard for the enrolled students is quite high, as this sample suggests:

Attendance policy: More than 3 cuts (out of 42 meetings) will result in an automatic F.

One gets the very clear impression that the Carnegie award winners have extraordinary expectations for their own behavior in and out of the classroom. Perhaps it is not so surprising, therefore, that these professors might impose some of these same standards on the students with whom they share so much. A final example (another syllabus note) reflects this standard on the issue of coming to class on time. Even though coated with a touch of delightful humor, the expectation is not obscured:

Please be punctual. . . . Chronic lateness annoys your fellow students and me.

Day one

Another important behavioral area examined involves activities associated with the first day of any class taught by the Carnegie winners. Each professor clearly regards the first class meeting as critical to getting the particular course off on the right foot. In response to the question, "What do you consider to be your most crucial first-day-of-class activity?" at least three prominent themes emerged.

First, virtually all of the respondents mentioned the importance of clearly conveying to students, with great precision, a description of what the course would cover (content), an explanation of the details of what would be required of each registrant (student roles), and the distribution of a complete course syllabus outlining deadlines, assignments, and grade weights (work expectations). As one professor put it, "I do all this on the first day so there will be no surprises." For each of these teachers, student involvement in the learning process is an essential part of each class. The likely success of this process is vastly enhanced by carefully laying out for the students the "how-to's" of their anticipated participation.

Second, these teachers want to know each of the students in the class. They want to know who they are as persons as well as who they are in the academic community. The actual practices vary among the different Carnegie professors and according to the size of the particular class. But, typically, biographical information will be solicited from each student, and the instructor will review that information after the initial class meeting and also later in the term. Great efforts are made to get to know the students' names and why they are in the course. That often-referred-to notion of connectedness, which is so important to this group of teachers, is particularly critical to them on the first day of class.

The third overriding theme related to first day activity has to do with getting the students' collective and individual interests piqued at the outset. Through a variety of means—enticing rhetorical questions, relating the course to issues critical to most students' concerns, delivering a spicy and high-energy lecture—the Carnegie teachers seek to get students to want to take the course, to get them excited about the material, and to intrigue them with the subject. They also have a tendency to get the students involved and working in the first class period. A few of the teachers, using an advance copy of the class enrollment list, send out a pre-class reading assignment accompanied by a list of questions that are to be addressed in the first day's discussion. None of the Carnegie professors regard the first day as a merely perfunctory exercise during which the roll is taken, the syllabus is passed out, and the class is dismissed. Each views this initial meeting as critical to setting the tone for the remainder of the term.

SUMMER ACTIVITIES

Finally, the Carnegie professors were asked about the nature of their summer activities. Probably it is not surprising that, although none of the respondents said so in so many words, one might have the distinct impression that these professors see the summer "break" as a time of renewal, refreshment, retooling, and refocusing on what they think and do. Further, it is probably not surprising that a group of individuals who have spent so much energy in intense relationships with their disciplines and students would need time to pause and relax. The words "pause" and "relax" must be used advisedly, however, because of the potential notion that summers may be periods of inactivity or, at least, reduced activity. Let there be no mistake: These teachers simply redirect their efforts to a set of tasks which differ only in that a less consuming intensity is required for their conduct. For example, there appears to be a great deal of personal and professional renewal at the center of each person's summer work. Virtually all respondents mentioned research (reading and writing) as his or her paramount concern. At least one of the Carnegie winners uses this time for lab work with students. Another directs special summer programs for pre-college students. While none of these very distinguished teachers is idle during the summer, it is a significant fact that none will be found in the regular classroom.

CONCLUSIONS

The major purpose of this essay has been to catalog, in terms as precise as possible, the actual backgrounds and behaviors of this select group of professors in the hope that those who aspire to become better college and university teachers will be left with a clearer understanding of what it takes—both inside and outside of the classroom—to succeed. It is not likely that the reader will have uncovered any startling truths in this essay. Some of the highlighted techniques and activities may be considered mundane or at least not very cerebral. But these are the techniques and activities of a group of individuals considered to be "best-in-class," and therefore these practices are noteworthy. While in the purest sense these behaviors are at best merely descriptive of what a good teacher does, it is difficult to resist the temptation to present these behaviors as a prescription for inspiring teaching.

REFERENCES

Baldwin, R. G., & Blackburn, P. T. (1991). The academic career as a developmental process: Implications for higher education. *Journal of Higher Education, 52* (6), 598-614.

Beidler, P. (Ed.). (1986). *Distinguished teachers on effective teaching.* New Directions for Teaching and Learning, No. 28. San Francisco, CA: Jossey-Bass.

Feldman, K. A. (1976). The superior college teacher from the students' view. *Research in Higher Education, 5,* 243–288.

Kinney, D. P., & Smith, S. P. (1992). Age and teaching performance. *Journal of Higher Education, 63* (3), 282–302.

Kremer, J. (1991). Identifying faculty types using peer ratings on teaching, research, and service. *Research in Higher Education, 32* (4), 351–361.

Pascarella, E. T., & Terenzini, P. T. (1991). *How college affects students.* San Francisco, CA: Jossey-Bass.

Simpson, R. D., & Frost, S. H. (1993). *Inside college: Undergraduate education for the future.* New York, NY: Insight Books.

21

What This Book
Teaches Me

JOHN K. ROTH

When the professors who contributed to *Inspiring Teaching* were invited to reflect on the exemplary practices that characterize their teaching successes, they were asked to make their reflections personal, practical, and philosophical. This book's success depends on its ability to lead more of us college and university professors to reflect on our teaching in those ways.

As the book's editor, I have lived and worked with these essays for some time. My thinking and teaching, even my sense of what a teacher's identity can and should entail, will be affected by their impact. But how might that process work? When it comes to teaching teachers, how can the essays collected here make a meaningful contribution? To illustrate what some responses to those questions can be, I want to identify and explain five lessons that this book teaches me, a college professor in his mid-fifties who still has a lot to learn. None of these lessons is entirely new, but each is a notable reminder, and all of them can reassure and challenge any professor who cares about inspiring teaching.

1. Outstanding teachers are similar

True, the places where they teach and their disciplines may be very different. In their approaches to teaching, some outstanding teachers are traditional, others more experimental. In their intellectual outlooks, some are liberal, others more conservative. These differences, however, do not obscure the similarities that outstanding teachers share. To the contrary, the differences put those similarities in bold relief and make them stand out all the more. Every reader may identify them a bit differently, but here are three clusters of those shared characteristics that loom the largest for me. How would your statement of them compare or contrast?

First, outstanding teachers share a contagious enthusiasm for the subjects they teach. They do so because their teaching emerges from the passions of their lives. Caring so much about the particular studies to which they are committed, they work to keep informed, to learn more, to master their subjects better, and, whenever possible, to advance the state of the art in their fields.

Typically, outstanding teachers do not regard teaching and research as two separate activities. One informs the other. Nor do they define their fields of study too narrowly. Recognizing that the world and its problems do not conform to the boundaries established by the standard departmental lines of colleges and universities, outstanding teachers are curious about many areas and problems, and they often enrich and broaden their specialized interests by connecting them to diverse disciplines and topics.

To communicate effectively, outstanding teachers plan assignments carefully and fit their teaching methods to their students' needs as well as to the subject matter. In particular, their communication styles put a premium on making the environment of every learning situation—the classroom, lab, office conference, tutorial meeting—a place where openness exists, honesty abides, respect prevails, inquiry progresses, and mentoring takes place.

Within these contexts, outstanding teachers challenge their students—and themselves—with high expectations, and then they collaborate with their students to fulfill them. Outstanding teachers fear few things more than the possibility that students may feel less positive about a course at the end than they did at the beginning. So they keep looking for ways to motivate and encourage students—the weak as well as the strong, the uninspired as well as the dedicated—and to extend their goals.

Second, outstanding teachers share the conviction that it is vitally important to know their students personally. They work to gain such knowledge—it includes basic items such as knowing the students' names—because such awareness enables them to teach their students more effectively.

Perhaps more than anything else, knowing one's students requires accessibility. Outstanding teachers take inventory of their practices in this crucial area. Going beyond holding regular office hours or even giving out home telephone numbers, the accessibility that outstanding teachers embody involves more than simply being available. Outstanding teachers turn accessibility into an active practice, which begins with the recognition that what we professors *are* speaks to students more emphatically than what we say. So accessibility means opening oneself to students by sharing one's life, as well as one's knowledge, with them. It means tapping into students' interests and concerns as well as encouraging them to plug into ours.

In addition, accessibility means showing students that learning is what students and teachers do together; it means making clear that teaching and learning are more like two points of view on a single event than they are two separate processes. When the times are right, accessibility also means being friend and parent. Such roles entail saying no as well as saying yes to what students think, say, and do; they also include making students aware of options, helping them to choose wisely, and fostering their independence.

Third, outstanding teachers share inclinations that are radical. I do not mean that outstanding teachers are extremists or revolutionaries. But they do cut to the chase, penetrate to the core, and get to the heart of the matter. As their detailed course syllabi often suggest, outstanding teachers have their wits about them: They are organized; they focus their concentration. While keeping their inquiries open-ended and their teaching flexible, they map where they are going. Often those journeys are intentionally risk-filled, and to reduce the chances of wasted time and energy, these teachers plan as carefully as they can.

When plans go awry, destinations are missed, goals remain unachieved, and successes are too few and far between, outstanding teachers have no immunity from discouragement, but their radical streaks defy despair by bouncing back to try and try again. The ways outstanding teachers try and try again include distinguishing the profound from the trivial, the fundamental from the transitory. They separate what is mixed up and integrate what needs to be brought together. They see that theory and practice are more like two inseparable sides of a coin than they are two separate realities.

Furthermore, outstanding teachers question assumptions that are taken for granted. They subvert beliefs that are uncritically affirmed. As they take learning to be a transforming agent, outstanding teachers are accountable: They check not only to find out what their students have comprehended; they also do their best to ensure that their students' understanding is neither faddish nor ephemeral but marked instead by lasting importance and value. Moreover, outstanding teachers put themselves as well as their students to these tests. They keep their students and themselves off balance so that no one gets stuck in ruts that are too comfortable or in grooves that are too predictable. Looking for ways to explore new ground that needs to be broken, they give the tried-and-true respect but never more than it deserves. They find it impossible—because doing so is dull and unsatisfying—to teach even a successful course in exactly the same way twice.

Thus, outstanding teachers are vigilant about change—from the technological and theoretical to the social and spiritual—that must be acknowledged and embraced if they and their students are to be the lifelong learners that a civilized and well-governed world needs. They look for every way that time and energy permit to help and serve the students they teach. They rejoice when major breakthroughs in student learning take place, but knowing that education is an ongoing, incremental process, they learn to watch for small gains, too, and to take heart from them when they occur.

In sum, this book alerts me: Outstanding teachers pay attention.

2. I am a good teacher

In emphasizing this lesson, I intend no self-congratulation. To the contrary, I stress this theme for reasons that point in quite a different direction.

If a professor must do all of the things mentioned above—and perhaps even more—to be outstanding, then I do not and cannot fit that profile. Here's why: Taken together, the essays in this book provide a professorial portrait so lofty and idealized that scarcely any real professor could possibly match it. Certainly I do not. Nor do I know of any other professor, living or dead, who has done so completely and perfectly.

Nevertheless, rather than being disheartened by such conclusions, they lead me to grasp two important insights: First, the lofty and idealized portrait has merit; trying to fit it is worthwhile. In addition, I can say—not immodestly but honestly—that at least in some times and ways, I do fit that profile.

As I study this book, I recognize something of my own combination of theory and practice as a teacher, not just in my contributions to these pages but, more importantly, in the words that others have written. I expect this experience will be widely shared by other readers, too. Because so many of us professors can, in one way or another, recognize positive reflections of ourselves in these pages, I take one of this book's most significant contributions to be that it can build confidence and self-esteem, which teachers need as much as students, and that by doing so it can help more and more of us professors to see that we are and can continue to be good teachers.

In sum, this book alerts me: I need to remember that I am not a perfect teacher, perhaps not even an outstanding one, but I am a good teacher. Nothing that *Inspiring Teaching* tries to show is more important than its fortunate implication that there are a vast number of us professors—and there can be even more—who fit that description.

3. I can be a better teacher

Even if I cannot incorporate perfectly and completely all of the inspiring teaching practices detailed in this book, my reading also tells me that I can and should go beyond the ones that my teaching already contains and emphasizes. I believe that other readers of this book will share this same realization, which can lead to constructive change.

Such a realization might lead one, for example, to develop completely new courses and to try substantially different teaching methods that one has never tried before. For me, however, the immediate impact of this book underscores some of John Zubizarreta's specific advice.

In his essay about teaching portfolio revisions, Zubizarreta suggests that it may not wise to try to change too much all at once. Just as learning takes time and tends to be incremental, it may be wise to let this book suggest certain areas where one can concentrate, say, to improve a particular course next year, or a specific part of a course next semester, or even some aspect of a course that is under way right now.

For instance, *Inspiring Teaching* leads me to mark three areas where I want to improve or add to what I do in several of the courses that I teach with regularity. Two of those courses, including the one on the Holocaust that I discussed elsewhere in this book, usually have enrollments of about forty students. This book and Dennis Huston's essay in particular challenge me to make a commitment to improve two specific aspects of those courses: 1) to learn my students' names faster than I have been doing, and 2) to find ways to make discussion more effective and meaningful in classes of that size. Third, this book and the essays by Sally Phillips and Mark Taylor in particular challenge me to make a commitment to include Internet resources and e-mail discussion groups in my teaching. I have not taken either of those steps before. Doing so will take me out of my comfort zone. That's one good reason, among others, to try them.

Having written down those commitments, perhaps I have also made a small start on another improvement I can make, namely, to keep my version of a teaching portfolio of the kind that John Zubizarreta described. In any case, now I will at least be able to look back and check whether I have been faithful to these small but significant responses to the challenges that this book has put upon me. Perhaps *Inspiring Teaching* can work in similar ways for other teachers who read it: For example, try thinking of at least a few improvements that it suggests to you, write them down, try them, and check to see how the effort turns out.

In sum, this book alerts me: There are specific, concrete steps that all of us professors can take—next year, next semester, right now—to make us better teachers.

4. I can regard my local colleagues with new appreciation
I knew a few of the writers personally before we worked together on this project, but I have not met most of them face to face. Nevertheless, I now feel that I know them well, for as we have communicated with each other and as I have studied their essays, my understanding of who they are, what they do, and why they do it has grown and deepened immensely.

During the months while I worked on this book, I often thought how exciting, challenging, and stimulating it would be to have all of these people as colleagues on a campus that we shared. Although that dream will never come true, what can happen is that I will have new appreciation for the colleagues I do have on my own campus.

I make that point because every person who has been named a Carnegie Professor of the Year probably wonders why. That wondering is right. For however accomplished and distinguished they may be, the Carnegie professors understand that we are not so much "professors of the year" as representatives of the tens of thousands of college and university professors who are dedicated to excellent teaching and who can be found on campuses and in classrooms all over the United States and Canada, including the ones where most of the readers of this book do their work.

In sum, this book alerts me: If I can learn so much about teaching from people I have never met, maybe I can learn more from my local colleagues, if only we will take the time to share with each other in personal, practical, and philosophical ways what we think good teaching involves.

5. I am different from other professors

As similar as I may be to tens of thousands of professors in the United States, Canada, and elsewhere, the essays in this book clarify that my combination of scholarly interests is particular to me, that no other professor's way of teaching is identical to mine, and that there are many suggestions in this book that I am unlikely to follow, even assuming that I were capable of implementing them.

On the latter point, for example, I am left in awe, wonder, and admiration when I read about Mark Taylor's teleconferencing, or the performance-based teaching of Shakespeare that Martha Andresen and Michael Flachmann have perfected, or the feminist pedagogy that Rosemarie Tong so persuasively defends, or the contractual syllabus development that Sally Phillips utilizes, or the camping-trip fieldwork that Harvey Blankespoor enjoys with his biology students, or the community-based student publishing projects that Patrick Parks has led so successfully, or even the dramatic class openings that Teofilo Ruiz uses to provoke important student questioning.

The list could go on and on, but I would not be honest with myself, nor of very much help to my students, if I changed my agenda to conform with the specific ones that those good professors have made their own. Nor should they be advised to conform to mine. Already I have emphasized how much I have learned from the other contributors to this book, but among the most important things they have taught me is that I would not be myself if I tried to mimic them.

If, as the saying goes, it takes a village to raise a child, then surely it takes a community of teachers to educate students. Education's quality depends on the competence of teachers; it depends, too, on the characteristics that outstanding teachers share. But sound learning also entails that students encounter dissimilarity in their teachers—a variety of perspectives, a multiplicity of personalities, and a diversity of approaches. We professors need these differences, too, because appreciation of them can educate us, keep us on the cutting edge, and stimulate us to consider more carefully what we can and should contribute to the educational enterprise, lest that particular content and approach be underemphasized, ignored, lost, or left out altogether.

In conclusion, then, the point of *Inspiring Teaching* is not to provide blueprints that anyone should copy. To pursue that goal would be foolish because inspiring teaching eludes such rigidity. The hope is that this book has done something else instead, namely, to offer adaptable suggestions and, even more important, to provoke reflection—personal, practical, philosophical—about how you and I can build upon and improve what only we can give to our students. We make our contributions in social settings and as social beings, for teaching and learning are always social activities. But within that context inspiring teaching depends upon our individual particularities as well.

Thus, to sum up once more, this book alerts me: My task as a teacher includes learning from others, but in that process my primary responsibility is to become most truly myself and not somebody else. Only to the extent that each one of us professors finds our own way, developing it with the help of others as skillfully and conscientiously as possible, will our teaching be inspired and inspiring.

Index